CIOs at Work

Ed Yourdon

Apress®

CIOs at Work

ISBN-13 (pbk): 978-1-4302-3554-5

ISBN-13 (electronic): 978-1-4302-3555-2

Trademarked names, logos, and images may appear in this book. Rather than use a trademark symbol with every occurrence of a trademarked name, logo, or image we use the names, logos, and images only in an editorial fashion and to the benefit of the trademark owner, with no intention of infringement of the trademark.

The use in this publication of trade names, trademarks, service marks, and similar terms, even if they are not identified as such, is not to be taken as an expression of opinion as to whether or not they are subject to proprietary rights.

President and Publisher: Paul Manning
Lead Editor: Jeffrey Pepper
Editorial Board: Steve Anglin, Mark Beckner, Ewan Buckingham, Gary Cornell, Jonathan Gennick, Jonathan Hassell, Michelle Lowman, James Markham, Matthew Moodie, Jeff Olson, Jeffrey Pepper, Frank Pohlmann, Douglas Pundick, Ben Renow-Clarke, Dominic Shakeshaft, Matt Wade, Tom Welsh
Coordinating Editor: Jessica Belanger
Copy Editor: Kim Burton-Weisman
Proofreader: Nancy Sixsmith
Compositor: Mary Sudul
Indexer: BIM Indexing & Proofreading Services
Cover Designer: Anna Ishschenko

Distributed to the book trade worldwide by Springer Science+Business Media, LLC., 233 Spring Street, 6th Floor, New York, NY 10013. Phone 1-800-SPRINGER, fax 201-348-4505, e-mail orders-ny@springer-sbm.com, or visit http://www.springeronline.com.

For information on translations, please contact us by e-mail at info@apress.com, or visit www.apress.com.

Apress and friends of ED books may be purchased in bulk for academic, corporate, or promotional use. eBook versions and licenses are also available for most titles. For more information, reference our Special Bulk Sales–eBook Licensing web page at www.apress.com/bulk-sales.

To Teddy

Contents

About the Author

Ed Yourdon is a computer software consultant and IT expert witness in his own firm, NODRUOY Inc., as well as co-founder of the Cutter Consortium and Editor Emeritus of the *Cutter IT Journal*. Working in the software field for more than 45 years, he has published 27 computer-related books and more than 550 technical articles.

Yourdon has programmed, designed, and tested numerous software applications and programmer-productivity products. He has managed numerous projects as a first-level project leader and also as a senior IT executive. He has also reviewed numerous software development projects for clients during his consulting career.

Acknowledgments

It's hard to imagine anyone writing a book entirely on his or her own—even a novelist would be hard-pressed to deny the inspiration, support, encouragement, and feedback from friends, neighbors, a spouse, or a "significant other." The same is true for textbooks and works of non-fiction; and it's definitely true of this book, *CIOs at Work*.

The most obvious people for me to acknowledge, of course, are the sixteen individuals whom I had the pleasure and honor of interviewing. Not only did they graciously carve a significant chunk of time out of their schedule in order to share their experience, their insights, and their advice, but they also shared their passion and excitement about the IT industry in which they work and to which they have dedicated a significant part of their professional lives.

Behind each of these CIOs there was at least one—and often two or three—additional people that I need to acknowledge. First, the administrative assistants who help their bosses organize their schedules and coordinate their interactions with a wide range of people inside and outside their organization. For every e-mail interaction I had with a CIO, I probably had ten with his or her administrative assistant; and without their help, I would never have even reached the point of having a conversation with the CIO. They tend to stay in the background, but play a fairly invisible role; hence, I hope they'll forgive me if I don't mention their names.

There were also several people who helped me identify, locate, and contact the CIOs that I eventually interviewed. The most important of these was my editor, Jessica Belanger, who enthusiastically suggested industries that I had overlooked, companies whose CIOs were likely to be particularly interesting to interview, and clever strategies for tracking down CIOs who often seemed to be doing their level best to remain hidden from sight. Several people at Computer Aid, Inc. were quite helpful in my search for CIOs, including Mike Milutis, Joe Hessmiller, and James Nicol. I also got some much-needed help from Leon Kappelman, Toni Nash, and John Baker, as well as several quasi-anonymous people on Twitter—and I am especially grateful for the assistance of @redmamba, who put me in touch with the

CIO of Parliament in the United Kingdom. Indeed, the CIOs themselves were of great assistance, often introducing me to their fellow CIO colleagues, or at least telling me how to track them down and get in touch.

When it came to the actual writing of the book, there were three key people who kept me on track and helped keep me from going insane. Kristen Ng did an unbelievably professional (and fast!) job of transcribing the audio recording of each interview into an eminently readable and coherent word-processing document. My editor, Jessica Belanger, worked with me tirelessly to edit several audio "conversations" into readable English without losing the style, personality, and "voice" of the CIOs who spoke to me. And Apress' Assistant Publisher, Jeff Pepper, carefully reviewed each chapter and suggested additional questions that would help round out each conversation.

The only hesitation that an author has when it comes to acknowledgments is that he might have unconsciously overlooked someone when compiling the list. There is no doubt that I am guilty of such a sin, as I had numerous conversations and e-mail exchanges with friends, colleagues, and family members throughout the several months that I worked on *CIOs at Work*. Some of those whom I've inadvertently failed to mention won't even notice the oversight. Some will shrug and I suspect a few will mutter to themselves that I've deliberately slighted them. I apologize in advance to all those individuals and promise that I'll do a better job next time.

Ed Yourdon

Introduction

For the past two generations of human civilization, we have been told that we live in an "Information Age." And for at least one generation, we have been told that our business organizations, our government agencies, and our day-to-day social lives depend more and more critically on computer technology. We no longer express any surprise about how rapidly technology is changing and evolving because it's something we *all* experience: every one of us has his or her own "war story" about how primitive things were—even a short five years ago.

Nowhere is this more evident than in the office of the Chief Information Officer of today's organizations. Ironically, that title did not even exist when I finished college and entered the workforce back in the Paleolithic Age of the 1960s. But those were the days when companies thought they were in the "widget" business—whether the widgets were automobiles or toasters or some other tangible product. Today, even the most Luddite executives realize that information technology (IT) is what connects their organizations and its products/services to the marketplace and the customers and their assortment of laptops, tablets, and smartphones. Equally important, IT is the "electricity" (or, as U.S. federal government CIO Vivek Kundra puts it, the "digital oil") that keeps their "factory" running 24 hours a day, seven days a week.

Consequently, CIOs are becoming an increasingly critical executive in both private-sector and public-sector organizations. As I confirmed in the interviews presented in this book, they almost all have a title of "Vice President" or better; many of them report directly to the CEO or COO of the organization; and some are members of the board of directors of their organization. At the same time, they are often difficult to identify and sometimes *extremely* difficult to track down and contact. Of course, it's not so easy to pick up the phone and make a direct call to the CEO of a large organization, either; but I was surprised to see how many companies had *no* public information about the identity, or even the existence, of their Chief Information Officer.

Indeed, I was surprised by how many CIOs were uninterested in talking to me about their opinions of how IT was being used to make their organizations more productive, more competitive, more efficient. After all, "information" is the middle initial of their abbreviated title; and, as one CIO put it, a more appropriate title might even be "Chief Communication Officer."

After several such unsuccessful efforts to contact CIOs within various Wall Street banks and financial services organizations, it finally dawned on me: in some of these organizations, strategic use of IT really *is* considered a competitive advantage. If these firms really do believe that to be the case, why on earth *would* they want to share that competitive advantage with anyone else? Why would they want to discuss it? Why would they even want to acknowledge its existence? It would almost be like the CIA or the National Security Agency opening all their secret files for public review and discussion.

At the same time, the secretive "closed" approach towards IT that these organizations exhibit reminds me of "closed" countries now experiencing turmoil on the world scene where attempts to shut down the Internet essentially shut down the country's economy. Wall Street firms are *not* the CIA, and in the long run, I believe their attempts to seal themselves off from the increasingly interconnected, Internet-enabled world will prove to be a failed strategy.

Meanwhile, some organizations are clearly proud of what they've done, and what they plan to do in the future, with information technology. They're not going to share their "secret sauce" proprietary algorithms (for example, Google didn't offer to share its page-ranking algorithm with me any more than Coca-Cola would have shared the detailed recipe for its soft drink) and they're not going to deposit all of their software in an open-source code repository. But they realize that their employees—who often number in the tens of thousands, sometimes even the hundreds of thousands—represent a society of their own, and that it's a *positive* thing to encourage their employees to interact with customers, suppliers, vendors, and business partners in the outside world.

Equally important, most of the companies I spoke with have finally accepted the wisdom of *The Clue Train Manifesto: The End of Business As Usual* [Perseus Publishing, 2001], which comprises 95 theses describing what the authors (Rick Levine, Christopher Locke, Doc Searls, and David Weinberger) felt was the new "reality" of the networked marketplace. A decade ago it sounded quite radical to suggest that "Markets do not want to talk to flacks and hucksters. They want to participate in the conversations going on behind the corporate firewall," (thesis number 62), or that "Companies need to realize their markets are often laughing at them," (thesis number 2). But today, more and more companies realize that the best way to confront these theses (which have turned out to be realities, not abstract theories) is to be honest and open, and to be pervasively and intimately involved in the activities of their markets and their customers. As Messrs. Levine *et al* prophesied, this cannot be done by having "flacks and hucksters" talk *at* the marketplace, but by having *everyone*, from the clerk to the executive, talk *with* the marketplace—via Twitter, Facebook, smartphone, blogs, wikis, and whatever new forms of interaction may come along in the next few years.

Clearly, all of this involves the IT department within an organization, and thus requires the vision, strategy, and leadership of the CIO and his or her team. But it doesn't tell us what the CIO *does* on a day-to-day basis. As I learned from my interviews, those duties usually break down into three major categories, the first of which can be described metaphorically as "keeping the lights on." I must confess that I didn't give this area much thought when I began the *CIOs at Work* project because I started my own IT career in the 1960s, when most organizations operated fairly straightforward mainframe computers in locked, air-conditioned, heavily secured data centers. As we moved into the 1980s and 1990s, of course, companies began acquiring thousands of desktop and laptop computers, and their solitary mainframe centers evolved into increasingly scaled-down, distributed, interconnected computers in every country, every manufacturing center, every sales office, and every nook and cranny of the organization. But my understanding was more intellectual than visceral. It didn't really make an impact on me.

Today, it's common to see CIOs overseeing an IT infrastructure that includes tens of thousands, perhaps even hundreds of thousands, of computers and servers and computerized gadgets—as well as thousands of applications and mind-boggling amounts of data. Bits and pieces of this infrastructure can, and do, break down from time to time; but as a whole, it's "mission critical" in the sense that if you turn off the computers (or, equivalently, turn off the network that connects them), you might as well turn off the electricity and send everyone home. It would be a sublime understatement to say it's a non-trivial task to keep all of this running smoothly; and what surprised me, consistently, was how calm and matter-of-fact today's CIOs are about this part of their job.

Perhaps because of my own career in the field, my "gut instinct" was that CIOs would be spending the majority of their time working with their peers and counterparts in the various business units of the organization, looking for ways to make the business more efficient, more productive, and more competitive. Part of that, of course, includes making the IT department itself more efficient, productive, and competitive by accomplishing more work with fewer people, and by carrying out system development projects in a fashion that's consistently on-time, under-budget, and free of the software bugs that drive everyone crazy. And because computer hardware is still an expensive part of the IT budget, CIOs are looking more and more closely at the benefits of virtualization and cloud computing—indeed, those technologies are a "done deal" in the majority of organizations that I interviewed.

But simply making *existing* business processes more productive and efficient is apparently not as exciting as it once was. After all, business organizations have been using computers, for almost 50 years now, to make the number-crunching, paper-pushing, mundane operational activities of the organization less time-consuming and expensive. There is always more that can be done, of course, but the main emphasis today seems to be shifting the IT emphasis from *inside* the organization to *outside* the organization—to connect the organization's employees, processes, and data more intimately to the consumers, suppliers, partners, and other organizations with which the business interacts.

Of course, improvements in these areas are not being carried out by the CIOs on their own, nor are they being carried out by brilliant IT technicians working on behalf of passive, technology-illiterate business people. More and more often today, the people in the business units are almost as computer-savvy as the people in the IT organization. They, too, are part of the "digital nation" that has been using computers since birth. Indeed, many of them learned to program when they were children, just as our IT wizards did, but then they decided to focus their energies on marketing, or manufacturing, or finance, or genetic engineering.

As a result, the most exciting part of the CIO work that I saw during my interviews involved true partnership efforts between IT professionals and business-unit professionals—as well as external customers, suppliers, and business partners in many cases—to find completely *new* things for the business, which simply did not exist before. New markets, new customers, new ways of interacting with existing customers, new products, new features for existing products ... the possibilities seem endless. And, of course, when these partnership efforts do conceive of new things to build, make, or do, everyone wants the IT department to carry it out as quickly as humanly possible. If there was ever any doubt in my mind that the "agile" approach to systems development would be widely adopted, it was certainly dispelled after the first one or two interviews that I carried out. The "waterfall" development approach may not have disappeared entirely, but it has certainly moved into the distant background.

Throughout my interviews, I asked CIOs what excited them most about new technologies and new developments they anticipated in the next few years—and I then turned the question around and asked them what their biggest concerns were, what kept them awake at night. Many of the answers were predictable: everyone agreed that we have only begun to see the impact of "mobility" as we continue building smarter and smarter handheld devices, at prices that can be afforded by people all over the planet. And everyone is concerned about security, ranging from terrorist attacks to traditional cyber-security to "inside-job" attacks. Almost all of the CIOs are already adopting the technology of virtualization, and most of them agree that "cloud computing" is a tidal wave that may or may not be sufficiently "bulletproof" (in terms of security, privacy, and reliability) to use for mission-critical applications, but which will eventually be a pervasive, if not "universal," technology.

Some of the CIOs' responses surprised me, though they often reflected trends that are visible all around me, and which I should have noticed a long time ago. Shortly after the September 11 attack on the World Trade Center, for example, I remember hearing my New York City friends and colleagues reacting angrily to policy statements from their employers that business-supplied cellphones and BlackBerries should only be used for business purposes and not for personal use. "If there's another attack," one friend said to me, "my first priority is not my company, but finding out whether my family is safe. If my company is going to insist on these ridiculous rules, then I'm going to need a second cellphone for my own personal use."

At the time, I remember thinking that this was an extreme but perfectly understandable response, and that it was a response to a localized phenomenon, not an indicator of a general trend. But that was ten years ago and now it *is* a general trend—not so much because of crises and terrorist attacks (though Hurricane Katrina, the Haiti earthquake, the tsunami in Japan, and dozens of other events have certainly reinforced the trend), but simply because people know they have more powerful technology available to them at home, and at affordable prices, than they have in their workplace.

That being the case, I was fascinated to hear how the CIOs of major companies are reacting to the trend. After all, a corporate ultimatum of "Thou shalt not use consumer devices!" is not likely to succeed. So what *do* the CIOs say to the employees who bring smartphones into the office, who have *two* BlackBerries (to ensure that the corporate security people don't spy on their personal e-mail messages), and who have far more powerful desktop PCs at home than the ancient clunkers they use in the office?

Equally important, how are the technology vendors reacting to this trend? As several CIOs lamented to me, they used to expect the vendors to come to *them* first, because technology was sold *en masse* to large companies, which then allowed some of that technology to "trickle down" to the worker bees at the bottom of the corporate hierarchy. Now, many of the vendors (think Google, Apple, Microsoft, and several others) are approaching the consumer market *first* ... and then waiting to see if a grassroots revolution causes the technology to trickle *up* to the top of the corporate hierarchy.

In addition to hearing their reactions to current trends, I was also interested in the advice that CIOs had to offer about education (is a computer-science degree better than a broad, liberal-arts degree?), project/work assignments, reactions to the corporate environment, mentors, and the skills needed to move up the career ladder to a CIO position. Here again, some of the responses and comments were predictable, while others definitely were not. If you've been dreaming of being a CIO someday but lamented the fact that you don't have a master's degree in software engineering from MIT or Carnegie-Mellon, you may be surprised at what the CIOs have to say in this area. Similarly, if you thought that your master's degree in computer science from Cal Tech or Stanford would guarantee you such a job in the future, you may also be surprised.

My final question to the CIOs was: *what's next?* The answers were correlated fairly closely to their ages: those who were approaching retirement typically viewed the CIO position as the culmination of their career and looked forward to a semi-retirement role as a consultant, professor, or board member. Those in the middle of their career were generally enthusiastic about their current position, and had mixed reactions to the idea that they might someday be promoted to an even higher position, such as CEO.

And those who were relative youngsters, still in their twenties or early thirties, generally relished what they were doing and looked forward to the expansion of challenging assignments as they work to make their organization all that much more productive, efficient, and competitive.

All of this was quite thought-provoking to say the least—especially for someone like me, who has already spent 45 years in the IT industry. My only regret is that I didn't conduct these interviews right after I graduated from college—it might have sent my career off on an entirely different direction! And I think the same possibility exists for today's readers of this book, whether they are in their twenties, thirties, forties, or older. The sixteen CIOs interviewed in this book represent hundreds of years of experience. Read what they have to say and benefit from their experience!

New York, NY

Ed Yourdon

June, 2011

Benjamin Fried

CIO, Google Inc.

Benjamin Fried is Chief Information Officer of Google Inc., overseeing the company's global technology systems. His extensive hands-on experience in technology includes stints as a dBASE II programmer, front-line support manager, Macintosh developer, Windows 1.0 programmer, and UNIX systems programmer. Prior to joining Google, he spent more than 13 years in Morgan Stanley's technology department, where he rose to the level of Managing Director. During his time there, he led teams responsible for software development technology, web and electronic commerce technologies and operations, and technologies for knowledge workers.

Ben received his degree in Computer Science from Columbia University.

Ed Yourdon: Let's start by asking about any role models or any early heroes or mentors that may have influenced you to get where you are now.

Benjamin Fried: I think there have been a lot. I've only had maybe four major employers in my career, three or four employers, but a lot of role models. I think I've been lucky in that in every job I've been in, there's been one or more people I've been able to look up to and learn from.

Yourdon: Hmm.

Fried: Kind of different depending on the situation. When I was working my way through school, I was spending a lot of time reading, guess what? I think it was classic computer science texts.

Yourdon: [laughter]

Fried: And everything from reading [Brian] Kernighan and [P.J.] Plauger's *Elements of Programming Style* [McGraw-Hill, 1978], the books of the Bell Labs guys, [Donald] Knuth's *Art of Computer Programming* [Addison-Wesley, 2011], and the stuff he did. Did you guys [Bell Labs team and Ed Yourdon] publish together? I thought I remembered.

Yourdon: Well, because it took two years to get my books out—in fact, because of Bill Plauger, we had the first nonacademic UNIX license in the country.

Fried: Really?

Yourdon: And I said, "Is it free?" And [Plauger] said, "Of course not, it's $10,000." That's what UNIX cost in the '70s, which he loaned us, interest-free. That's why I thought, "This guy is serious." And we got a typesetter, on loan, and we were in the publishing business with TROFF.

Fried: Wow. Really? Wow. The typesetter's workbench? Is that what it was called? The document workbench? Impressive.

Yourdon: Yeah, but the book that he and Brian Kernigan wrote was certainly one of the major books in the field.

Fried: Yeah. I'd say that, the corpus of books that came out of Bell Labs—Brian's and Rob Pike's and others—were really influential, as well as Knuth's books. I guess I had a lot of time when I was a kid. I spent a lot of time teaching myself computer science in high school and in college, and so I had a bunch of academic and computer science heroes and people that I learned from. And then in jobs, there was always someone who was a mentor or someone I could look up to and learn how they were doing something, trying to understand what they were doing. I was very, very lucky. I spent almost 14 years at Morgan Stanley, in one place, and I think I learned a lot there about operating in a big company—what it means, the differences between great engineering and providing a great service.

Yourdon: Mm-hmm.

Fried: And a whole lot about how … "reality" is a better way of putting it, but that great engineering without the ability to communicate and understand what people want [or] understand how to negotiate and compromise and discuss and so on … the great engineering on its own does you very little good if those other skills aren't there, and there were a lot of people I saw who were able to work with that. So, I have a lot. It's hard to pin it down to just one, but there've always been people who I've looked up to for things. I think that's just … part of my personality.

Yourdon: Okay. That's good. And how did you end up here? You were at Morgan Stanley for a long time.

Fried: Well, I was lucky enough that I had several friends who joined here, some of whom joined the place fairly early on, in 2000, 2001 or something like that.

Yourdon: Mm-hmm.

Fried: As Google grew and grew, they said, "Oh, you should come and interview." Even in 2004, for Morgan Stanley I worked on building a lot of the technology that was used to run Google's IPO, which was interesting. I met a bunch of people who worked at Google, visited Google a bunch of times as part of that. And then in 2005, my name was submitted again … after the IPO experience, I came and I met a lot of people here. It was really, really interesting, but at the rate Google was growing at the time, they said, "You seem like a really interesting person. You know, we don't have a job for you, we don't have a particular role we're trying to fill, but come on, come through the process, and if it works out, we'll figure something out."

And meanwhile, I had a great job at Morgan Stanley, where I knew what I was . . . and I thought, you know, this is a small company … they're growing. That's great, but they don't really know what they want me to do. And so it wasn't that interesting. Then, although in retrospect it was probably a mistake, but in 2007 … the same recruiter called me back up and said that [the Google] CIO was moving on to a different role. … They said, "We are looking to find a replacement … and we thought, maybe that's something you'd be interested [in] talking to us about." … [T]hat began a long process of many, many interviews and I thought, well, they have a job for me now. And that led to my meeting with a lot of people here and ultimately getting the job.

Yourdon: Now had you been a CIO at Morgan Stanley?

Fried: No, I wasn't. I was not. And I honestly never thought I would be—this is probably an important thing to know about me—I had never thought I would be a CIO. I thought [about] the roles probably, the traditional CIO roles, even in Wall Street, where technology is this incredibly important part of competitive advantage and they're very, very aggressive about pushing the envelope. I had never thought I'd be a CIO anywhere.

I was really interested in the engineering and computer science parts of IT. I thought of myself as someone who was the gearhead in the back, who was the person trying to bring engineering and computer science and so on into industry and that I thought I'd always probably be, as I was at Morgan Stanley in my last role, a direct report to the CIO but with more of a technical focus to my job. But it was the way that the CIO role was constructed at Google—I thought, well, that's a CIO job I might actually like, I might actually be qualified for.

My observation was, and maybe it's a bit cynical, was that most CIOs carry a heavy burden because they're typically one of, if not *the* largest cost centers in their organization. Because so much of their jobs is operations, operationally oriented and execution-oriented. It's this combination of things: you always have to be super, super good at kind of understanding the financial picture of IT because it's such a big expense. You have to keep systems running really, really well all the time because the company depends on it, and that's incredibly important. But I didn't find the operational part of it alone to be that compelling. And then, finally, you're only as good as your execution, right?

And I thought that those three—you know, any two of them were kind of interesting, although I hope our CFO would forgive me for saying this—this "running the books part of it" was by far the least interesting. I saw a number of CIOs on Wall Street and in other industries who I almost felt had a bulls-eye painted on their back as a result of being the large, enormous cost centers. And I thought, I just don't want to have to worry about those things. You know, my passion and my excellence is in computer science and engineering and in building things, and in solving problems. And in building software and doing systems infrastructure and that kind of stuff. And I thought, CIOs don't get to spend a lot of time on that stuff. They manage big portfolios, etc., etc., etc. But they spend a lot of time on governance, they spend a lot of time on things that are important, but not interesting.

But Google has constructed the CIO job, because Google views IT as an engineering discipline. . . I report to an SVP of Engineering, who reports to the head of Engineering and Research, and I sit in an engineering executive group with the people who run Google Search and Google Apps and Google Enterprise and Ads. I thought, while I think of this as an engineering discipline, this seems really interesting to me, and they have a strong, strong belief in building software.

I think the other trend I've observed is that there's a lot of great IT departments and great CIOs who are really all about buying things, which is great. That's fine, it's one of the ways IT can be transformational, but not so much—you know, buying is great, but building is also where my passion is. I think it's part of the advantage I can bring to the table: I can help; I can create an environment to manage engineers well. So Google defined the IT job very, very differently. There's a real strong belief in building software. I thought of it as engineering—whereas at Morgan Stanley, I was kind of the gearhead in the back. I thought that at Google it would be the nontechnical skills that I had acquired at Morgan Stanley that would serve this engineering function. I thought they were asking me to serve really, really well—the ability to negotiate, create forms for governance, the ability to communicate well. I thought it was interesting that at the same time I'd still be able to kind of exercise my interests and passions as an engineer and someone with a computer science degree, too.

Yourdon: Okay. Well, that's a good answer. But, clearly, one of the things that distinguishes Google and Microsoft from the typical "XYZ widget company" is that you guys are not in the business of building widgets or tangible things. You're in the software product business—products or services.

Fried: Yeah.

Yourdon: So you tend to give a different kind of answer than I have been getting . . . [last week] I spoke to the CIO of a utility company. They're in the business of making electricity. Now, clearly it depends a lot on IT, but historically, they still go back to the days when they thought of themselves in the business of distributing electricity around the country. And that leads into my next area of questions of, basically, how does IT and the work you're doing as a CIO make Google more successful, more competitive, given that you're in the business of building software and services?

Fried: That's a really interesting question because, I'm not responsible for any Google products. I have peers who are responsible for all the products.... Yet at the same time I think IT here plays this incredibly important role in a number of ways. I think one of them is—I actually think a lot of this ties to the mission of IT, but I think it gets lost in the noise of the other parts of the conversation with CIOs—what's amazing about technology is its ability to transform a company. To do things to a company, to be an influencer on an organization. And I think what's great about IT is that having technologists at the center of a company who can fuse the understanding of a company, what differentiates it and what it seeks to be, with the opportunities of technology and understand what this incredibly rapidly moving, advancing area can apply to it.

That's this amazing opportunity, and what does that mean for Google? There are a few ways in which I think IT is important at Google and differentiates it. Number one is that we're a very young company and founded by people who grew up in the Internet Age and who are obviously all computer scientists. And there is this deep-seated cultural belief here that we want to change the company very, very quickly. In all kinds of ways we want to change it at a moment's notice and we don't want the company to...

I think all too often CIOs or companies make a decision that they will embody some best practices implemented by their ERP vendors or something like that: "We'll, we'll adopt the HR processes and technologies provided by the products that we bought to solve these problems." Whereas I think Google starts by asking itself and frequently re-evaluating: "What do we want to be and how does, what does technology need to do to support that?" So as material examples of that, we have very unusual hiring practices in Google Engineering. Hiring managers actually have very little voice in hiring the people who work for them. There are standards set for Google software engineers, there is standard training for interviewers, there are panels that aren't composed of people or are primarily not composed of people in the hierarchy of the job that you might move into.

Yourdon: And by the way, did I read somewhere correctly that you had 75,000 applications in one week recently?

Fried: Yeah. . . that is true. We have a corpus of millions of resumés, millions of job applications, I should say, that have come to us over time. We get many, many, many thousands of applications every week, sometimes every day. That in itself is a unique problem, I think, or a rare problem. I'm sure Walmart has some version of that, too, right? But we hire people in different ways. We value very much having an unbiased evaluation of someone's skills as an engineer before we decide to place them into a job, and in fact, typically, people are made an offer to be a software engineer and then after they accept that offer are they placed into a job.

Yourdon: Oh, okay.

Fried: So, this idea of a consistent bar and the processes that support that and that maintain high standards—these are very, very important. So we hire people, and then there's a series of reviews and approvals of offers to make sure that we're hiring people in consistent ways and keeping consistent standards. That's interesting.

Yourdon: Well, this sounds like it might be part of an answer to this question I had raised, which is how do you use IT to be more competitive?

And part of it is, "We hire the best damn people in the universe."

Fried: But I think it's interesting that what we decided is, "Here's what it means to hire the best people. Here's how we have to do it. And now let's build the software that will make this process work."

Yourdon: Oh, okay.

Fried: And similarly, we have, I'd say, unusual approaches to performance, and to how we do 360-degree performance management. We both incredibly value the signals about someone's performance that come from 360-degree evaluation while at the same time understanding the enormous impact it makes, it takes on a company to have everyone doing evaluations. Everyone has to stop what they were doing and do these other things. Not only that, but we're always trying to tune it. What can we do to create better signals about how people are actually performing and how they need to improve, and so on over time. So the performance management systems here are very much tuned to these ideas of the skills that we value and to making it incredibly easy to produce these signals about people's performance and capabilities. And we change what we want to measure and how we measure it and how we'll gather information every performance management cycle. By the way, we have four performance review cycles a year.

Yourdon: Is that for everybody?

Fried: At least in engineering. I don't know what the other departments do. But I think that that's unusual. And, similarly, we take differing approaches to how we do compensation management. And how we compensate people, and interesting approaches to the philosophy and different kinds of components to the compensation. These are all places we've defined to get to the question of what is the role of IT at Google?

One of the roles is to enable Google to be the kind of company that it wants to be without the constraints created by pre-existing systems and to allow us to rapidly change. This element of allowing the company to rapidly change and redefine what it wants to be is prevalent in other parts of what we do, too. So the people who provide technology support, fix your laptop when it's got a problem, giving you software and so on, that's also part of my organization. And that same philosophy of allowing the company to change rapidly is embodied in how we do end-user support.

Often I'm seeing end-user support to be considered an activity where you rapidly try to manage as many costs out of it as possible, get it down, limit options, get it down to basic scripts, offshore as much of the work as possible, and get it so it can be done by people who don't need to have a deep understanding so that you don't have to pay them for that. Whereas our approach is: technology is always changing; we want to be able to make rapid changes to the technology environment here for a whole host of reasons. Sometimes it's because we want to experiment with new Google software before we give it to other people. Sometimes it's because we've observed that the world has changed or security requirements change rapidly and we want to implement those changes really, really quickly or we want to . . .

So the computer support people that we hire are generalists with deep skills. And the general approach is that the person you bring your problem to—and usually it's in person, it's a place we call it TechStop—bring your laptop and then you can ask them a [question].

Yourdon: Like the Apple Genius Bar?

Fried: Yeah, exactly, they should be able no matter what it is, that person should work with you and solve your problem with you, and they should have the skills, not that they can necessarily do it all themselves, but they can figure it out with you. They call upon other specialists. And that's a very different model. It allows us organizationally to rapidly change the environment. There have been numerous cases where we've had products that we experimented on with Google, we got a lot of feedback on and we decided not to ultimately launch and maybe we shut them down. And being used in some cases by thousands of people, and we wanted to rapidly go from having thousands of people using them to shutting them down and moving on. That's one of these cases where having generalists in the support organization has allowed the company to move really, really rapidly and change rapidly. So I think that that's also an element of what IT is. I mean, I'm very fundamental now. When I think about IT, I think it's about maximizing the productivity of your people in any number of ways.

Yourdon: Hmm.

Fried: So that philosophy and approach is that people who work at Google can choose to have a Linux machine or a Macintosh or a machine running Windows. And that's because we believe you probably know how you can be most productive, and we want to give you the toolset that will make you most productive. And, I think that's a very different kind of social contract from what you see in many other IT shops, where the philosophy is more along the lines of, "We've made a set of decisions that we, the IT leadership, believe are optimal and we will educate you, support you, and so on around the set of decisions we've made for you," whereas we believe, "You probably know how to work best." That doesn't mean you go and buy a computer at Best Buy and bring it in to work. We do purchasing, we support Mac OS and Windows and Linux here, and we have teams who are experts in it, but by trying to give you a toolset that is one you would choose to use, the difference in the social contract is also that because you've made a choice about how you want to work, you probably don't need the same kind of support as if we've given you one way of doing it that's our way, not your way.

Yourdon: Good point.

Fried: So, users end up getting more personally involved in solving their own problems because there's some level of recognition that, "Well, I chose this."

Yourdon: Right.

Fried: "I wanted to use a Mac," or "I thought Windows was best for me." And I think that recognizes the fact that there's something you'll refer to later on, one of the great generational differences we're exposed to is now it's not just the first generation of people who grew up with computers in the workforce. But it's the first generation of people who grew up with computers *and* with the Internet *and* with e-mail *and* with instant messaging are in the workforce. Whereas when I first entered a large enterprise in 1994 or something like that, expectations were completely different. People often first saw a laptop when it was given to them [through] work. Or first saw Windows when they got it at work.

Yourdon: Yes.

Fried: And the best computing experience you could expect to have would be the one that your company provided for you. But that's all changed.

Yourdon: Oh, absolutely. There's no question.

Fried: And, you know, we very consciously recognize that IT has a different role as a result of those changes, and I think that the role is about enabling the individual. It's about creating maximum individual performance. It's about allowing users to choose how to work. It's about enabling an organization to rapidly change what it wants to be and kind of what's important to it. I think that the opportunity that CIOs have, that technologists have, is to use technology to positively differentiate the organization that you're part of. That isn't just about competitive advantage. Competitive advantage and making your company more competitive is part of it, but there are lots of ways in which organizations, nonprofits, governments, and companies want to be different. They all have some sense of identity or they have some sense of individuality and identity. And I think we have to recognize that technology should be a part of it. It often is. Every company has some piece of internal technology that's become a noun or a verb that's entered the language, the jargon of that company.

Yourdon: Mm-hmm.

Fried: And I think that's in part evidence that technology can have these sorts of roles. What IT leaders need to do is recognize that that kind of differentiation is really important. It could be about making your company more competitive and productive or profitable. But it could just be about accentuating the differences that define your organization. And I think that, having CIOs, having IT departments at the center of a company that can recognize and enhance and create those opportunities, is kind of the core, the core of what IT's mission should be, and it's the only thing that will be durable given that the technology landscape is only accelerating the rate at which it changes.

Yourdon: Yeah, that certainly is true. Let me ask a related question if I can. You said that you're not responsible for the Google products per se. But obviously the Google products run on server farms of hundreds of thousands of servers in various places. Are you responsible for that kind of day-to-day operational aspect of it?

Fried: Uhh, no. There are one or two small corner cases where we are, but we don't operate those servers. It's relatively well known that Google designs and builds its own servers. And I have a team that's responsible for the supply chain and inventory and asset management of that manufacturing and repair and deployment work.

Yourdon: But in terms of keeping the lights on, that's not your job?

Fried: No. I have groups that are responsible for keeping the lights on for things that operate what Googlers use.

Yourdon: Right, like her laptop [pointing]?

Fried: Her laptop or maybe even the server that it might be talking to.

Yourdon: Okay.

Fried: The servers that drive things that Google "corporate" uses, yes. The things that drive Google commercial products, no.

Yourdon: Okay, and that's what I would have expected. I scribbled down a word also that came from Microsoft's Tony Scott and I'd be curious to see whether you were involved in [it]. His word for it was "dogfooding." And I'm sure you know what that means.

Fried: Yeah. I know what that means.

Yourdon: Do people look to you and your IT department as the first dogfood eaters for some new product that may be coming out?

Fried: Dogfooding is an enormous landscape within Google. And there's a bunch of different flavors of it. It's an incredibly important part. I've seen others refer to it as "drinking your own champagne" and "eating your own cheese." But I'm a partner in a sausage-making company, so, maybe "eating your own salami." So dogfooding is an incredibly important part of what we do. But there's a bunch of dogfooding that happens without us. Keep in mind that Google is predominantly a consumer products company, a consumer services company.

Yourdon: Right.

Fried: And so in the realm of the consumer services that we offer, often it makes the most sense to have an un-intermediated conversation between the product management and engineering teams responsible for those services and people who work at Google who can evaluate them as individual consumers would. You know, one of the differences is … Microsoft has an incredibly large portion of its business devoted to serving enterprises, large and small, right? We have an important enterprise division. It's not as large a percentage of what Google does as it is at Microsoft and what they do.

Yourdon: Though it's growing rapidly.

Fried: Yeah, it is. It's growing tremendously; it is thriving. We all think it's an incredibly important part of what Google does, and where Google products are doing things that relate more to enterprise uses or organizational uses of technology, my organization is much more directly involved in dogfooding and providing feedback.

Yourdon: That would make sense.

Fried: And we also often get involved in looking at how we can come up with enterprise uses of consumer technologies, and we're willing to be fairly experimental in trying out dogfooding enterprise uses of technologies that we're aiming at a consumer audience. Because I believe this is one of the interesting opportunities and missions of my organization because of the company it's situated in. Because one of the macro factors that made me believe Google was an incredibly important company was the dominance of consumer IT over enterprise IT that's come about in the last 10, 15, 20 years.

I think everyone has observed or recognized that technologies often started out serving corporate purposes that had buying power and moving their way out to the consumer. I think that that's changed with the likes of Google and a few other providers, whereas now you have all this innovation and R&D going into consumer products that find their way into enterprise uses. And, honestly, a lot of what Google Enterprise does is take Google consumer offerings and make them viable inside an enterprise. And it's hugely successful for that. There are a lot of reasons why. You asked what are the great macro phenomena affecting technology.

Yourdon: Yeah.

Fried: I think that this is one of them. This is the one that I think is probably the most important. The rise of consumer-driven technology, consumer-driven computing, consumer-driven software-as-a-service offerings. I think that because there's this motion from consumer to enterprise, I'm very focused on having my organization be in the avant-garde of trying to understand where there are new enterprise uses for previously consumer offerings. As one example, we've spent a fair amount of time trying to take Google's consumer video chat product and turn it into corporate videoconferencing.

Yourdon: Okay.

Fried: And we now actually do that in partnership with the corporate videoconferencing group, the product group at Google who are doing that. But it's something we've been working on for a long time. It's one of these things that, if you think about it, seems quite obvious. So, you asked about dogfood, and I monologued on you for a long time.

Yourdon: Well, I see the distinction you're making between dogfooding of things that are either already in the enterprise or moving in that direction, as opposed to consumer products.

Fried: No, we do often find ourselves in the position of having to provide some amount of question and answering for people who are dogfooding consumer-oriented products, They may just walk up and say, "I don't understand why this isn't working," or "I can't do this," or whatever. And so you have to have support—this gets to the idea that there's so much technology entering the environment that's experimental, having support people who can react to that and learn on their feet is really, really important. I don't know how we would survive if we tried to move to script-based, outsourced, level-one kind of support.

Yourdon: That certainly makes me realize a question that I would not even know how to ask a lot of the other CIOs that I'm talking to. For me, one of the things that I found so intriguing about Google [is that] for a period of ten years or so ... every one of your products [was] a beta product.

Fried: Yeah.

Yourdon: And that you're proud of it. Now I think that's begun to change a little bit, but what that says, on so many different levels, is just mind-boggling, and I always thought that it was just a stark contrast from the old-fashioned IBM model ... or actually it was a German company that I remember. Ten, fifteen years ago, I was over there consulting for them about a software engineering tool. And I'll never forget a project manager who said, like the old TV commercial, "We ship no product before it's ready." And I said, "By the time you do, no one's going to care anymore." And he said, "I don't care." You know, it's this Teutonic kind of mindset.

Fried: Yeah, the precision engineering.

Yourdon: And you guys totally reversed that. Does that reflect an IT culture that is still a big part of Google?

Fried: I think you touch on that when you asked about agile. You have an interview question about agile methods.

Yourdon: Yes.

Fried: I had looked at that question as a great observation. ... [T]here's a document I believe called "Ten Things We Know to Be True"[1] trying to describe Google's core values, and one of them is the value of this idea of launch and iterate. That great products often become great through triangulation.

Fried: And those are my words, not, not the words of the authors. But this value of launching and iterating—releasing what you think is right, what you think is good, getting data... We have a deep, deep belief in being data-driven in our decision making, including decision making about even subtle features about applications. There's a story somewhere—and I'm sure this frustrated the user interface people to no end—that we actually did experiments to understand which color blue in an icon people responded to

---

[1] Google, "Our philosophy: Ten things we know to be true."
www.google.com/about/corporate/company/tenthings.html.

the best. And the UI designer probably was not happy [about] who thought this was an expression of their artistic creativity. But there was actually data that we could get about which color blue people clicked on more, or were responding to more, and that was how we made a decision to do that. And so this idea of being data-driven, of realizing that the world is changing, you can't be perfect, and you have to launch and change and change and change—and have an environment where you can do that—is absolutely core to us.

There's a very deep part of the understanding reflected in the question that you asked, which is that Google is predicated on the notion of software as a service, where we're running the software on servers that we control and we deploy it on a timeframe of our choosing—whereas all traditional technology companies are predicated on the idea of software that customers installed on their laptop, or on their personal computer, or in their own data center.

And the pain of doing software installation, doing upgrades, and the necessity of it, all the difficulties in it lead to a "better get it right" mentality. I don't think it's even consciousness so much, but I think it finds its way in the DNA and the muscle memory of organizations even if consciously they understand that it's a web world and even traditional downloaded, traditional shrink-wrapped software can be updated through Internet downloads. But there is this very deep industry muscle memory that comes from customer installation, whereas we don't have that. We've virtually never had that. We have a small number of things that people install on their computers, but even the products like Chrome that you do install are essentially designed to give you the always up-to-date model of software and service of the software you installed yourself.

Yourdon: That is true. Fascinating. Well, I'll have to give some more thought to that. I might come back to you with a follow-on question or two.

You had already started touching on a couple of things on my next major area: what are the significant new trends that are likely to influence Google and ultimately all of us over the next few years?

Fried: So … thank you for such good questions.

Yourdon: Any one of these could keep us going for quite some time.

Fried: So the technology trends that I see shaping the next few years. The one that was the most educational to me was understanding the domination of consumer-oriented technology over enterprise technology coupled with the enormous economies of scale only available to enormous software-as-a-service providers like Google. You know, these terms like the "cloud" have been hijacked by everyone. They can mean almost anything.

So the ... phenomena we've already talked about: the fact that personal expectations of technology and the role of technology [are] defined by people's expectations outside of the workplace, instead of people's experiences inside the workplace. I think that that's number one, and there are all kinds of interesting corollaries from that. And often you'll find the most advanced technology people encounter now is their home technology. The best computer they use is the computer they bought, not the computer that their work provided to them, as companies have had to do things like go from three-year depreciation cycles to four- and five-year depreciation cycles.

Yourdon: Right.

Fried: And personal computer equipment, more and more consumers would never stand for having a five-, four-, or even three-year-old computer.

But then the expectations extend to these free software-as-services, software as a service powered by ads and other mechanisms. Those offerings—like Gmail—could never be successful if you had to have an enormous customer support organization around them. So ... this is an interesting observation and this is what makes it such a powerful force in the enterprise, that traditional enterprise software is incredibly complicated and feature-rich because enterprises have asked for all those features, but the result of that is you can never separate yourself from an incredibly expensive support cycle around those things. Outlook is an incredibly complicated piece of software. It does many things that many, many enterprises have wanted for a long, long time. Microsoft is doing all the right things, it's being responsive to their customers' needs, they add features to it. But the net result is a piece of software of such enormous complexity that it's almost unimaginable that you would not need a support infrastructure for it. On the other hand, with Gmail, you don't really need it—many, many millions of people use Gmail on their own without any customer support, every day.

Yourdon: Right.

Fried: So that allows you to do something different. So part of the changing world of technology and the scale parts are just—without going into the numbers—because Google has so many computers and such large data centers, you can't get the pricing of computers and ... resources that we get if you're not of the size we are. It's just not the same, and I worked at a large Wall Street bank that had a lot of very advanced computing, and we got great pricing from our vendors, but we were not comparable to the kind of pricing that Google gets at all.

Yourdon: Well, the thing that you just said a moment ago, I've not heard yet from any other CIO. And I think I'm going to have to keep it quiet and see if they volunteer it.

In terms of the fundamental worldview change of free stuff: I'll tell you just a quick story because it's in the news right now. In 1992 I was in Cairo at a conference with my friend Tom DeMarco, and he and I turned out to be the only Americans there. Somehow I got into an argument with somebody who was saying, "Why doesn't Microsoft provide more support in Africa for its stuff?" And I, being the smartass that I am, said, "Well, if you guys weren't stealing so much software, maybe they would." And he said, "You don't understand. One copy of Microsoft Word is the annual salary of a university-educated person here, anywhere in Africa."

Fried: Yeah.

Yourdon: And he said, "How can you possibly think that we're going to pay full price for that?" And, of course, now, they've got Google apps.

Fried: I had a lot of "Aha" moments just like that over the last ten years prior to my joining Google. I had a very similar moment. It's fascinating you described that. Morgan Stanley was considering buying a company in China, and I don't have the precise numbers in my head, but consider these to be directionally correct. We looked at all the costs, the books and all that. We got a lot of pushback from the business development people trying to do the deal. It looked like the cost of one Morgan Stanley PC plus all the infrastructure required to support it was about equal to the average annual salary of the employees of this company, right? And that furthermore, if we wanted to take a Morgan Stanley front-line technology support person and move them, and put them there, then those costs, that person's salary and the cost of putting them there, were greater than the combined payroll of this entire sixtyish-person company.

Yourdon: [laughter]

Fried: And this is not in any way a commentary on Morgan Stanley having bloated costs. It didn't. It reflects exactly the phenomenon that you observed.

Yourdon: Yeah.

Fried: Meanwhile I saw the rise of, "Well, if I was doing this from scratch, I would just get an Internet connection or I would just get a computer that could connect to the Internet and then I wouldn't have to worry about having a private network and having to provision file servers and print servers and a whole personal computer software stack in the developing world." The thing that I thought was a great opportunity for this Google-like world we were in was that all of these companies trying to find new sources of revenue in the developing world, being faced with first-world cost structures. It struck me as this incredibly important impediment that was actually probably slowing down things like business development and revenue opportunities in the developing world.

What I really wanted to be able to do was have the technology offered and say, "All right, you want to open an oil exploration office in Kyrgyzstan," or "You want to try to do something in Ho Chi Minh City, right? You know, all we need for you to go out there and be successful is an Internet connection and some very basic personal technology and you can have everything you need: apps and telephony and videoconferencing and everything, but at reasonable costs." And allow companies, these first-world, cost-driven companies to actually be far more experimental on how they approach new markets, and I think they can be.

Yourdon: Well, in terms of the next few years, though… We kind of drifted off. Do you see just more of this phenomenon that we started experiencing in the last couple of years or any radical changes?

Fried: I think that these changes are a tidal force, but they have not yet had their full effect because there's been a tipping point that hasn't been reached due to what I believe to be generational demographics.

Yourdon: Really?

Fried: You still have enough decision makers in large enterprises who are—you know, either IT decision makers or the people above IT decision makers—who arose through the previous mindset, one of those "my vendors comes to me, I tell them what I want, they try very hard to sell to me, my wants go into their R&D, the money I pay them funds that R&D," right? I think that generationally you have people who grew up in that model: "I control everything that my people use. I build our data centers. I work with software vendors that do exactly what I tell them to do because I'm paying them and if I didn't pay them and the other people like me didn't pay them, they wouldn't do that."

Yourdon: Yeah.

Fried: And I think that generationally, there's a generation of decision makers, check writers, who are still of that mindset. But the world's changing around them, and I feel that the water's rising around them, and I feel that at some point either they will start to retire or there will be companies that are able to move to this new model and demonstrate competitive advantage that these other companies don't have that will cause a tipping point. It seems to me this is inevitable. I couldn't tell you exactly when, what it is that will cause the tipping point.

It's interesting—when I joined Google, I couldn't have predicted the emergence of Chrome OS, for example, but I think the idea of a personal computer that has no state on it, that you never have to worry about having viruses, that is always up to date, that you never have to worry about the data that enters and leaves your company as a result of its being on it, that is incredibly easy to support because it's just running a browser, and that is furthermore lower cost because not only is the hardware needed in it to run a browser really well, that's incredibly appealing to a CIO, right? It eliminates so many of the security concerns; it dramatically reduces support costs; it dramatically reduces equipment costs. Maybe that will be a tipping point. That will be one of these things I couldn't have predicted... that as a tipping point and people being attracted by that model will lead them to more rapidly embrace this pure web delivery, software-as-a-service model.

I don't really know. But I couldn't predict when it's going to happen, but I do still feel that these are tidal forces that will change our industry. It's just a matter of when. In the same way that the first Apple IIs entered industry to do real work, and came on a typewriter budget.

Yourdon: Yeah, exactly.

Fried: But at some point then it became IT's business to provide microcomputers, right? It will happen. I don't know when. But the fundamental truths of what's driving it are, are inescapable.

Yourdon: I also usually like to ask about what you think are the most significant landmarks looking back over the last five or ten years that have radically changed the way we do things. You know, I tend to think of Google itself.

Fried: Yeah.

Yourdon: Just the original Google search engine as an example, and the Internet and the Web, obviously—but are there any other not-so-obvious things that you can think of while you were growing up or in college, or the first five or ten years out of college?

Fried: I don't know if I have any new things to report that others won't have observed. The creation of the ARPANET, the creation of DARPA, without which we wouldn't have had the ARPANET, without which we wouldn't have had the NSFnet, without which we wouldn't have had the Internet, without which we wouldn't have had Google, right?

Yourdon: Yeah, that's true. That is a good point. No one has mentioned that, and that obviously is a social or human creation, that led to all this other stuff.

Fried: And there's this other unique—I'm a big fan of Steven Levy's book, *Hackers* [Doubleday, 1984].

Yourdon: Mm-hmm.

Fried: There was this unique point in time where our culture was created that we now see evidenced in Linux and open-source software—and in a dramatically lower cost to compute that comes from that. And as a result now people talk about open-source hardware as well, but this notion that people should be able—if you believe what Levy has in the book, it came out of this belief that computers should be open, that anyone should be able to use them and experiment with them and learn to program.

It strikes me as we're all kind of lucky. Everyone in the industry or affected by the industry is lucky that that ethos took hold there and installed the ability to create the Free Software Foundation. I think you can connect the dots there to open-source software, free software. The Free Software Foundation, open-source software, Linux, a whole bunch of things came from this interesting and unique place and time. Like I said, we're lucky. If things had been a little different, we might not have had that. Some of that is open funding, Cold War–driven open funding, large, large checks being paid to research universities to support computing, giving great access to people. It's interesting when we can see such good coming out of things like the Cold War. I think part of it is this ethos that emerged at MIT, some of which came from the fact that a lot of these people were originally model railroad hobbyists and…

Yourdon: TMRC, it was called. Tech Model Railroad Club.

Fried: Yeah. So, there have been these major junctures in the road, right? Timesharing, the personal computer, computer connectivity, inter-computer connectivity, Multics led to UNIX led to Linux—we're incredibly lucky that that happened. We're incredibly lucky that Steve Jobs visited PARC.

Yourdon: Mm-hmm. [laughter]

Fried: And, you know, they thought they were onto something there.

Yourdon: Now there's one last aspect of that, which occurred to me just a minute ago and I'd like your take on it. Arguably, one of the next steps along the way of from Multics to UNIX to Linux to whatever is epitomized by Wikipedia, is described by a couple of books that you've probably heard of. One is called *Cognitive Surplus*, by Clay Shirky [Penguin Press, 2010].

Fried: Clay—I found him fascinating.

Yourdon: There's apparently a new YouTube video, which I haven't seen yet, called "Minds for Sale," which talks about the next aspect of everything we've already discussed: we've got six billion people on this planet now with lots of available brain power that they're willing to contribute for good causes, whether it's Wikipedia or Linux or whatever. And we now have this incredible Internet infrastructure that supports it. Is Google tuned into that? I mean, you guys are making wonderful products, but are you trying to take advantage of that phenomenon?

Fried: I think it's easier for me to be a departmental spokesman than a company spokesman. We believe democratization of access is an incredibly important part of our mission. If you look at what we've done with Android, for example, in creating an open-source phone operating system, which will be the dominant computing tool of this next generation. To make them actually be phones that interact with the Internet really, really well; that are open; that people can collaborate with; that run really good software. So we really believe that we have a role to play there. We believe that the Internet is something that we need to do our part to get in and make better. I think that the belief that you expressed there about creating the opportunity for the world to collaborate with itself and for a community to find itself and for the cognitive surplus to be created—these are concepts that I believe in many ways are echoed fundamentally in other things that we do.

Yourdon: Hmm.

Fried: I never heard us state, "These are our explicit goals of Google as an organization," but I do see very similar principles in all of these things that we do, and so many of these things that we do right. I mean, making a great free web browser. Making a great free smartphone operating system. In general, we have a deep, deep belief in things like the power of the Internet for collaboration. And if you look at, the major metaphor change, the paradigm—after Thomas Kuhn[2] and all, I hate to use the "p" word—but I

---

[2] Note: Kuhn is the author of the book *The Structure of Scientific Revolutions* (University of Chicago Press, 1996).

think the paradigm change of our productivity applications, like Google apps, is that the first principle is that people *collaborate* on these things. It's not features. They're designed first around allowing people to work together—that documents whatever flavor are a product of collaboration. So it starts with making collaboration work.

Yourdon: That's a good point.

Fried: I'd say that I see those same values expressed in a different way. We believe that we have this incredibly significant enabling role in enabling responsibility.

Yourdon: Well, let me turn 180 degrees around now and ask about that "dark side," about the problems and concerns and issues that you see confronting us in the IT world and that keep you awake, if anything keeps you awake, at night as a CIO.

Fried: I have three small children, so they're keeping me awake.

Yourdon: [laughter]

Fried: But I'd say the first one for me is security. It's the downside of the interconnected world we live in. The opportunity for compromise, for attack, I think one of the metaphors for the second half of the 20th century and now for this 21st century, is that society trails technology. Society evolves slower and the conventions of society and its mechanisms evolve far slower than technology does across a broad landscape in technology.

Yourdon: Right.

Fried: And I think this is true in these areas related to information security, information warfare. These things are deeply concerning to me, because, the technology's evolved at such a rapid rate and these are powerful, powerful tools with a powerful, powerful ability to be misused, with many, many opportunities for attack. I'm really concerned about vulnerabilities and people's ability to take advantage of them. Yeah, security worries me. Google's security and the world's security worries me. One of the lessons I took away from the attacks on Google that were spoken of so much in January of 2010 was the power of organizations with significant resources at their disposal. The attack surfaces of the software and internetworks that we use today are broader than we could have imagined; that even very, very significant users can be vulnerable; that there are very, very, very sophisticated attackers out there.

I've always tried to stay abreast of the literature, but I've found attackers to be way more sophisticated than I had thought. And the general level of awareness in the industry in the broadest sense of the word—not just the technology, but industry's ability to recognize that this was taking place and respond to it was very far behind the state of the art of the attack. The state of the art of the defense and companies' abilities, organizations' abilities to respond was very far behind, very, very far behind. So, not much keeps me up at night. Not as much as it probably should keep me up at night, but I do find security to be one of these, these big things that we all need to spend time thinking about.

Yourdon: And, of course, every single CIO has said the same thing, in maybe slightly different ways. But I'm particularly interested given what you were saying earlier, that you are so influenced by the consumer level of use of technology and obviously consumers, generally speaking, are far less sophisticated about security issues than your typical big company.

Fried: Yeah, exactly. It's interesting. There's a whole set of technology offerings these days where "bring your own computer to work" is the part of the meme. And, one of my concerns about it is it makes security presumptions that are very much more backward-looking than forward-looking. Attacks that we know of in the past, really we think we can defend against, right? In the same way that we think that anti-virus is dead, we just don't want to actually announce that it's dead, right? But the traditional signature-based anti-virus is a technology that is just of minimal protection today.

I worry that's there's the same retrospective element of the security propositions made by these "bring your own computer to work" technology offerings. So I do have some concern that the end state of the domination of consumer-oriented technology is one that somehow makes enterprises vulnerable. Maybe not ours so much. We're very lucky in having the most impressive computer security organization I've ever encountered. And we're very, very lucky—we're certainly not invulnerable. We have many, many very, very deep and capable thinkers. So there is this set of concerns I have that one recognition of the dominance of consumer-oriented technology is let them bring their own technology to work, let them bring whatever they want—it could lead to a world of *less* security because we don't know what the set of attacks might actually be specifically against "bring your own computer to work" sorts of offerings. Honestly, we've only begun to explore the possibilities for evil of these enormous botnets.

Yourdon: Yeah.

Fried: I mean, the largest distributed computing environments in the world are these botnets. Wait till we get a few world-class distributed computing people and a few world-class malware hackers together in thinking about what they can do with hundreds of thousands or millions of interconnected machines and, uhh, eww. Scary.

Yourdon: It *is* scary.

Fried: Anyway, you can't let yourself be driven off by that. One has to develop a plan of action and follow it as opposed to just let these things dominate one's nightmares and one's dreams. But of the things that worry me, I'd say security is one, is definitely one of them. It's the one that's most industry-specific.

And there's a bunch of things that keep me up at night I'd say, or I spend a lot of time thinking about that. I think other CIOs probably do, too. You know, do I have the right kind of governance, the right mix of governance for my organization. Do we provide the right set of services for our customers? Are we engaging with them correctly? Those things definitely do sometimes keep me up at night. They're common concerns among the people with my title.

Yourdon: One of the other common concerns that I've heard from a lot of the CIOs is the following: They say, "Here I am, running the technology part of our business and I've got a whole bunch of business peers around me that are responsible for various products or various services, and they've risen to their position of authority because they're very good, obviously, but also because they have very strong personalities. And they feel that obviously they know how to run *their* business better than anybody else and, in fact, they even think that they know how to run *my* business in IT better than I do. And since my technology pervades everything they're doing, I find myself butting heads with these people quite a lot—either trying to persuade them to do something that I think they need to do, or trying to prevent them from doing something that I think would be a disaster. And, of course, I can't order them because I'm not their boss. So the problem or the concern is: how do I influence these other peers of mine about issues of technology that I probably do know more about, whether or not they believe me?"

Fried: Yeah, so, I think it's one of the great universals. If you want to talk about larger-than-life personalities, I think Wall Street probably has a disproportionate number of them.

Yourdon: [laughter]

Fried: And I did work in Wall Street for many years…

Yourdon: And that's where I first heard the concern…

Fried: Wall Street has this particular flavor of the problem as well, that you may have a profit-generating line of business that can just hire and [better pay] the people it wants to do the very, very specific sorts of things it wants.

Yourdon: Right.

Fried: There's the whole class of people called "quants," who are people with computing skills who sit next to traders and other people and make bets and kind of assist them in the technology to do that. And in fact, at hedge funds, typically those people may be the traders in a Wall Street bank, they might sit on the side. So anyway, that's one of these concerns that we had on Wall Street, but I think it's a universal. I think it's always been there. It's been there for a very long time. In one way or another it always will be there.

I do think that that problem is getting worse as a result of the rise in consumer technologies because at least 30 years ago, maybe IT was the first person to put a computer on your desk, whereas nowadays that's not the case. You go home and buy your own computer and have your own opinions about the stuff. So I think that those people are more empowered. I think that CIOs have a forward-looking problem, which is that this model of the software enterprise hardware R&D cycle that I'm participating in and deploying to my users is going to be rudely interrupted by the person whose opinions were all generated by modern technology. And it grows rapidly at the top and they didn't actually use any of the things I provided, right? You're not needed, and I didn't use you. You're not needed.

Yourdon: Arguably that's been going on since the introduction of the PC.

Fried: Yeah.

Yourdon: But not to the extent that it is now.

Fried: Exactly. And it's certainly with people buying Apple II+ on their typewriter budgets so they could run Visicalc, so they didn't have to rely on the overnight cycle of the mainframe to do the books. But it's gotten tons worse. The set of activities that people can perform without needing central IT offerings has grown. So it's one of the hardest parts of the CIO's job. On the other hand, here are my beliefs about it. There's always going to be some technology among your client organizations. It's a question of how much and what, and the number is never really going to be completely zero, and generally you shouldn't expect it to be. It's a question of how much technology they're going to want or have or control. You have to think about what's right for them as part of it. The other thing I think is that at least in the United States, in a post–Sarbanes-Oxley world, you look at the scandals of the last 12 years, you look at the regulations that have come up in the world, and enterprises are more regulated than they were before and that, literally mandates having more standards than would be maybe necessary, and so when CEOs and CFOs can go to jail because their attestation about the accuracy of the books and records of the company was incorrect, that has certain repercussions for what happens with technology. So, I think CIOs have overplayed that card, to tell you the truth.

Yourdon: Oh, okay.

Fried: But that said, it's a changing reality that does define certain hard limits to the parameters of what organizations can do on their own. And I think that the final piece of it is, the thing that is painful but good, is that it's far better to have technology offerings that win on their merits rather than are forced upon your users.

Yourdon: Good point. That is a good point.

Fried: Now, it's difficult in conversations about matters of security. At some point you may need to get the CEO or top corporate leadership involved in setting the parameters or frameworks around things like security, around protection of physical security, computer security, protection of intellectual property. Things like that you probably need to have corporate policies on that that need to be centralized in their enforcement. But in general, it's better that you woo and win your customers. It's probably better that way. The environment is harder for you to do that, to woo and win, than to be the sole provider. That's not to say that it's efficient or good to have multiple competing providers for the same set of things. But it's as they say, better to win in the marketplace of free ideas.

Yourdon: Okay, interesting. One last question in this area, and then I'm going to go on to the generational thing. This whole question that I had about agile development: since the CIO is usually the one that's in charge of developing new at least internal systems, this transition from a waterfall approach to an agile approach has initially been seen just as a methodology issue, but the more I see it, the more impact it seems to have on how you go about managing people and organizations. A lot of CIOs that I've spoken to say that that's been a problem for them. And, of course, everything you guys do, I suspect, has this overwritten thing of this agility on it, so maybe that's just part of your DNA.

Fried: I'd say it *is* part of the DNA. So, in general, it's the right thing to do, right? Especially for internal software, I think that it's much better to start off with the implicit assumption none of us really know what it is we need to do here, but let's do enough so that we can actually define based on evidence and feedback and data what it is that we need to build. Build a front, build a slice of the application front to back—does this solve the problem, is that what you wanted to do? You know, observe how it works and either change that piece until it does what you want or if it was right, then move on to the next piece. I think that it solves a huge number of problems for us, which is … like waiting for Godot, waiting for the software to appear, in the traditional waterfall model.

Yourdon: Mm-hmm.

Fried: And that's just not acceptable. I mean, business changes faster today than it did 30, 40, 50 years ago when this was considered to be state of the art, and we have to realize that with long, long delivery cycles, no one can actually assure you in most cases that the software at the end of that delivery cycle will need to do the things that it needed to do on the day you kicked the project off. So, it's absolutely necessary. That said, here are the things that are hard about it. On the one hand, there are large classes of users I experience who don't want to look at just a single front-to-back slice of something even if you're on a weekly release schedule and they can see another version of the thing, a week from Wednesday. There are a lot of people who are just more comfortable seeing the whole thing.

Yourdon: Mmm.

Fried: I think that in technology we've generally embraced and understood the advantages of this, but I think our users are catching up to it, especially being agile in the early parts of the development of an app, when you really don't have very much to show, but it's even more critical that you take those agile approaches. I think that that's part of it. I think that a more recent conclusion that I came to about agile methodologies is that it's easy for them to devolve into a rapid-release cycle that doesn't actually appear to change much. So there's a whole art in planning the scrum, in understanding what goes into the next release, and I'd say that it's very easy to embrace the philosophy and embrace the rapid release and all that comes with it, but if you don't also embrace the notion of focusing on what's going to change, rapid releases that don't seem to actually have any difference to your end user produce an interesting pathology that is obvious when you think about it, but you might not have expected when you went down this path.

Yourdon: You keep mentioning this point about getting real feedback with real metrics. So we're beginning to see agile projects in regulated industries with distributed project teams and all kinds of things where people had previously said, "Well, that will never fly."

Fried: "That will never happen."

Yourdon: And it is, it is.

Fried: That's really comforting. That's great to hear. I guess another pathology of agile—and an IT framework in particular, as opposed to a product framework—I think is your users can become kind of pixel-level negotiators.

Yourdon: Mm-hmm.

Fried: It doesn't actually work well if users are telling you what color to make radio buttons or "that needs to be left-adjusted not right." But it's all too easy for agile to enable that because you can make the turnaround so rapidly, so it's another pathology to avoid, that there has to be some kind of art to avoiding. I'm not a dilettante about any particular agile methodology so much as the overall results that you get. I also think I'm a big believer that enabling rapid releases produces a result in tooling and testing that ultimately leads to higher-quality results. In order to be able to release rapidly, with any quality at all, you probably have to embrace automated testing.

Yourdon: And regression testing and so on.

Fried: Exactly. Unit regression system testing, smoke testing—all these things have to happen as part of the release cycle. As a result, you get to a better state in terms of quality than you would without a significant investment otherwise.

Yourdon: So, let me go on to the generational issue. Is there anything else you would like to say about the good things or bad things of the whole generation of workforce, whether we call them digital natives or whatever, that are not just coming into your IT department, but they're coming into the entire workforce—with their toys and gadgets and their social media?

Fried: And with a different set of expectations. And they don't want work to give them a cell phone, right? Or work to give them a separate smartphone. And the technology is still catching up to that—catching up rapidly but still catching up. It's not just Google and the consumer landscape. It's other companies, too. Tablets are redefining people's expectations of what their personal technology's going to be. So I think you probably phrased the situation more articulately than I do. I think there's another generational concern that you hint at in your questions here. That is the decreasing number of computer science graduates.

Yourdon: Hmm.

Fried: It's a huge problem for us. And I think that academia has struggled with what the answer is, with what to do about it. You know, trying to make computer science more relevant to practice or specializing it, changing the curricula. I've never attempted to validate this, but one theory I've had for some time is that there was certainly a point where studying computer science was a way of getting access to technologies that were otherwise impossible to get access to.

Yourdon: Yeah.

Fried: And I think a number of people kind of entered the field—they were curious, they had heard about computers, they entered, they took a class because they were curious about it, and they got hooked, whereas today you don't need to take a class to get a deep exposure to computers. I met a surprising number of people who were great programmers, great software engineers, but who hadn't majored in computer science because, why would I? I can just go do that on my own. I don't really need that. I think that this generational change in access to computing may be also partially responsible for the difficulty in attracting people to the discipline.

Yourdon: Hmm. That's interesting.

Fried: And it's demystified it. And I think the mystique was, for some, part of the attraction. I think I was always interested in it, but one of my first jobs was working in the university computing center at Columbia and it was all about—that was the only place in the world where I knew there was an Imagen laser printer that I could possibly get access to—and getting access to a laser printer, too. Access to technology that was unavailable in any other way was one thing that drove me into, uhh, the discipline. And it's not needed anymore. But that's a very, very deep problem that we have because we need a lot more computer programmers than we're producing.

Yourdon: Well, there's a variation on this: the superficiality and glibness of the current generation with regard to technology. Of course, you have access to whatever you want on the Internet, but it's something I've noticed having written a whole bunch of books: nobody wants to read a book anymore. Nobody wants to spend more than ten minutes focusing intellectually on anything. Nicholas Kristof wrote something saying that in today's world you could never read *War and Peace* because who's got time for a 1200-page book, whether it's a novel or a computer science book?

Fried: Yeah.

Yourdon: Who's going to read Donald Knuth's four volumes?

Fried: Yeah, I just got the new one, the 4A just came out, right? So, that's interesting. There had been this period of time when many of us had thought or hoped that the prevalence of e-mail would lead to a second great, generation of letters, of people of letters. But of course, what happened instead was instant messaging and tweets and so on—more and more sharding of one's attention. I think it's a trend that technology's created. On the other hand, I was incredibly skeptical of e-books. I didn't want others recording in their logs what I was reading, and I liked the idea that books represent the cash of ideas.

Yourdon: Hmm.

Fried: Right? They are—cash, not cache, right? Books are liquid, they are untraceable, and they represent the ability for people to transfer and share ideas and thoughts, and they have all these properties that cash has and is this great and enabling thing. So on a personal level I was very suspicious of e-readers, because it seemed to violate these cash-like principles that I thought were important to books. But then, I got an iPad, and the convenience—I just read more, I actually read more books, and not all small books, you know? But I read a lot more after I got that than I ever had before.

Yourdon: Hmm. Interesting.

Fried: And so I have some hope. I have some hope that I didn't have before. And I see it, not just in me, but my son is six and, you know, highly digitally enabled, enough to make us all kind of uncomfortable.

Yourdon: Hmm! [laughter]

Fried: He just goes and starts reading books on the iPad or Google books on my iPhone—we'll be in a restaurant or something and he'll be bored and he'll read Google books on my phone. He just read a book called *I Am Number Four* [by Pittacus Lore (Harper, 2010)]. It's a book aimed at teens. He read it all, on his own, over the course of several weeks. He found it on my phone with the little screen here and he read it, the whole book!

Yourdon: That's amazing.

Fried: You know, interspersed with many other things. It definitely sharded his attention, but like that gives me hope. And he knows how to find other books in the Google Books apps and download the free ones and ask me if

I'll type in my password so he can download a paid one, and I think he reads more than he would otherwise.

Yourdon: There's a collaboration aspect to that that just terrified me when I saw it on my Kindle. You're reading along in the book and all of a sudden you see this thing saying, "Ten other people thought that this phrase was really significant." And I thought, "Well, I don't care what they thought." I'm not sure that's a good thing, but it's obviously, it's a part of the process.

Fried: Yeah, it's a—I have a friend who's responsible for the whole digital books thing at Amazon, and I should talk to him about it, because some of these things are distracting. Get a dictionary, right? So double-click on a word and you get a definition.

Yourdon: That part's good.

Fried: Like for my son, he's in first grade—who knows how much of the book he read he was able to figure out on his own, or he wasn't able to figure out on his own? Things like that are, are game-changers. I wonder what the Folger Library editions of Shakespeare are going to look like in this digital era, right?

Yourdon: [laughter]

Fried: You know, you won't have the facing page with the kind of "this is what they mean." You can just kind of integrate it. And the e-reader can integrate it into the text in new ways that are probably less intrusive.

Yourdon: Let me ask you just one last question, and it's the obvious kind of final question: where do you go from here, you know? Or if you have any plans or dreams or thoughts?

Fried: No, no plans or dreams. My last job I thought was a great job and could have been the last job I ever had. And then they called me here and I thought this was an amazing thing that I wanted to try, the only CIO gig I'd ever heard of that sounded appealing to me. So I don't know…

Yourdon: Well, that's fair enough. You know, when I interviewed the CIO from Detroit [DTE] Energy last week, she said she had never gone looking for things, but opportunities always presented themselves, and so she had no idea what the next opportunity would be, but she had an existence proof that there would be one, at some point.

Fried: I'm sure those things will emerge. By personality, I'm someone who tends to spend a lot of time thinking about how to make things better. So I always tend to think that there's more opportunity than what I've been doing, and it's been good for my career. It's worked out, right, so, we'll see.

I don't have an aspiration to politics or anything like that. Google is a unique company at a unique point in its history at a unique place in time, and I'm thrilled to be … here in that place in that time.

Yourdon: Well, you're very much at the crest of the tidal wave, so, you know, you might as well stay on top as long as you can. It makes sense.

Fried: It's pretty all-consuming.

Yourdon: I can imagine. Well, thank you. Listen, I really appreciate your time.

Tony Scott

CIO, Microsoft

Tony Scott *joined the Microsoft Corporation in February 2008 as Corporate Vice President and Chief Information Officer. Under Scott's leadership, Microsoft IT is responsible for security, infrastructure, messaging, and business applications for all of Microsoft, including support of the product groups, the corporate business groups, and the global sales and marketing organization. Scott champions IT as a value-added business for Microsoft and works with all the company's groups to identify opportunities, structure IT solutions, and deliver measurable returns to the business. Scott is also the executive sponsor for Microsoft's Operational Enterprise Risk Management efforts and supports the integration of management principles from the Quality & Business Excellence team, which drive continuous and breakthrough process improvements across the company.*

Before joining Microsoft, Scott was the Senior Vice President and Chief Information Officer for The Walt Disney Company, where he led planning, implementation, and operations of Disney IT systems and infrastructure across the company. He also held the position of Chief Technology Officer, Information Systems and Services, at General Motors (GM, where he was responsible for defining the information technology computing and telecommunications strategy, architecture, and standards across all of GM's businesses globally). Previously, he was Vice President of Information Services at Bristol-Myers Squibb, and his professional experience has also included assignments at Marriott International Inc., Cadre Systems LLC, Sun Microsystems Inc., and PricewaterhouseCoopers.

Ed Yourdon: Let me just ask the basic questions about how you got started in the field after college. Did you start right off in IT or did you start through another path?

Tony Scott: I graduated high school in 1970, and there was a belief at that point that because of advances in technology that somehow the work week was going to be significantly reduced.

Yourdon: Ha-ha.

Scott: And that what we would all struggle with was going to be how we were going to use our leisure time, you know, that we were all going to have this abundant amount of time on our hands. So that's the career I started off in. It was called Parks and Recreation Administration. The discipline was called Leisure Studies and it was going to help us figure out how to use all of our spare time.

Yourdon: Did you have any role models or heroes that you were sort of looking to as you went through this early stage?

Scott: I worked in the field and actually did a lot of leadership training, because part of the Parks and Recreation core discipline was all around developing leaders and people who could lead activities, in the spirit of "what are we going to do with all our free time?" And so in that discipline I had a number of role models. One was a guy named Rick Bunch, who was actually the first guy who got me to come work for him in that field.

Yourdon: Well the obvious next question for me is to ask you then is how you got from that kind of start into the computer field and into IT?

Scott: Well, what happened was after two years, I figured out that this was pretty much not going to happen. If anything, the result of all this technology is that people are not likely to reduce their work week; they are likely to just take on more work. That was my conclusion, so I changed fields kind of by accident.

I had moved, by this point, from the University of Illinois in Champaign to Silicon Valley. And I began to work in Silicon Valley—still working for the Parks and Recreation Department, but I began to see and meet people in technology. People who work for HP, people who worked for some of the chip companies, Texas Instruments, and various others. So my general awareness of technology started to ramp up pretty significantly. And finally the critical event was that I decided to get married and my wife-to-be also worked in the Parks and Recreation Department. They had a rule that they didn't allow two people that were married to work in the same department, so it meant that one of us had to find another job. So I ended up taking a job with Marriott ... which was opening a theme park called Marriott's Great America in Santa Clara, California, in 1976.

Yourdon: Oh, I've been there. We may have been there at the same time. I was doing work at Amdahl at that point.

Scott: I was on the team that opened that park in 1976. The area I was in charge of was Games and Arcades. It was all electronic pinball machines and arcade games, you know Pong, and all the racing games and Atari was one of the big suppliers. You'll probably remember all this.

Yourdon: Yes, absolutely.

Scott: Well, it turns out that the theme park industry had a couple of pretty big problems to solve in terms of managing its business. One was that these are very labor intensive businesses and a reliance on part-time labor, much like a McDonald's for its restaurants, its retail stores, its games and arcades, its rides. You need labor to run all these things. And the amount of labor you need is highly dependent on how many people are going to show up to the park on a given day.

Yourdon: Right.

Scott: And also the time of day they are going to show up. And your profitability is highly dependent on whether you correctly forecasted your labor needs on that given day. So right around early '78, as I had gotten a year or two of experience under my belt in this business, I got put into another position, which was to do planning and forecasting for the business. And I discovered a little company called Apple Computer. They had an Apple II+ computer, and it could be programmed in BASIC and Pascal and all kinds of things.

I thought, hmm, I wonder if we could write software to do attendance forecasting and help with planning. And as a benchmark I bought a time share service from Computer Sciences Corporation [(CSC)], which was selling labor modeling software to toll roads and telephone companies and other entities who had similar kinds of problems that needed to be able to accurately forecast the amount of labor they were going to need based on external forecasts and projections, and so on.

So I got the CSC terminal and understood how their particular software worked, and we began to develop sophisticated computer models with CSC to help us better forecast the labor and attendance, and in parallel to developing, writing software actually on the Apple II to do the same thing. And within about three or four months, discovered we were beating the pants off of the CSC program on a pretty regular basis in terms of doing a better job and so on.

I didn't do this by myself. I had some people from the IT department. They were better at programming, and I was better at sort of figuring out the math behind some of the stuff. But anyhow, I taught myself to program. They would write the basic program and I would tweak it, you know, and put in some of the math models and all that sort of stuff. To the point where we bought a whole bunch of Apple II computers and a Corvus disk drive and started using the Apples for lots of things. Um, created a bunch of different databases, and we just got hooked. And so everything just sort of took off from there.

Eventually I went to work for Sun Microsystems, finished my degree, finished college at the University of San Francisco in information systems management, and went to law school at Santa Clara University while I was at Sun. Then I worked for Pricewaterhouse, and Bristol Myers, and General Motors, and Disney and then here. But it all started with the need to solve some attendance, forecasting, modeling, and labor scheduling kinds of problems that were real business problems that I was confronted with.

Scott: That is the long story.

Yourdon: Yes, but it's a fascinating one, and interesting for me. Like I said, I was in the same area at about the same time, and had Apple II computers for my own kids. Well, at the end of your story, you're here now obviously at Microsoft.

What you do as a CIO at Microsoft. What duties and activities that the job entails—is there some way you can summarize what your key responsibilities are as CIO at Microsoft?

Scott: Sure, I divide it into three big buckets. In the middle it is the sort of the same thing any CIO at any large company would do. We have any number of internal systems that we run the business on, and so in our case that includes sales and marketing systems, financial systems—we have probably the same collection of systems and software that any other CIO at any other company would have. We have payroll, you know, blah, blah, blah.

Yourdon: Sure.

Scott: And in that sense, I wear about the same hat and shoes and everything else and have the same concerns and issues as any other CIO. What makes this job different are two other pieces. On the left-hand side, we work very closely with our product groups, and it starts with defining what the product is going to be in the first place, all the way through.

Once we are into the development process, IT supports a lot of the product tooling the product team uses to make the product. So code source repositories, code signing technology, all kinds of things to help build the product and quality check and that kind of stuff all sits in IT at Microsoft. And then we also play an important role which is: once a product is in its early stages of development and is complete enough to start deployment, we start deploying it internally at Microsoft in small quantities initially—and then as the product matures and gets closer and closer to its release date, we have typically broadly deployed it inside Microsoft. It even has its own name: we call it "dogfooding."

Yourdon: Oh, yeah. That phrase has been around for a long time.

Scott: And so we are the number one filer of bug-fix requests and enhancement requests and so on, more than all the rest of Microsoft customers combined because of that important role. But we are also one of the groups that signs off and says that the product is ready to ship, so it is a little bit of an usual role for an IT organization, and particularly one we take seriously. So that kind of on the left side of the main role ... is pretty classical.

On the right-hand side, I also spend—and my teams spend—a fair amount of time with our customers. Virtually every customer who comes to visit, to do an executive briefing, or whatever, wants to know how Microsoft does IT. It really is: "how do you use the products for Microsoft, how do you integrate them together, what lessons have you learned with whatever the latest is?"

Clearly that is one of the focuses of the dialogue with customers, but they are also very interested in how we do governance, our IT lifecycle management process, how we're organized, our internal metrics of success, things like that. We aspire to be a trusted advisor on how to do IT and the question I proposed not only to myself, but to my organization—we aspire to be the world-class benchmark for IT, and we ask ourselves every day: if not us, who would it be? And if not here, where else could any IT organization aspire to be that? And if not now, when? You know, that kind of thing. We seek that role, we practice it every day, and we get a lot of very positive feedback from customers in terms of the value they get out of that dialogue.

Yourdon: You know 30 years ago, it would have been IBM's role to do that sort of thing. Do you think that what you described represents kind of a technology shift that everybody assumes that they will be using Microsoft products and the distributed kinds of computing tools rather than main frames today?

Scott: I think that's one of the elements of it. Certainly Microsoft has a breadth of products that probably no other tech company has today.

Yourdon: That is a good point, yes.

Scott: And it is a leader in several of the areas in terms of where people want to go—whether it is cloud or whether it is mobile or any of those kinds of things. We're in the game in a whole bunch of different spaces that not many other companies are. So I think that's one element of it. And our sweet spot is certainly central to where most IT organizations are, and I think that's a part of it as well.

Yourdon: I've obviously been following many of the things that Microsoft has been doing in the marketplace, and I would imagine you can just give me a general answer on a lot of these topical issues, like cloud computing and so on, you've got or Microsoft has got white papers or position papers. Do those tend to come from your group or are they influenced by your group?

Scott: Well, it is really collaboration. Just like the dogfooding and things I was describing earlier. For example, cloud computing group, we have played a key role in helping shape the product from an architecture perspective and from the perspective of, "here is what CIOs are going to look for in terms of capability, and manageability, and how they think about the business case for the cloud and so on." We have been one of the major contributors to that whole discussion for sure.

Yourdon: Ok, well that is very interesting. Maybe one last thing. One of the things I am quite interested in myself is the generational issue. How is the up and coming generation of kids coming out of college viewing IT and technology, as opposed to my generation or yours?

Scott: We do think that relevance to Gen whatever-it-is—the millennials, or whatever you want to call them today—is something that is certainly relevant. So we do a lot of work with customers in terms of our own models around that.

Yourdon: One of the big topics obviously is social computing. How do you think about that? And should you think about that as a CIO?

Scott: We have a really good model that we use that essentially evaluates anything like that along two different vectors. One is value and one is risk. And depending on where you fall in that matrix, you can either embrace it, ignore it, manage it, or exploit it—those are the four different ways we think about it in that space and each of those strategies would have a certain set of characteristics and an external company might choose to put a specific technology in a different place in the matrix, which is fine.

But what we have given them is a model to say here is how you can think about this stuff, and you can make your own judgment call based on your company profile and your regulatory environment, and so on, which bucket you will put things in. And it is leadership like that that we think is a role we can play in terms of helping develop useful models and frameworks for the industry.

Yourdon: I've got a bunch of questions that I can't avoid asking because I'm sure everyone will want to know—and that is the question of whether Bill Gates or Steve Ballmer hired you or promoted you into your position, or whether you have any other tidbits, you know, about them that you want to talk about.

Scott: Well, I actually worked for Kevin Turner, who was our Chief Operating Officer at Microsoft, but Steve was a part of the interview process, and I'd actually worked with Bill on a number of different things even before coming to Microsoft—so it's probably the only job where I've gone into the job knowing the senior executives and the company reasonably well before coming to take the job. All the other times, it's pretty much an interview and then a surprise as to who the execs are and all that stuff.

Yourdon: Well, being interviewed by the COO is a good enough big name for anyone, I'm sure. Was there anything else unusual about the interview that got you into Microsoft?

Scott: Well, when I interviewed with Steve three years ago, the obvious question is, how do you see the future? I still have the little piece of paper that Steve sketched out where the company was going from a cloud perspective and phone and all that sort of stuff—so I have to say, it was pretty impressive. And I was impressed at the time with the plans, and I've been impressed with the investment and the subsequent realization of the vision that Steve laid out a couple of years ago.

Yourdon: Very impressive. Well, that leads to a related question. If you had one piece of advice that you could give to aspiring CIOs, whether it was somebody who was dreaming one day of being the CIO of Microsoft or possibly the CIO of any other organization, what would that one piece of advice be?

Scott: Well, it's probably the lesson I've learned over and over and over again—which is, nothing is ever as good as it seems to be or as bad as it seems to be. Every time as I've gone into the role, I heard about all the things that are broken and all of the things that are going well, and there's usually a little exaggeration on both sides, in terms of how bad it is or how good it is.

Yourdon: Well, that's certainly interesting advice. Another related thing—and these are little segués in a sense—I've now talked to maybe a half a dozen CIOs, and one thing I've heard in common from almost all of them is the importance of the team that they've assembled to just help them get through the day. I'm curious as to what kind of key qualities you look for in someone who's going to become a member of your team that you work with on almost a day-to-day basis.

Scott: Sure. I think there's three in particular that I look for. One is just pure leadership capability. These are big, complex, challenging, physical organizations that we're managing, and to do that well, you need a lot of leadership capability. You have to have somebody who enjoys that role and who sees as a core part of their being developing other leaders in the organization. So leadership is probably the number one thing that I look for.

Two, I think you need to be technically astute and competent, especially if you're working in a technology company like Microsoft. There's a whole set of things that we do every day where technology does make a difference, and being technology-literate and making the right choices is fundamental to what we do. And these are big architectural decisions that we end up making, and so that skill is pretty important. And probably the third one that I look for is just basic integrity in terms of not only telling the truth, but representing the truth and dealing with people and situations in a very honest, transparent, straightforward sort of way. People that can uphold our values and represent them well, so that integrity factor is critical in all of our leadership roles, if not in life, then certainly in leadership roles people play.

Yourdon: I heard a variation on that yesterday from a CIO whom I interviewed who said one of her key things is that everyone on her team, has each other's back, so to speak. They realize that they all have to succeed, and so rather than the competitive backstabbing that you might allow or even be expecting in some situations, her team won't let any other member of the team fail if they get into trouble or get overloaded. And I guess you could argue that's one aspect of integrity.

Scott: Well, I think it's also part of leadership.

Yourdon: Yeah, good point.

Scott: Part of what I look for there is an element of that, where we all have to work closely together to succeed, and it's not even about our team winning . . . especially at Microsoft. It's about Microsoft winning, but also enabling people in the world to reach their potential, to paraphrase our mission—and that's a fairly lofty thing for us to shoot for, but we all carry that weight. You know, at Microsoft in particular, if we all don't do our jobs well, we're hindering the world from reaching its full potential in a certain way, so we have to shoot for a pretty high goal, I think, and that usually means more than just individuals winning. It means a broader purpose.

Yourdon: Ahh, good point. Are you guys helping out in Egypt at this point? Maybe that's a little off target, but, boy, that's amazing watching. I'm sure you and everybody else are just glued to the television to see what's going to happen there.

Scott: Yeah, it's pretty incredible. Well, I think what you'll see when all the dust settles, what we've seen over and over and over again is, our Microsoft team is in there as quickly as possible helping rebuild and re-establish the necessary infrastructure for a country or a region to function. So whether it's an oil crisis or tsunami or floods or snowfall or earthquakes, Microsoft always responds and is there to help rebuild, at the earliest possible opportunity.

Yourdon: You know, I hadn't thought of that, but I now recall seeing a similar thing from the CIO of FedEx and the CIO of Delta Airlines about what they had to do immediately after—well, not even after, but in the midst of—Katrina, and basically, any high-technology company these days is going to need to and want to step in to help out with whatever rebuilding of whatever infrastructure they're involved with given a natural or political disaster. So, I guess that's something that every CIO has to be prepared for. If you turn on the news and see that all hell's breaking loose in some part of the world you never cared about, it may still have a huge impact on what you have to do tomorrow morning.

Scott: Sure, exactly.

Yourdon: That's very interesting. Okay, another very interesting question. I'm sure you and every CIO I've spoken to ends up having to interact with a lot of very strong-willed peers who may not be in your empire itself, so to speak, but literally peers in other business units—or, in your case, product groups. They think they know how to use IT. They not only know how to do their job, they probably think they know how to do *your* job better than you do, and you can't boss them around, because they don't report to you.

How do you go about influencing these people and get them to do what you think is right and to avoid doing what you think is wrong?

Scott: Well, I use a principle I learned many, many, many years ago when I was a playground leader. And I was taught this by another playground leader. If you're leading kids' activities on the playground, there's always some kid hanging on the sideline. Maybe he's a bully or maybe he just wants to tease or be disruptive or whatever. And the technique that I was taught was put him to work, make him a solution rather than a part of the problem. And I've followed that principle throughout my career, and so if you have somebody who's strong-willed or has a strong opinion, first of all, they might be right and you have to consider that possibility.

Yourdon: Sure, yeah.

Scott: But second of all, put them to work and get them engaged and make sure they're a part of the solution. And so what I've found is that one of two things happen. Either they get engaged and contribute, or they shut up very quickly and run the other way, and one of the two doesn't happen.

Yourdon: Of course, one thing that's different about your peers and which you would also find in other computer companies or high-tech companies, but which I don't see in some of the other places, is that your peers in the product groups or business groups, are presumably all extremely proficient with technology. It's not just that they're stock traders or automobile designers. Obviously, all of these people know a hell of a lot about IT, so that you're in even less of a position to boss them around and tell them that you're the only person who knows the complexity of what you're dealing with. So that's a very good strategy to deal with, you know, kind of get them involved with you.

Scott: Well, yeah, it turns out that with our product group, they can be as opinionated as anybody. It's usually about somebody else's product, though. They usually think that their product is great and everybody else's has got a problem— but again, the same strategy: put them to work. We actually have a significant number of people who are not technology-literate. They're in traditional business functions like finance or HR or whatever it happens to be. And they just want something that works for them. They're not as enamored by the new feature or the new capability, maybe as somebody with a more technical background, so part of our challenge as we're developing applications or creating user experiences is to satisfy both the technical and the nontechnical in terms of what we do and how we do it and the services that we offer. That's part of the fun at Microsoft.

Yourdon: Now, there's an aspect to this that I had expected to hear more about and that is the situation where these peers and their respective business units are able to get their hands on technology by themselves because it's so cheap and so pervasive. The PC version of that 25 years ago was just going down to Radio Shack to buy something. And these days, they can just download an app for their Android or iPhone or whatever, and start using technology that you're not even aware is in the office, until it gets big enough to be noticed. Is that kind of a problem area that you run into a lot?

Scott: No, we don't think of it as a problem, really. What we have is a model that we use to figure out how we think about any given application and it basically is a matrix that results from on one side, the threat or the risk associated with that application, if any, and on the other part of the matrix, the business benefit from that application. And the result is four quadrants that either allows you to say, "We have to contain this. We have to embrace it or we should embrace it. We should allow it and not mess with it at all—it just exists. Or we should ban it, and effectively block it."

And so there are some things where's there no business value and a high business risk either in the form of viruses or some sort of threat, IT threat or whatever, that we just block. But there are many others, like a lot of the social network capabilities, the better ones, where we say, "Not only are we going to embrace it, but we are going to fully utilize it for the business benefits that it can bring." So everything falls in the matrix somewhere and every company can make its own judgment on any given thing about which part of the matrix it falls in. But we use that framework really to evaluate things and then put in place either the appropriate measures or not, as the case may be.

Yourdon: Well, that certainly makes sense. The aspect of this that I've heard from most of the other CIOs that makes eminently good sense is that somebody might bring a new toy, a new gadget, a new smartphone into the office without your knowing it, but sooner or later—and it's usually sooner these days—they want to access your data, and they want to connect to your infrastructure. And that's something you've got control over and you're very concerned in terms of risk—obviously security and privacy, and so forth—so they can't get very far, so to speak, without running up against your protection or evaluation matrix that you've put in place. So I guess maybe I was over-worried about that one.

But why don't I move on then to the next obvious question: what are the main problems and concerns and issues that you worry about that keep you awake at night? I assume security is at the top of the list, but are there any others as well?

Scott: It is. I mean, Microsoft is one of the most attacked companies on the planet in terms of every hacker trying to earn his merit badge seeing if he can get in, so out of necessity we had to try to be at least very good at the security thing. So, while you always worry about that every single day, on a daily basis we don't end up having much issue in that particular space.

I suppose one of the things I think about a lot is what I'll call "macro-architectural threats," and let me explain what that is. Over the years, the quality of the components that we build things out of has just gone up and up and up. And you see it across the landscape. Cars are better. The quality of everything we buy and use has just gotten better and better and better over the years as the broader quality movement has taken hold. And so, it's not very common anymore that you see product failure in the same way that we used to see it, maybe a few years ago. Or defects show up in a particular product, because most manufacturers—whether it's Microsoft or hardware people or whatever—have gotten pretty sophisticated at building a quality product or component. Where the new opportunity is in the architecture that is built up from all of the pieces. So it's still possible, for example, to build something, a solution for an end user that, while the components are all of high quality, the way they're put together may be vulnerable or may have some architectural flaw in the way it's created. And because of the complexity of many of these things today, it's hard to actually see these architectural flaws. We've seen examples of this in the nation's electric grid.

Yourdon: Right.

Scott: Where in some cases accidents happen because of some unanticipated event that exploits an architectural flaw that was latent in the system. The Internet is a Petri dish, I think, in some respects for some of these architectural failures to not only happen, but also the magnitude of them could be enormous at some point as we build up solutions and capabilities out of all the components that exist. And I don't say that in a way that should be interpreted as we shouldn't use the Internet or it's dangerous, but I think we have to be prepared for some of these bigger failures to occur, and we will recover from them relatively quickly, but they will occur, like the stock market crash.

Yourdon: Oh, the "flash crash" last year?

Scott: We keep having these long, deep depressions that once were the case, but we're still having these events, and I think of threats that we may face in the technology space in much the same way. They will happen, we will recover reasonably quickly, but they might be rather prolific in terms of their impact.

Yourdon: I can certainly tell you that the Defense Department and various other government agencies spend a lot of time worrying about that, simply because there are people who are trying to deliberately exploit these things as opposed to accidental architectural defects.

Interestingly, one of the ways that I earn a living is working as an expert witness for lawyers, trying to figure out whose fault it is when some huge system doesn't work. And it often has to do with these architectural problems between vendors. So, the Microsoft product is fine, and the XYZ product is fine, but there's something about the architectural interface that can either be exploited or has some limitation that nobody ever thought about. I don't think that problem is going to go away in the short term, and, indeed, if anything, it may get worse. So that's a good one to bring up, because I think that's probably something that every CIO is either already worrying about or really ought to be.

Scott: I totally agree.

Yourdon: Because if nothing else, all these CIOs are usually the final stage of approval and endorsing some of these huge architectural complexes involving vendor software. So they're the ones who are going to get the blame if it does all come crashing down on their heads. Okay, let me just ask a couple final questions. These were prompted by some of the things you said in our first conversation. You had told me about how your IT department works with several of the product groups when a new product is being developed. And I'm curious to know whether your IT group takes a proactive role in terms of interactions with other departments, or do you wait for them to come to you to start talking about new stuff that they've started doing?

Scott: No, we're very proactive, actually, so as each product cycle begins, we're in the early stages of the design—putting our two cents in in terms of what features it needs, what capabilities it needs, how it should work, all those kinds of things, and we follow that all the way through the whole life cycle, including upgrades and subsequent patches that may occur. So we live with the product groups through the entire life cycle, and we have a very active program that measures the health of that product relationship.

Yourdon: And, and I would assume that might even start with the kind of early exploratory prototyping?

Scott: Oh yeah, absolutely.

Yourdon: Well, I think that's a good thing for people to know about, that these products don't just sort of spring out of the Microsoft firewall without a lot of internal stuff going on with you guys.

Okay. Well, I could go on all afternoon, but I'm sure you've got a long list of things to do, people waiting outside your door at this point, so I should wrap things up.

Scott: All right. Thank you.

Yourdon: Well, thank you. I really appreciate it again, and good luck with everything else.

CHAPTER 2

Monte Ford

Senior Vice President and CIO, American Airlines, Inc./AMR Corporation

Monte Ford is Senior Vice President and Chief Information Officer at American Airlines and its parent company, AMR Corp. He oversees all aspects of the company's information technology strategy and operations. Widely regarded as a leader in the field of information technology, Ford joined American Airlines at a time when the airline needed to regain its technological prowess. Ford's leadership has been critical in restoring American to the forefront of technological innovation—one key element to the long-term success of one of the world's largest airlines.

Prior to joining American Airlines, Ford held senior management positions at The Associates First Capital Corporation and the Bank of Boston. Mr. Ford has served on the boards of two public corporations and is currently on the board of directors at Oncor, one of the United States' leading energy transmission and distribution companies. He is also a member of The Research Board, an international think tank restricted to CIOs of the world's largest corporations, and the CIO Strategy Exchange (CIOSE), a selective multi-sponsor program for chief information officers from "forward-looking" companies. He is active in community programs, church leadership, the Baylor-Grapevine Board of Trustees, and the Dallas Children's Medical

Center Development Board. Ford has a long history of community involvement in both Dallas and Boston.

Ed Yourdon: One of the questions that I've asked everybody at the very beginning, particularly because I know there are lots of young IT professionals who dream and hope that someday they're going to end up in your position, ... is basically [about] how you got to where you are now. Is this your first CIO position? Or have you kind of come up through the ranks of technology to end up where you are now?

Monte Ford: I started on the vendor side or the supplier side of the business, working for supplier companies, like Digital Equipment and IBM.

Yourdon: Oh? That's unique amongst the people I've spoken to so far. I started with DEC[1] also, by the way.

Ford: I thought that was a fantastic company, but I ended up being hired by my customer in Boston at DEC, and took an executive position with the customer organization. I was about to take a different job at Digital, a more senior job at Digital, and I went to tell my customer, and he asked me to come work for them.

Yourdon: Oh.

Ford: Which I did. I went to work for them and became a customer of Digital Equipment and IBM and other companies at the time and then continued on along the technology track from there. So I came into this side of the industry reporting to a COO that also was a CIO and moved from there to take a job in Texas ...with the intent of being the CIO at that company, which I did [become]. And then I moved from there to being CIO at American. By the way, I did have marketing and technical jobs when I was at DEC as well.

Yourdon: Ahh, okay. By contrast, I was always in the techie department. I worked at the old [Maynard, Massachusetts] mill, originally on

---

[1] Digital Equipment Corporation, a vendor of computer systems, software, and peripherals that merged with Hewlett Packard in 2002.

the PDP-5[2] and then on the PDP-6[3], in the early days. But it was quite a place to work. [laughter] That's for sure.

Ford: Sure was.

Yourdon: Anyway, the question that I was about to ask was whether you had any important mentors or role models along the way.

Ford: I have had mentors and role models along the way. In both sales and marketing and in technology, I have had mentors and role models and people—I continue to have mentors and role models and people that provide me the opportunity to grow and develop in what is always a mutual relationship. At least I try to make sure that every relationship I have is mutually beneficial, but I have had them along the way, inside the professional range and out.

And I know this book is about technology, but as an African-American in this industry, this business, I've had the opportunity to have role models that counsel me on how to function within the technology world, as well as people that counsel me on what to do about technology. Technology is really the culmination of a set of common-sense functionality, if you will, to me, that is applied to solving business problems and business needs based on circumstance. The technology business, though, is as much about people as it is about technology, maybe more about people than it is about technology. So my focus, and the role models that I've had, and my focus over the years has always been on the people, and a lot less so on the technology.

I think if you get the people part of it right, the technology part will come. Technologies come and go. They change—I've been through several technologies that are supposed to save the planet.

Yourdon: [laughter]

---

[2] The PDP-5 was DEC's first popular minicomputer, introduced in 1964; it was the predecessor of the far more popular (and more miniaturized) PDP-8 minicomputer.

[3] The PDP-6 was DEC's first large-scale computer, introduced in 1965 and aimed at the scientific/engineering marketplace. Its design was based on a 36-bit word of memory, and it thus competed fairly directly with IBM's 7090/7094 computers. It was the predecessor of the PDP-10 and DECsystem 10 computers.

Ford: And make programming incredible and make the world incredibly easy, which I know that you have both lived through and written about over the years. And you know, every so often, you hear another technology's going to change everything, and often technologies do change things, but there's always another one coming. The thing that allows you to make it through all those changes and iterations and capability and lack thereof around technology has to be the people you work with and grow and cultivate and manage and develop. So my focus around technology is really on people.

Yourdon: Yeah. You know, that's something they certainly don't teach you in college, at least not when I was in college. I didn't have a chance to learn it for several years after college either. But I think that's a comment I've heard fairly consistently from everybody in terms of their mentors and role models. And one of the reasons, by the way, I had to put that question on the list is that I knew, for example, I was going to be interviewing the CIO of Microsoft, and I had to ask him whether Bill Gates was a major role model for him and so on, and I've gotten a variety of interesting answers.

One last question in this "getting started" area: once you started moving along this career path, did you find the need for any additional education? Did you go back to get an MBA or anything of that sort?

Ford: You know, I've had several opportunities to get an MBA and including sponsorship to get a full MBA and multiple opportunities for executive MBA. And I did not. I chose not to.

I think the most important role model for me … from a technology standpoint—and I think this will stand the test of time—is a guy named Jim Cash.

Yourdon: Now where have I heard that name before?

Ford: Well, he was dean of the business school at Harvard. He ran the *Harvard Business Review*. He was a professor at Harvard in the business school. He ran their executive MBA program. He's a technologist, he's written books, he's on the board—well, I think he just got off the board of Microsoft, he's on the board at GE, Walmart, he's been on the board of Knight Ridder, he's on the board of Chubb, he's on the board of Tandy, which is originally Radio Shack. He's done a number of very strong, highly qualified things. Early indicator of what outsourcing would be to India.

Yourdon: Ahh.

Ford: Early indicator of real-time and just-in-time inventory management and did consulting around those things. Early indicator of just a number of things—social networking. Early indicator of a lot of things that technology would evolve to. He's just an incredibly bright, well organized, very well socialized person.

Yourdon: Very interesting. Really, it's the heart of your day-to-day life in a sense—and that is, how you see technology and IT contributing to the success of an organization like American? I think everybody knows the story from the early days of just what an enormous impact [American Airline's reservation system] Sabre has had business-wise and technology-wise, but what's the story today, in 2011?

Ford: I think that the business that we're in is a technology business. We're in the information business, I should say. We do transport things on airplanes. We make the world smaller, certainly. We transport things on airplanes, but the thing that people need most, whether it's transporting cargo or themselves or somebody else or something else, they want information. You know, our routine day is transporting 33,000 people someplace on an airplane that they weren't at earlier in the day before getting on our plane. And it happens on time the vast majority of the time, around … 84 to 87 percent of the time, which is a pretty incredible number actually across the industry. … And that's great. If you look at all the things logistical and otherwise that need to go in to get a plane off the ground, it's a minor miracle. Never mind luggage and all the rest of those things.

Yourdon: [laughter]

Ford: So we transport 110 million bags or so a year, and we lose, literally lose, less than a couple thousand out of 110 million. And the tiny minority of those bags, less than three tenths of 1 percent, arrive late, and 80 percent of those come in on the next flight.

Yourdon: Right.

Ford: So when you think about that, 110 million times—now, if it's your bag, it's late. That's another issue. It feels different. But less than three tenths of 1 percent is a big number. So on a routine day when everything is fine, at the airport and routine flight, everything is fine, everything is great. We're measured by what happens when things are not routine. When there's a dust storm that shuts down Dallas, like it did a couple of weeks ago.

Yourdon: That's right.

Ford: When there's the most incredible weather in recent recordable history in the Northeast and in Chicago. What happens when you've got thousands of planes and hundreds of thousands of people who are impacted? And when it happens over a two- or three-day period? How do you recover? People want information about their flight. They want to know what's going to happen, what do I do, what are my options? All of these are built around and driven by technology. Technology is at the center of everything we do, and information technology, information specifically, is at the heart of that sensor. It's the core of that sensor. So we play a pretty significant role, and probably even more so than we did back in the Sabre days, because even with Sabre, a lot was still manual and otherwise, and with today's volume and today's technology, you just cannot do that.

Yourdon: You know, I heard a variation on this in a speech by Theresa Wise, the CIO of Delta, who said one of the things they now try to do is stay in touch with their customers almost 24 hours a day, along the lines of what you were saying. And what I see as a traveler, I'm getting things on my iPhone saying, "You can now check in on this flight," or "Your flight's been delayed"—I got that on the way to the airport a couple of weeks ago—"and here are your options." So I certainly agree with you that generically, maybe one of the things that has changed over the last 30 or 40 years is the opportunity that you have with technology to provide this information everywhere and anywhere, anytime to a degree that just wasn't possible back then.

Ford: You know, Ed, our philosophy, our goal, is not only for customers and employees, but we want to meet the customers and employees where they want to be met, which we don't get to dictate. And—do you have American's iPhone app?

Yourdon: I do, yeah.

Ford: So what we're trying to do, with all of the things we're doing with iPhone and Android and other platforms that we're working on, we want to be able to meet people wherever they want to be met. And you'll see some other examples of this coming up. And we don't get to dictate that. I mean, in a world of social networking, in a world of social media, social technology—we don't get to control everything. The world has gone from being very vertical to very horizontal.

Yourdon: That certainly is true. Absolutely.

Ford: And in a horizontal world, you don't want the hierarchy. In your business, I used to sit around every morning and wait for the newspaper kid to come, and I would hope that he wouldn't throw it—when I was living in Boston—hope he wouldn't throw it in the snow.

Yourdon: [laughter]

Ford: And hope that he doesn't break a window or bang the front door with it, and I would sit there and wait patiently for the newspaper to tell me what my world was and what was going on in it. Now I get the newspaper on Sunday, the *New York Times*, just because I like laying down on the couch and opening up the newspaper and having paper everywhere and reading it. But the world has been voting to get information instantaneously. My kids won't read a newspaper.

Yourdon: Right.

Ford: They read it online. But they won't physically read—you know, it's kind of sad to me actually, because I'm a newspaper guy. But they want the information when they want it and where they want it, and they're not going to wait for the paper guy, paper boy or the paper girl. And the information flows horizontally at a rate that we can't control and manage. So, three years ago or so, I don't remember the time, a plane set down in the Hudson, and the way the news media found out about it was on Twitter.

Yourdon: Yeah, it was on Twitter. It was about a mile away from where I'm sitting right now. Out on the Hudson River, that US [Airways] flight. That was an amazing thing to watch—on Twitter.

Ford: On Twitter! You know, and the first pictures came from some guy with a smartphone. So nobody knows their names. Who was tweeting about it first. I mean, none of that is really important. It wasn't breaking news from CNN. It was breaking news from Twitter reported on CNN. And so, in a horizontal world, people go to each other really very quickly to get information. So the hierarchy of waiting for the newspaper or the hierarchy of waiting for American to tell me what's going on in my world isn't going to happen. So we supply all kinds of information through the Internet. Our customers aggregate that data faster, as fast as we can supply it, so they know and can understand what's going on.

Before we had the capability that we have now, we started sending information out over the Internet about flights and this and that to other service providers and other information providers and the like. And before we started doing this ourselves, I was standing at a gate and the flight was delayed. And I knew what was going on with the flight because I called the Operations Center to find out. I was at the airport walking around, seeing what was going on. The Operations Center told me, "Okay, we're just making a decision. Hold on a second. Okay, we're going to change gates. We got a new plane coming in. That one's broken. So we're going to move down three gates or two gates, or wherever the new one is. And we'll be getting that information out shortly." Well, as soon as they put that information out, it's broadcast across the Internet.

Yourdon: Right.

Ford: So I'm sitting there. I see a bunch of people looking at smartphones and handheld devices. All of a sudden, about 20 percent of them, 25 percent, pick up their bag and walk down two gates, just as the gate agent is announcing, "We'll have more information for you shortly. Just hold on." Those people already had the information. The irony was we sent it. And at that moment, I said, "You know, I know we have all these things coming, but I am not going to put our employees in this position." And we emphasized getting real-time information out to people as quickly as physically possible, at least at the same time that we get it out to customers.

Yourdon: Interesting.

Ford: And now, we're the best aggregator of data of anybody. We see the smartphone implementations and other things. And the responses to it—in our app, we've embedded technology and information into the functional features of the device. So it's not a website experience. It is a functional experience that takes advantage of the device. And you'll see this continue through GPS, the concept of presence, the phone. So at DFW [airport] here in Dallas, one of the most difficult things for people is parking someplace and coming into another terminal [thinking] "Where did I park my car?"

Yourdon: Right.

Ford: Now you can take a picture of the place where you parked, of the location number where you parked, and it's embedded into the app. And you pull up your flight and the information comes up on the phone with a picture of where you parked. It's embedded in the app, taking advantage of the features of the phone.

Yourdon: That's fantastic.

Ford: It pushes—for an Android, for instance, it pushes flight-status notification. And you can imagine that it's not too far-fetched to think that, well, since we know where you are—I mean, customers are willing to share information. They know nobody has any privacy anymore—about when they're on, what their location is, and what their GPS position is—so if I know that you left Dallas a couple of days ago, and the application knows that you're coming back, and the application then realizes you're in Dallas, it ought to just pop up the picture of your car and say, "Remember. You parked at B23" or whatever it is.

Yourdon: Yeah.

Ford: And those are things that the public is just not going to stand to wait for. And those are the type of things where I think we have the right mindset. I'm biased, but I'm willing to test this. We have a superior mindset than most companies like ours about what the function of technology is and the capability is and how to embed that into the thinking of the people that implement it. And not just customers, right, but the people that implement it, so customers and employees. So we have—CRM.

Yourdon: Right.

Ford: And CRM is customer-relationship management, as you know. Well, we have something called ERM, which is employee-relationship management, which focuses on the same concepts, right?

Yourdon: Aha.

Ford: Employee-relationship management—our employees live the same way our customers do. So our employees work the same way—our employees work the same way our customers do. And it's unrealistic to think that our employees, who live in a very horizontal world themselves when they're outside of work, will get to work one day and all of a sudden have to be vertical. Have to be in this hierarchical structure, with this technology that doesn't allow them to work horizontally the way they work everywhere else. It doesn't make sense. So we have to be as focused on the employee, à la my airport day experience I just told you about, as we do for the customer, or we've only got half the equation. And most people don't think of things that way. We focus on the information our employees get, and the social networking aspects, social media, social technology aspects of what they do. They will by definition be of more use to the customer.

And if it makes it sound like I'm doing a little bit of bragging, I guess that I am, but that's not the point. The point is, technology in our environment is the leading-edge indicator of what the capabilities of the environment and the workplace are. People will almost let them pay us to do the work. So here's the deal. You can fly on a flight that costs $10, and you go to the airport, stand in line, get your ticket, whatever. You can fly on the [same] flight, it will cost you $12, but you do the work yourself and go through a self-service machine. You'll pay the $12.

Yourdon: Just because you feel you're in more control.

Ford: More control. You've got all the information. You've got all the things you need yourself. In a horizontal world, nobody's going to stand around and wait for the hierarchy to wait their turn in line. Tell them, "Here, okay, I'm going to give you information." "No, I want it all. I can do it myself." Nobody's going to wait for the newspaper boy.

Yourdon: Very interesting. Now, a lot of this involves giving customers and employees the opportunity to do things that they basically could not do before. Is IT in your organization expected to be the originator or creator or the source of new ideas? Or does it come from all over the place?

Ford: Yes, we call it the "art of the possible." But it's a three-pronged approach. Part of what we do at American is we take some of the best businesspeople … throughout the organization—they're in revenue management, they're in capacity planning, the person that is the president of the Advantage program, our frequent-flier program… You take the best employees in the company—some of them, anyway—and we run them through the IT organization when we can, as part of sort of corporate property, if you will. I take them here, give them a total frontal lobotomy, and then retrain them from scratch about everything from how to start a project, how to manage a project, how to run a project, the IT aspect—because their job is information.

Yourdon: Right.

Ford: They're only as good as their ability to implement the next-best technology solution within their business unit. And so we take them here, we don't park them. We take them here, they go through regular jobs in the IT organization like a career IT person, and then we push them back out into the business.

That philosophy works beautifully if you really believe that the world revolves around IT. Because your people can be great managers, great thinkers and this and that, but if they walk into the room and say, "Okay, we're going to talk about everything about the business and every aspect in the business, except that IT stuff—I'm going to throw that over the wall to the programmers. I don't understand that IT stuff." It's perfectly acceptable in some places to walk into a room and say that, but unacceptable to say, "Uhh, numbers, financials, budget—I don't understand that budget stuff. I'll leave that up to the financial guys." Nobody's accepting of that. But in some places it is still acceptable for somebody not to have a thorough background and training and understanding of technology.

Yourdon: How much of that is a function of the generation? You know, you still see older managers who won't read their own e-mail, but it's much less common, isn't it, with the younger generation?

Ford: It is with the younger generation. That makes it more challenging though. It doesn't solve it, because IT is still evolving. The younger generation is pushing IT in a very horizontal way. It's pushing IT to places it's never been pushed before. So social networking, social media, horizontal stuff, is part of the continuum, not the end state. So, the, the people driving—I'm talking about young people—are driving things to another place, to another level. So, for instance—what's the best way to articulate this? The places where we have to be are ahead of where we are today. So when we bring people into the organization, bring young people into the organization, they expect instant messaging and social media and socialized technology and this horizontal world. That drives a set of requirements and a set of things that set the future of the next generation of things that we have to provide that is head and shoulders above where we are today.

And so our job is to figure out how things like mobility, what things like mobility and the concept of mobility mean. So we can't develop applications anymore that are "stateful" applications. Even mainframe-like applications or client-server-type applications, certainly not cloud-based applications, you certainly can't develop them in a way that doesn't contemplate mobility. You can't develop them in a way that isn't agile in nature, or an agile development methodology, because they're not going to sit still for six months of requirements that they'll see a year and a half later when the project's done.

Yourdon: Right.

Ford: It's not how they work. So while they are driving some of the things we do on an implementation basis today that we live with, what's not happening is, they're not contemplating and thinking about, "Okay, what is the future going to be? What kind of cellular or wireless network am I going to have to have when everything is on, when everything, everything is an Internet-based function, an Internet-based protocol?"

Yourdon: Interesting. Now you've actually touched on a couple of things in the next area that I wanted to discuss, in terms of the new trends in … IT that are likely to influence … your organization over the next few years. You mentioned cloud and mobile are the two ob-vious ones. Are there any other new paradigms or new trends that you see coming along in the next few years?

Ford: The real implementation is agile computing. Not just the talk of it and not just—but the real implementation of agile computing.

Yourdon: Interesting. Okay. I have not heard other CIOs emphasize that quite that much.

Ford: I'd be interested in any comments you might want to add here, such as: what kind of development projects are you now doing in an "agile" fashion, and how much of what you use is older legacy apps? How are you dealing with the legacy apps—are you refactoring any of it? What issues have come up, and how do you deal with them?

Yourdon: Okay, well, that's a good one to add to the list. Let me turn it around 180 degrees then and ask about the dark force. You know, what are the problems that keep you up at night and the things that you really worry about in terms of IT over the next few years?

Ford: This is part of what I was saying is challenging IT. And I don't think I articulated it well, but the days, the hierarchical days, of big American Airlines or even some of the technology providers deciding what the future of technology is—that's gone. Consumer-based technology, in a horizontal world, consumer-based technologies will dictate what big corporations do and how they provide it and what they provide and when and to whom. It will dictate what your employers demand. It will dictate what your customers demand. I don't care what project we have going on, if it's not based on what consumer-based technologies are driving people to have the capabilities to do—and when I say "consumer-based," individual technologies that people can have and use—then it's useless.

So one of the challenges we have is we don't get to determine all the rules anymore. We don't get to go to the mainframe gods and tell everybody what they can network to and what they can do and what they can't do. I mean, DEC made a living off of helping to open this up.

Yourdon: Yes. It's true.

Ford: So we don't get to do that anymore. We have to look at and be predictors of the trends and technology and media and stay much more ahead of where things are and … where we think things might be going in order to provide the capability for people to do that. So to do what they demand to do, because if you can't connect to people on their BlackBerry, they're just not going to talk to you, irrespective of how good you think your application is. So you better build it in a way—in an agile way, I think—you better build it in a way that works mobilely and you better be able to make sure it works up and down quickly, in the cloud, and you better be able to do it nimbly, agile.

Those three things go together, significantly go together in my opinion, and are a troika, like a three-legged stool that cannot be broken apart functionally, for the future. The difficulty in all this is how do I predict what my budget is? How do I predict what the next things are? I can't do five- and ten-year programs very often anyway, at least not the way that I used to. They've got to be smaller component-part things. I've got to be able to turn left and turn right quickly. I've got to be able to do a lot of things that I didn't have to necessarily do before, and I have to be a pretty good predictor of where we spend money. And then how do you, how do you budget an agile-developed project? You have standup meetings every day, you have the scrums every day, ten-minute standup meetings in the mornings. You're having these agile work sessions where what you started with, where every two weeks you're coming back, or three weeks or four weeks you're coming back with a prototype, and what you started with six months ago is not where you are now.

Yourdon: Right.

Ford: But it's a better place, but you thought your scope was gonna be XYZ. Now scope is ABC and XYZ, or you thought it was going to be XYZ, now it's just Z. So how do you manage technology in a predictable way in that environment? And we're cutting our teeth on that, and I don't think the whole world has figured that out, but I absolutely believe that's where it's going and that's what we're doing. I don't think that most CIOs … that are not technology providers—I can't speak for them—but I don't think that most CIOs in businesses are thinking about things that way. And that's absolutely how we have to think about things.

Yourdon: So you see that as one of the big challenges. Well, I certainly would agree with you. I think everything you've said makes eminently good sense, but it's interesting that you focused on that as the first and foremost item as opposed to what I've been hearing from almost every other CIO, whose first and topmost concern that gives them nightmares every night, is security. Not that I'm suggesting you're ignoring it at all, but that wasn't the first thing that you mentioned.

Ford: But that's a given. You can't stop the train unless it's just egregious, but you can't stop the train because the horizontal world provides different security concerns. Of course, it does. I mean, in the news business, authentication of stories is much more difficult, and there have been a bunch of people saying, "Stop this horizontal stuff, because you can't trust the stories." Well, that's not stopping. Security has to catch up with—it has to be not the tail wagging the dog, but the other way around. Security has to function in a way that we need it to function to be effective. And people like me have to think about security differently. When we first started this cloud computing thing, we had 150 reasons why we couldn't do it, 'cause it didn't look and feel like the mainframe, it didn't look and feel like the client server, it didn't look and feel like the data center. It's not going to look and feel like that, so what things can we do and how can we change the security paradigms, and we can by the way, to adapt to what the needs of the people are, because, remember, the consumers are dictating this stuff, not us. And people are always going to provide things that they can sell, and that's what people are buying, this horizontal technology, not the vertical stuff. And security better figure out how to catch up ... security to me is a given.

And by the way, when I talk about this three-legged stool, you know, this ... agile development methodology, mobile computing, and cloud technology, we're dragging the vendors along with us, we're dragging the suppliers along with us and demanding that they do things in the way that we need them to do. So it's not just us following technology trends. It's suppliers to companies like mine. And ... CIOs don't have this nailed, they don't have this licked, they don't have this figured out as well, and we're having to do this together, at the same time.

Yourdon: Interesting. And I think that's kind of different from the popular story that you see in the press, where the impression is that the vendors are leading the way, and you're saying it's really not that way at all.

Ford: Not that way at all. No, you may hear that from the supplier guys, but, of course, they're supplier guys, so they think they've got all the technology. It's not that way at all.

Yourdon: Hmm, okay. Well, that is interesting. So you're saying security is just a given. One of the things that I've been interested in, though, is the level of concern that I've heard from some CIOs.

Ford: Oh. I don't want to, Ed, I don't want by any means to minimize the importance of security. We are all over security. We're all embedded with the government, TSA. You know, we're 20 percent of the air commerce in the United States. If something were to happen and our systems were to shut down, that's pretty significant. I mean, we have *a lot* of personal information.

Yourdon: There's all the privacy stuff, too, yeah.

Ford: I mean, we've got to PCI-a-go-go everything we do. So we *are* security-, security-, security-focused. Absolutely. Incredibly so. My only point was, you have to just be that way. It has to be part of your existence. Not to focus on the future of technology is shutting things down. Or the focus on the future of technology is security. If you can focus on security, you can focus on shutting down things that happen as opposed to what you can allow to happen in a secure manner. It's a different mentality.

Yourdon: Okay. That does make an awful lot of sense.

Ford: And things that we can't do securely, by the way, we just don't do. But so far, there have been very few things that we've not been able to do. That's one of the places where we're dragging the vendors along kicking and screaming.

Yourdon: Aha. Interesting. Two more areas that I want to ask you about before we run out of time. We've already touched on this whole topic of the younger generation or the digital natives or whatever else you might want to call them. And, of course, they're not only coming into your IT department; they're coming through everywhere, in all business organizations. Do you have any concerns about the younger generation in terms of how they use technology or what their expectations are?

Ford: No. My only concern is if we can get enough meaningful information from them. If we can sit them down long enough to get enough meaningful information from them to be able to chart the course of our future. They're a tremendous resource all over the company, and if we have our way, we're not trying to limit the technology or the people who understand the technology in the organization.

If I have a company full of technologists that work in business and do the job in business every day, I'm happy. That's why we transplant people from the business unit into the technology organization and then send them back out. Even if they're technology-savvy, it's a re-quirement to work here, to have technology background, if you're coming into the management training program or whatever. I don't view that as a limitation or an issue or—I'm not afraid of it at all. One of my first jobs, when I got hired by my customer, the first thing they said [was], "The first thing you've got to do is this e-mail stuff, [it] is getting out of hand."

Yourdon: [laughter]

Ford: "Now we've got to shut this down. People are using it during the day, you know, they're hacking off. People could be using it—my God, they could be sending e-mails out all day instead of doing their jobs! You've got to shut this e-mail thing down and figure out how to get it under control. And the other thing is, these PCs are out of con-trol. Personal computers are just causing people to do their own work and, you know, just people have them at home now. They're starting to be in their homes. This is crazy. Shut it down."

So the first thing I did was look into this. And I thought, "You know, these guys are crazy. We're not going to shut this down." So I came back with this report that said, "The way you really get control over it is you let people do what they want to do." And they said, "No, no, no." And I convinced people that we should do that. And we opened it up, with some measures and some security and some control and all that, and the response was incredible. I mean, we got more value and understanding about what we need to do as a company by doing that than by everyone else running around and trying to shut things down.

I think the same thing is true with people coming in. Unless you think they're all stupid, you really ought to take advantage of them. They're the ones that made this stuff really popular and really work and caused the companies that are supplying the technologies to them to focus on what their needs are and what they want to do and how they want to do it. The best ideas from YouTube come from … people using it and saying what ought to be the next thing. Not, you know, the genius of some big corporation.

Yourdon: That certainly is true. Absolutely.

Ford: If you really believe that the world is horizontal and becoming more so, you have to embrace it in how you live your life every day, including the people you employ and how you manage them. And by the way, it's not just technology. How do you manage these guys? How do you manage these people? They're not going to sit around and listen to you dictate all of the—you know, we've got to be sensitive here, because we're in airlines, so we need structure, right?

We need a bunch of things because safety is first and foremost in everything we do, so you've got to have structure. But how do you manage a bunch of horizontal employees coming in to a historically vertical organization? You'd better manage them differently, or you won't get as much out of them, or they'll leave. So it's a set of problems that are, that are interesting and different—but a tremendous opportunity.

Yourdon: That reminds me of a question I wanted to ask you about, because it came up in an earlier interview this morning. Have you seen many instances of younger people being hired into your organization as a team and insisting on remaining together as a team?

Ford: No.

Yourdon: As opposed to just individually?

Ford: No, and I don't know how tolerant we are of that in our work environment.

Yourdon: Well, as I'm sure you know, it's always been common in the IT industry that if a project team works together and bonds, they want to stay together on the next project, which runs afoul of a lot of HR policies. But this idea of being hired right out of college as a team. I heard this about a month ago from the CIO of Marriott, and I got it confirmed this morning by the CIO of Arizona Public Services, and I had not heard it before a month ago, so I was just curious.

Ford: That they hire people as a team right out of college?

Yourdon: Well, the kids insisted on being hired. They said, "You either take all four of us or none of us."

Ford: I would take a pass, and I'm not sure how long those kids would be around anyway. And I would take a pass because, we view people as individuals, and if you think about it—though, if you're doing agile development, you have to focus on teams more, you have to pay people differently, you have to have a better, greater emphasis on teams and the value of teams, because that's how you get the work done. But I don't subscribe to that philosophy at all, and when teams of people come in and start to dictate to you what you can and can't do and what they will—'cause the next thing they're going to say is what they will and won't work on. I'll take a pass. I have a very different philosophy. We break up teams routinely—high-performing teams.

Yourdon: Hmm.

Ford: And it's the best way to get more high-performing teams. Once a team hits a stride, and they're cruising and they're just loving life, "and this is great, and we're really high-balance, high-performance," you know, invariably there are other places that are not working as well.

Yourdon: Right.

Ford: So you take the leaders from that team and either create new teams or put them where they will be more effective in taking those traits and characteristics and learnings and things from the team that they were on, and propagate that across the organization, proliferate that across and throughout the organization, and invariably you get better people and better teams, with better people that are cross-pollinated, number one, and that culturally and functionally put the kinds of attitudes and culture and philosophy out there, spread out throughout the organization, that you would not have had as much of had you not done that.

The other thing that it does is … it proliferates the concept of team, because what happens with really high-performing teams that demand to stay together and that kind of thing, after a while, it's not necessarily them as a team, but it's the overall team. How much of a team do you have if you have people that pride themselves on how well they do versus other people at the expense of everybody else as opposed to how they make the entire organization better?

Yourdon: Ahh, interesting.

Ford: How do they make the entire world better? 'Cause what you have then is "us against the world," or haves and have-nots, or thems and those, and, you develop these little cocky—especially if they're working on new stuff, right? You develop these cocky, internally focused, "my way or the highway," "just us," "I'm only focused on me," "I do good work, but, you know, the rest of the organization—never mind them." When you routinely break those up, you get a team effect that's greater than the sum of the parts. You get a synergy that exists that otherwise you wouldn't by sending them across the organization.

Yourdon: Okay. Very interesting. Okay, I'm going to ask just one last question, and I think it's kind of an appropriate question, and that is: where do you see yourself going from here? Do you expect to be a CIO for the rest of your life, or is this just one of many opportunities along the way?

Ford: I was thinking about starting a career writing technology books. What do you think?

Yourdon: [laughter] It doesn't pay very well these days!

Ford: But as ex-DEC guys, maybe you and I can team up and go to some publisher and demand that we stay together as a team.

Yourdon: There you go. [laughter]

Ford: But I really don't know. I've never really managed my career. There will always be a need for technology people. So I'm on the board now for—I've been on two public boards and one board that's sort of a utility—and boards are going to continue to need good, strong, qualified technology people that have experiences like I have in a significant way. And I can only do one board at a time while I'm here. So I would do more than that, but for the time being, the world needs leadership that is open-minded and open-thinking and not shutting things down. The world needs to understand how to implement horizontal technology in, in a large enterprise environment. And that's something that I think I am extraordinarily good at and may be narcissistic or conceited about it, but I think that part I get.

And so I'm not really focused on it, but I know that if things keep going the way that they are, that there will be people like me that need to help get it there. And I'm not the only one, obviously. There are a whole bunch of people that understand this stuff. But I'm just one person. But I think I can help get people to where they need to be.

Yourdon: It's a future path that I've not heard other CIOs mention. And as it turns out, I've been on a couple of public boards also, so I completely agree with you that obviously in places like Silicon Valley, maybe everybody on the board is a technology person. But not in the typical Fortune 500 companies. You've got strong marketing people and financial people and so on, but, you know, having a real strong voice for technology—what a great career.

Ford: And I'm a very strong believer in all kinds of diversity, and I think some of those Silicon Valley companies would be a lot better off if they didn't have just technologists on the board.

Yourdon: Oh, absolutely. Yeah.

Ford: Think about it. Not a lot of them have CIOs on the board.

Yourdon: You know, I've been surprised how infrequently the CIO has been on the board of all the companies I've been trying to track down. You're right, absolutely.

Ford: You know, they absolutely should. People understand the organizations and the structure and the things they're trying to do, they're trying to sell to. No matter the size of the company, they want to sell to a big company. It legitimates them, it will standardize them, it will get them big contracts, all of that. And as much as even the companies that say, "We are so anti-big company," the first thing they want to do is sell a contract to a big company.

Yourdon: [laughter] Right.

Ford: And it makes sense. It makes sense to have that same expertise. I also am a firm believer that just as right now, because of not only security, but also all these other things that we talked about, because today on public boards, as you know, you have to have a financial expert.

Yourdon: Right.

Ford: It makes all the sense in the world to me for any significant board to have a technology expert. I don't, I don't know if it will be a sort of requirement, Sarbanes-Oxley, like that you're got to have one certified and all that, but if you're a forward-thinking CEO and you don't have a technology person on your board—I don't care what business you're in—how real forward-thinking are you? You absolutely have to have technologists on your board, or at least one, if you're going to live in the free world today, irrespective of the product or service.

Yourdon: Well, I completely agree with you, and I think that is a wonderful general suggestion as a career path for CIOs at some stage, maybe later on in their career. Wonderful. Okay, well, I'm going to wrap this up so that I don't interfere with the rest of your day of meetings.

Ford: Thank you.

Mittu Sridhara

CIO, Ladbrokes plc

Mittu Sridhara is Group CIO at Ladbrokes PLC. A leader in the global betting and gaming market, Ladbrokes transacts more than £16 billion each year— making it a pure, cross-channel digital business on a global scale. Customer experience at Ladbrokes is delivered by a combination of trading, banking, streaming-content, and gaming platforms personalized by channel. Ladbrokes' innovative KickOff app won the Future Mobile Award for Mobile Gambling 2011.

An international visionary, Mr. Sridhara has an outstanding track record of building high-performance teams, products, and industry-leading customer experiences. He is recognized for his customer-centric approach and passion. Mr. Sridhara's career has encompassed Senior Leadership Technology and Product Marketing at Sabre; CIO at Versapoint NV, a broadband telecommunications company; and Group CIO at Avis Rent A Car System, LLC.

Ed Yourdon: I usually start off the same way. I don't need to ask where you grew up or where you went to university, but people were not born into the position of CIO, so I'm curious to know how you got to where you are now. Were you a CIO somewhere before?

Mittu Sridhara: Yes, I was. I actually tell people about who I am, because how you do your job, especially on a global scale in a global organization does, I think, add flavor to it.

Yourdon: It does, and it's something I had not anticipated. And I hope for your sake that it's very different for you, but some of the organizations I've spoken with have said, whenever there's a crisis anywhere in the world—of which there are many today—"We get a phone call at three in the morning because our organization is global." Now I hope you don't have global crises, but I can imagine you have a global scale, so that it makes things different than a lot of people would expect.

Sridhara: I think probably most CIOs at scale have operations to run 24/7. I mean globally. So, something can go wrong at any point in time along the way. But also how you implement and influence, culturally and across geography, is also relevant to the context. Because, who you are and how you perceive and how you message are quite fundamental in how successful you are in getting things done. And you get things done through people, not through technology. You also get to customers through solutions that have elements of technology that is derived through an understanding of what the customer wants. I believe the global aspect has been a significant part of the job and I've operated globally for pretty much most of my career. I've been in business now for 22-odd years. So I consider myself a "young body with high miles."

I started with American Airlines in what was the decisions group, which then became Sabre Technology.

Yourdon: Separate business. Yes, I remember that story. That was one of the, I think, the first big case studies of information being more valuable than the parent company that spawned it.

Sridhara: We built an ERP system for what was the travel business as a whole, and earned my stripes going from being one of the 'coders' to leading the project because the lead got stuck in a previous project at Southwest. And by default, I assumed leadership and delivered an ERP for travel agencies. I'm going back a decent period of time, but that product is still there on the marketplace. It was built in a very agile manner, with customers in the same room. Locked into helping drive deliverables, literally cutting a version of the product every day. In about nine months, we built a product that was the ERP for the travel agencies business process, the ability to take your reservation, process it on the GDS in the back end. And then provide you with all the services you required.

I came into the business process side at American and very quickly was noticed as somebody who understood technology but also understood business process.

I was starting to manage teams as a whole, but more importantly, I understood what the customer wanted. And we were able to translate that into the requirements, or the user stories, as you call them today, in agile terms, for what needed to be built. So, yes, there was not a traditional technology part then, but I ended up then using technology to enable solutions for business.

Yourdon: One of the questions I've asked in this early stage of just about everyone is whether they received any formal education along the way. Did you go to CIO school or get an MBA, once you got on this track that was about to lead you where you are now?

Sridhara: From an educational point of view, I've been a CIO for, at a group level, for about ten years now, so it's been a school in and of itself. But in terms of building up to it, it was a progression of different roles and responsibilities—jobs and different career spans and spans of control, I should say, that gave me the experience to help execute as a CIO.

Yourdon: Well, it's interesting how few people have said, "Well, yes, at a certain point I had to go get my MBA" or "They sent me off to learn about finance and accounting and so forth." There has been a lot of emphasis on broad education at an early stage, but after that, it seems to be very much on-the-job training, as you rise up through the ranks.

Sridhara: Mark Zuckerberg didn't go to school to learn how to build Facebook. So the answer to this is, I think for all of us, especially for me, learning is big every day. I come in to work every day to keep learning. So it's a daily and a career aspiration. To learn literally every day and every year, to take on responsibilities that help you learn, grow, refine. And you also learn through building other people and building businesses. So you're constantly learning.

Learning is such an important thing to me, I went and signed up with London Business School and got some of the finance and marketing sides. I was kind of completing my portfolio of tools that I use every day. But I do believe in applying them practically.

The magic sauce to me is not just in the theory of what you need to do, but it's also in understanding how you do it. And how you refine it as you do it to get the job done, and these are three very separate things.

You can be a consultant up front, and a very good consultant at seeing what it is that needs to get done, but understanding true context, and then starting to deliver it, and then refining the plan as you deliver it to be the right result—you could think of it as agile, it's strategic agile, but in organizational delivery terms.

Not just the technology, because often CIOs, I think, are enabling businesses to do more, or they differentiate at a lower cost overall. I should probably talk to you about strategy.

Any simple strategy boils down to three things: differentiate and grow top-line revenue and differentiate and drive more value; drop costs and do more for less, while you currently run the business that is in play.

Yourdon: Very quickly. One last question in this sort of "getting started" area. And that is the question of whether you had any significant mentors or role models that helped shape who you are today?

Sridhara: I've been very fortunate, very, very fortunate, because in many of my jobs, I've had people that I've worked with where several people stand out. What's interesting to me when I reflect on your question is not only were they mentors back then; they continue to be friends/mentors/role models to this day.

Because I look back at them when they were young managers, and I still look at some of them today and look at how they've chosen the basic life decisions they've made, and not just career decisions. And you learn from them, and continue to learn because these relationships last a lifetime. There are several people that come to mind.

I've always looked at mentoring not just in a business context but mentors as role models.

Yourdon: Now you mentioned a moment ago, the next major area I want to get into, which is how you see IT here at Ladbrokes. For example, achieving the objectives you mentioned of competitive differentiation and driving value and just keeping the lights on. And everybody has had a slightly different story to tell me there. Why don't we start with the first part, about differentiation? How do you see IT achieving that, or how are you using IT to achieve that?

Sridhara: Fundamentally, I think, differentiation. It's probably worth taking a moment to describe the business, so that you understand the context. Ladbrokes has more retail outlets than Tescos in the UK. The market capitalization is £1bn ($2,000m). It's not our true turnover. If I reported like Tesco's, I would be reporting 15 to 16 billion in stakes yearly. So when it comes to the solutions in IT, we service every single penny of our £16 billion.

My can of beans is electronic, my shelves are electronic, my prices are also going to go electronic. And I was out at Gartner now ten-odd years ago, probably nine years, talking about real-time systems. Nowhere else in my entire career have I been somewhere where real time is truly, truly real time. In this business, if there's an example on the betting side of our business, if a horse leaves the gate, and you place a bet two seconds later, we might have a problem. So two seconds can make a huge difference.

You could be viewing it on-screen on what is effectively streaming media on the wall in a shop, and you could place a bet on a handwritten slip. If we capture that bet incorrectly at the wrong price, we could be out millions of pounds.

So that ability to digitize what is manual, in subseconds, but to get the right price, to match up with the video feed, with the right product is critical. Across channels we are a customer experience and entertainment company and delivering a rich entertainment experience to you, the customer, if you'd like to bet or game. And we've got to bring all those together in real time, and the technology underpinnings is what does it for this business.

By real time we're talking about 20 milliseconds of latency making a big difference. So it's about ensuring the price to be right, but also ensuring the pinning enablement is all correct. It's also about operational processes being automated because you're doing this for fun, the sooner we actually give you something back, the sooner you have a choice. You have a choice to put it back in or take it and walk away.

The whole industry is in the process of understanding the customer, and what the customer wants is key. I know you come to this question a little later in your series of questions around what are the big differences and emerging trends.

The smart mobile device for us, not just the mobile device, but the smart mobile device, is an interesting opportunity, because suddenly it's immersive. Before it wasn't, you know, your flat text message. Yes, you can engage, because we're in the space of providing a rich piece of entertainment to you, which includes content, it includes price, it requires streaming video or stats around a game, a price, around you. A smart device now suddenly starts to make that possible.

So that's where you have really rapid convergence coming our way. And we are at the forefront of most industries, because others have to deal with it as well. Convergence is coming to us much quicker than it is to anybody else because the only physical thing in our business is cash, and even that is going digital.

Because the iPhone 5 is expected to have a digital wallet, thus new battleground for the Googles and everybody else around payments. The reason it is a new battleground is because of convergence.

How do I then ensure that everything is consistent and engages around regulation as well, which is another key element for us. We are strictly regulated, more so than the FSA[1] on what you can and cannot do and what we're required to do as well. We cannot always do what another retailer can do.

So it's just a fascinating space, because we are in the Web 3.0 business in that our customers are already watching media, socially interacting in-store, and buying product. It's now about how do you make the technology—the technology's come alive for the segment—how do you then apply it effectively to the business processes you already have?

Yourdon: One of the things that you just said intrigued me, in terms of being aware of a customer profile. Obviously, there's a real-time aspect to that too—but how fast would my profile change and to what extent can you anticipate my future profile and perhaps offer me opportunities or games or transactions that I might not have thought about on my own?

Sridhara: That's what I call "more 'e' than Amazon," as a tagline. Why more 'e' than Amazon? It's more than just product. It's a product where the price is varying by the second. A large range of products, where the product has to be delivered through a web channel but also has to be delivered in-store, also has to be delivered on the smartphone, and all of those things have to be cohesive and coherent, rather. To deliver a seamless customer experience while you're performing trading.

As a bank, because we are, we have traders. We have people aggregating and disseminating content around understanding you, the customer. We've always looked at our platforms, and we've grown up in the silos of retail and a web-emerging web channel, but we've never really looked at our business and said, "Oh, look, this is just one business really."

It's a betting business and a gaming business in its core constituent parts. They're all technology enabled, and you don't need to do them separately and differently. Yes, you need to deliver them differently around who, you, the customer is and what you want, but in the past we've done it very differently, and we've grown up very differently.

What we're in the process of doing is automating the underpinning business processes, but also, building the platforms around you the customer, to where, as we understand you better, we deliver the personalization.

---

[1] The Financial Services Authority (FSA) is the regulator of the financial services industry in the UK.

The average customer is looking for an experience. It's our ability to give you what you need and when you need it, the way you need it. And that's what we're in the process of building right now. And building it in a cross-channel manner, so wherever it touches, it looks and feels consistent to you.

On the other hand, if you do not wish to be known, then we will not only respect that, but we will ensure that this is the case, and we will interact with you as such across channels. So we're going from this 'push it all out and some of you will take' to this 'push-pull engaged,' but again, it's engaging in real time.

Yourdon: That's really fascinating. The third basic part of the overall objective that you mentioned a moment ago is something that I characterize as keeping the lights on, just running stuff. And from everything you've just said, you obviously have to do so in a very high-performance fashion, where every nanosecond counts. And I assume also reliability and availability and all those sorts of traditional parameters are almost as important as they would be for a nuclear reactor or an air traffic control system. Umm, is there anything special you all do in that area, other than just redundancy and huge numbers of servers all over the place?

Sridhara: We can't afford huge numbers of servers. This is a bank without the cash to do it all.

[both laughing]

Sridhara: We have the same challenges without the same budgets or investments. We're not capable of making the same investments in these areas. So we have to be very innovative in how we underpin all this technology and how we build. We're in the process of building a trading platform, which is actually a banking platform effectively, but some of the systems integrators refuse to bid at the prices I was asking for.

However, we are delivering those platforms on industry-standard technologies at a fraction of the prices that most banks would pay. To deliver exactly the same thing.

I've got the economies of scale, and as a result I'm able to build a good level of redundancy into how we deliver it. And that's the good thing about technology; it's getting cheaper as well.

There are other, new technologies that are coming down the road. Computing power, as a whole. The buzzword is always *cloud*, but, you know, being able to do it securely is key.

We are very "spiky"—we'll go from 600 bets a minute to 6,000 bets a minute just before an event. Now, a bet in our business is about the same as Visa or MasterCard transactions. It's not only the payment, it's not only taking the cash out of your wallet and putting it back in; it's also about getting the right prices, getting combinations, managing liability behind it. So it's not just a sale, it's a sale which then has to be transacted, monitored, and re-computed for how much you may win to manage liability.

So one transaction typically means six different things that have to happen. So we are pretty "peaky" in how we have to transact. And so how affordable computing is, and the high end of computing, is key and also the virtualization of that capacity.

Computing power will get cheaper, faster, and smaller and for Ladbrokes, in simple terms, it's about coming back to strategy, differentiation, and value.

Yourdon: Okay. But there seem to be quantum jumps, where a 10 percent decrease in price or a 10 percent increase in CPU cycles isn't going to make a whole lot of difference. But there's some point where things that were simply not possible before suddenly become possible. And I assume that's going to happen in your case, although I'm not sure what form it will take.

Sridhara: But it's about you as a customer and your experience. So with a smart device, you're starting to expect that you have live streaming, as an example, and you have come to expect that it is as good as, if not better than, what you may be receiving sitting and watching television. But you're also expecting to transact on it and look up other things in additional windows while you're watching the video. Now, that requires a certain amount of computing power on the front end.

It's compressed, it's streaming, and it needs to compute. But on the back end, you've got to then be able to deliver all of that at scale, so you will never know how many people are going to be engaging with you on mobile devices, and that will continue to increase pretty dramatically.

Which is why the back-end ability to process all of it is key. So in our business in particular, our ability to continue to deliver the experience that the customers are looking for in an affordable way is absolutely key.

Yourdon: There is one aspect of what you've just said, this whole idea of mobile computing becoming more widely dispersed. In many areas it's gotten to the point where computing activity is essentially free. It may be supported by advertising or something like that, but whether it's free or almost free, it has suddenly opened up entirely new markets. Whole continents [that] could not afford computing at all before now can—and therefore, I assume, have become potential customers for you. That might not have been the case before. I don't know how much more there is to go on in that direction, although I suppose it will go on for another five or ten years. Not everybody in Africa has a cell phone yet, by any means at all. Let alone China or India. Do you see that multiplying by another factor of 10 or a factor of 100?

Sridhara: Well, it's certainly a factor of 10x. But also in our market, it's about regulated markets, so not every market is available. When the markets do become available, you will have phenomenal steps in growth.

Yourdon: Interesting. One of the points that has been mentioned to me by some of the other CIOs is that as the overall cost of computing has dropped and, we now have a phenomenon that one of the American authors refers to as a "cognitive surplus," an example of which is Wikipedia. We now have the computing power available, and people have enough spare time and good thoughts in their hearts that they're willing to contribute some of their surplus cognitive power to, to do things like open-source computing or Wikipedia or any number of other examples. Is there any aspect of that that's relevant in your world?

Sridhara: It's relevant, once we can open up what we do, to saying, "Hey, look, if you're a games developer," as an example. "And you like building games, I'll provide you a development toolkit to build games. Yes, you can go ahead and build it. You don't need to have the horsepower to run it."

"We will run it for you, and then you can become part of an app store." Games are an example, and we do run different versions of games, different versions of games take in marketplaces, customers like different games, they like variety. It will happen at a much bigger scale as time goes by.

Yourdon: What about the whole area of data visualization? I would imagine that some, if not all, of the things that you're dealing with involve the possibility of presenting enormous quantities of data to a trader or a player. Where it would be wonderful if there were some way of boiling it down to, a more understandable digest, so to speak.

Sridhara: Very much so. We're in the process of automating our entire trading floor. And they're actually in test runs going live right now for some markets and then we'll continue gradually adding all markets. But there's a lot of visualization and can have 20,000 different things possibly coming into setting up an event.

So that gets visualized for the trader. They can make decisions based on that, but also, if you go to our current website, you will see stats for how a horse performed or how a footballer performed at a previous match or what their history was. That's already there and making it more visual is clearly going to be a turning point.

On the gaming machines, we are in the process of testing a game in China. And the Asians more so than us and some of our customers here and other geographies, like to see and understand the patterns, understand what's happening. So visualization is a key element of the experience—for certain customer types.

Again, being able to provide that and then in some of the platforms, we're looking to roll out. I won't say more than saying they're going to engage you visually.

Yourdon: And, of course, a lot of those areas are, just by their very nature, going to require vast amounts of additional computing power to be able to do the back-end computation and presentation to the user. That is going to be interesting.

Sridhara: But it's also about the tolerance as you talked about earlier. I got a mobile device, not just a server, which is a foot next to the other. So it has to have a price update at the same time. And all able to fit on a small screen, too. So it's about getting it right for who you are and what you want.

Yourdon: Well, let me change from all the wonderful futures and opportunities to the dark side of the force—the problems and the risks. What is it that keeps you awake at night, if anything?

Sridhara: You never have a problem, you always have an opportunity. It's a question of how you address the problems. So when something is an opportunity, you go about it differently because you go about it and say, "Okay, is this an opportunity to address something now in a different way, so that it does not become an ongoing problem?"

Sridhara: So it's often an opportunity to go in and fix, but the way you fix it is as important as what you fix. You've got to look at what the customer wants, what broke, and how do you ensure that it doesn't break again? Or if it does break, is it okay for it to break, because it may not be that the customer sees that as the most relevant thing to your experience. You may do it in such a way that it's safe-fail as opposed to fail-safe.

Yourdon: Usually when I ask that question, the answer I get almost immediately revolves around security. And I would imagine in your case, the mismatch between dealing with the technology of security threats while also being constrained by all of the regulatory things that you have to live under, which usually moves a lot more slowly than the technology. How do you balance those two things?

Sridhara: Frankly, I'm coming from regulation, which is something you've got to comply with. It's not optional. And everything is designed to be secure and compliant, PCI-compliant or the gambling acts and everything else, so it's always designed with compliance right from the start.

That's one. Second, security is always a threat to anybody right now in operating in any electronic form. We've got things like DDoS[2] protection, we've got 24/7 monitoring alerts that go out should patterns change, automatic blocking that goes in place.

But DDoS attacks and security, or the way people come at you can continue to change and become more sophisticated, so it's something you're constantly looking for, constantly reviewing where you are, how you're doing it.

It's certainly something that I constantly re-evaluate, saying, "That's how we were choosing to address the problem yesterday. What has changed? Can we address it differently today?"

Yourdon: The way you just raised this a moment ago took me back to a comment made by the CIO of one of our universities, who said that, in terms of re-evaluation, he looks to his students because he said, "I don't know everything, my peers don't know everything, and we're not always able to keep up with everything. But we have this constant influx of new students who are smarter than us and more inquisitive than us, and we look to them in a way, as people on the edge of the frontier." Is there anything equivalent in your case? I can imagine it could be some of your customers, for example.

Sridhara: Our customers, absolutely. Our customers are looking for different types of services. It's industry peers. It's some of our partners as well. Because of our geographic spread, often an idea in one geography for regulation purposes cannot be applied in the other, but you have lessons learned that can be applied. So we have innovation or ideas coming out at us in so many different ways, and we also foster innovation and an open culture here to where every idea is a good idea. It's a simple thing: fail, fail fast, but succeed faster.

Yourdon: And get data about it, yes. I agree. One last thing that has always struck me, because I've been in the field for 45 years. Forty-five years ago,

---

[2] Distributed denial of service.

much of what we dealt with in technology was very expensive and very scarce and therefore controlled very diligently. But now, of course, so much technology has become cheap to the point of almost being free, and pervasive to the point where our employees—not just in the IT department, but employees everywhere, or customers in your case—may well have better technology at home than what they're going to find in the office. And yet the control structure that I've seen in a lot of IT organizations, led by the CIO, still seems to be this top-down hierarchal kind of mechanism that's just completely out of place.

And I'm just curious as to your thoughts about, you know, how to deal with that.

Sridhara: And that has to do with what worried me earlier. You've got to look at everything as a service, starting with the customer. Bringing them services that matter. And then, as you progress, so if you're a trader, those trader apps and perhaps you're trading as a trader where you do it, is completely secure today and will always [be] in the future. So you draw rings, concentric rings, if you will. You've got to hammer security and apply it in layers.

So the average user is just coming in and doing Word documents and e-mail. As long as they're not extracting customer data, we'll have a different amount of security and it will be a different boundary than deep down here, where there's lots of customer data. And trading information, as an example.

If you're a trader, yes, I will choose to provide you with a laptop and anything else you need and have it completely encrypted and wipeable remotely.

It's also about business process—which is why solutioning is an important thing, x role in y, the organization is now looking for something greater than what they should be looking for. They need levels of authorization for customer data. So if you look at it again from the "what data matters?" [standpoint], you can address some of these opportunities differently.

Yourdon: That's a very good point. What I have found with all of the CIOs I've spoken to is that they're focusing on all these technology issues that we've been talking about—but, of course, they're also interacting with their business peers, heads of business departments or product departments, who are very smart people and very competent people and often have very strong opinions that have helped them succeed.

And they not only think they know how to run *their* business better than you do; sometimes they think they know how to run *your* business better than you do. How do you go about achieving the kind of influence you need to avoid risks and to take advantage of opportunities that hopefully you do know more about because of your expertise?

Sridhara: Excellent question. I think you probably know the answer and where I was going to come at it from. In every business I've been in, I've been very, very lucky. I seldom had many challenges in working with my colleagues to get the job done. And I think part of it is, if you look at it from a customer view, fundamentally, and you understand the end customer, then they're all partners, they're all partnered together. I'm incentivized as much as they are to deliver business results and shareholder value by driving customer growth. So if I'm addressing the same problem they're trying to address, we're on the same side. Now, we may have different views of how we think we may address it, but we're fundamentally trying to solve the same issue, and it often is the ground of convergence, as a result, because you're comparing notes on how best to solve it and often find, "Yes, they've got great ideas. Let me combine these with the ideas my team can bring," and together you come up with solutions that no one person would have come up with. So that bringing the sum of the parts together—you know, what I used to call "2 + 2 = 5," but I increasingly think "2 + 2 = 22."

And that's very, very important. In a fast-moving world, no one area can see it all. So it's about people combining and collaborating now even more so than before.

Yourdon: I certainly agree with that. Now I think one of the reasons it's been a problem in some of the other situations I've seen is that the CIO has sometimes only been in his or her position for a short period of time, so there's this element of trust that has to be built up—because even though your business peers may think you're all trying to achieve the same objectives, they might not necessarily agree with your particular perspective or your solution or your priorities.

Sridhara: I'm not sure there is a quick way to win trust. I think you can get going quickly, but trust is something that is earned both ways. Over time, by doing what you say and saying what you do. About being trustworthy, about having integrity, competence—clearly, if you're incompetent, they may trust you, but they may not trust you'll get the job done. So it goes without saying that competence underpins all of that, and all those only can be established with some time. Now the key thing is to ensure results—because this is where agile comes in, because if you focus around the customer in agile, you can deliver to your end customer, to your mutual customer, and do so quickly and you build trust, because you're doing that in dialogue.

Yourdon: Exactly. And that's the common answer I end up with. You know, when I first got started in the field, you often didn't have anything to deliver for seven years. And you can only rely on trust during that period because you had no intermediate results or prototypes or daily builds.

Well, let me switch gears to the two last areas. I'm very curious about everyone's opinion about the "new generation," whether you call them digital natives or whatever. And, of course, they're arriving everywhere in the organization, not just in the IT department, but everywhere. Armed with their smart mobiles and their different attitudes. They've grown up in a world of Google and multimedia. Is that something that you see a lot of around here? Is this something that you think it's good or bad or irrelevant?

Sridhara: I think it's good. We increasingly see a lot more of it coming into our workplace. Overall it's good in that it always challenges how you keep your own employees engaged, but with them they bring, because of the space we're in, our customers are in the same space. It's a good representation of what I've got to solve anyway and solve for externally, and having that on the inside just brings good ideas—right inside our building.

So they're a part of the team and this is part of encouraging innovation right through the workforce, but also improving how we drive what we do. And it's an exciting place given the challenges we have. It tends to really lend itself to new ideas, looking at things differently, and driving solutions that work, by default, work for the person who's come in but also result in driving the right customer experience.

Yourdon: Well, that is a very good point. I've been even hearing about that in banks, where their traditional IT people simply don't know how to reach a generation of college students that the bank wants to get as bank customers, but they've got young programmers who are on Facebook who can reach out and effectively communicate. That is a very good point. Any negatives? Any concerns about the new generation of digital natives or digital whatever you want to call them?

Sridhara: No, not really. I think they're all different. Again, they come in different flavors. Yes, you can do a pattern and say, "This is what they all want." They are looking for places that have values and core ethics. That's important to the new generation as it is to everybody else, I suggest. They place different emphasis. They want to understand more about what they are doing and how they do it. The question of work-life balance is a bigger question for them than it was for some other generations.

Yourdon: One of the people I interviewed was the former CIO of the American Defense Department. He's very concerned with what he regards as the superficiality of the younger generation, their inability to spend a lot of time really focusing and concentrating on, on some intellectual question for long periods of time because they've grown up in a world where they can find something on Wikipedia right away, they can Google something right away, and they don't ever have to spend more than ten minutes thinking about anything. Is that something you see at all?

Sridhara: I think they adapt to the workplace with time—if you provide them with good mentoring and structure. Yes, that's a good thing. They can find an answer to at least 80 percent of the questions you ask them very, very quickly, which is great. All of them aren't going to fit into a mold. Some of them will take to program management; some of them will take to customer experience.

They will take to different roles as you start understanding their strengths. And I think they bring a valuable perspective, you know, contribution and energy and also make every manager and the world think differently as well.

Yourdon: One last question, and then I'll let you go. It's the obvious final question: where do you see yourself going from here? After life as a CIO, is there a future life?

Sridhara: Is there a future life? I think there is. Well, first of all, let's answer the latter one. There is a future life, and I think it will continue to evolve because I think increasingly technology enables the business and the running of the business are fusing even closer. When we're in roles like the ones I've held and I've had the luxury of holding, they're always closely associated with the front end, customer end, and the solutioning of the services.

So every role I've had has been technology-intense with the customer at the core. Delivering product platform and solutions to enable enterprise value, shareholder value and customer experience. Effectively, I've been on both sides of the fence as being a pure "CIO" and running technology and product marketing for a B2B and B2C. So, increasingly, I think, roles will fuse and will evolve. I think the people who want to grow and evolve will continue to have fascinating roles, especially when you come at it from a solution view and you get technology, and you get the customer. I certainly expect to have a lot of fun over the next 15 or 20 years.

Yourdon: Okay. Well, can't do better than that. All right. And with that, I think I will turn this off. I very much appreciate your time.

Steve Rubinow

Executive Vice President and CIO, NYSE Euronext

Steve Rubinow is Executive Vice President and Chief Information Officer of NYSE Euronext, parent company of the New York Stock Exchange (NYSE), where he is responsible for all aspects of technology as well as global innovation for the leading stock exchange in the world. Previously he was the Chief Technology Officer for Archipelago Holdings Inc. in Chicago, where he was responsible for software development, quality assurance, operations, customer connectivity, and technical support for the Archipelago Exchange (one of the original electronic communications networks to officially serve as an institutional stock exchange). The company merged with the New York Stock Exchange in 2006, which then merged with Euronext in 2007 to form NYSE Euronext.

Previously, Dr. Rubinow was Chief Information/Technology Officer for NextCard Inc.; Vice President and Chief Information Officer at AdKnowledge, Inc.; and Vice President of Corporate Management Information Systems at Fidelity Investments in Boston. He began his career as a systems analyst at the Continental Bank in Chicago.

Dr. Rubinow has a BS and an MS in Chemistry, an MS in Computer Science, an MBA in Marketing and Finance (where he ranked first in his graduating class), and a PhD in Chemistry.

Ed Yourdon: The questions I thought I would start off with are the more strategic ones. I can certainly imagine IT is "strategic," though I don't want to say "weapon" here. But what element of your IT is strategic? And how?

Steve Rubinow: It is interesting that you said that because a lot of times in the past, people will talk about our industry as an arbitrary battle ground. So yes, war terms are quite common here though we don't want to use "bull's eye."

But if you talk to certain people on any given day, they will tell you that this is a technology firm that happens to run exchanges, as opposed to an exchange firm that has something to do with technology. That is for a couple of reasons. One is that without technology there is no firm. Certainly, the open outcry system with people exchanging slips of paper, that's from another era, everything is electronic. The vast majority of trading takes place with servers talking to servers. Humans are the trading model builders but they are not there in the middle for the most part where it takes place, except for on the floor downstairs. That is an important, but smaller, part of what we do.

The other thing is if you were to define our business as we do, we put it into three segments. One is the cash trading business. That is what people first think the New York Stock Exchange is for. It is important. Second is the derivatives trading business—we have a healthy global business in both cash and derivatives. The third one, which is the newest one and the most interesting, is the technology business. Every product and service that we build or create for ourselves we are certainly willing to sell to others.

Finally I would think it's one of the most promising businesses we have. We said to the world last year that within five years we would be a billion dollar business. So the technology feature of the company's services is a big part of the business in terms of becoming a technology vendor, which I try to point out to our vendors. I remind them that we love that they are our vendors. We love what they do with us. But also in some small way—and maybe big ways in the future—they are our competitors. So it is an interesting focus.

Yourdon: And I was just thinking about the kind of things they show people on television, with human traders waving sheets of paper, even though that sort of thing has been out of date for five or ten years.

Rubinow: A relatively small percentage of our volume goes to the floor and sometimes people ask me what's the floor for, or why do you still have a floor? So many exchanges throughout the world no longer have a floor. They have largely disappeared. I say what sounds like a company line, but makes perfect sense: The floor will be there as long as there are customers who vote with their dollars and support it. I think the floor is a small but significant portion of the trading that goes through here. The customers support it. It makes money for us. It is a service that offers yet another option for the customer.

As long as that model still is viable, we keep it. If it ever changes, we may reevaluate, but it doesn't look like it is going to change. And it makes a great platform for CNBC, Fox News, and all our in-house media outlets broadcasting from here, rather than broadcasting from a lifeless place like some of our competitors.

Yourdon: At the other extreme is a whole phenomenon that I was unaware of is the high volume of the high-frequency trading business. I was staggered to see what a large fortune we are all seeing. Will that continue growing?

Rubinow: Yes, it has definitely, the trend has happened for a number of years in the United States, and it is becoming more pronounced in Europe. In my mind it is really just a matter of time before it becomes the norm in Asia and the other continents, too. That is something I wanted to point out to people, from the technology perspective, it is one of the most interesting things we do. Designing something in an industry that is concerned with micro-second response times. In order to develop that, we have to not only understand how to write good functional software, but we also have to know how to write efficient software and you have to understand the operating system, the network, the hardware and all the resources in a computer environment.

When you finally develop the software, you have to realize all these things make it an interesting job. But it is the only way you can do it with microseconds here and there. And then, of course, you have to do it in high volumes. Some of our systems, like our market data systems, run at millions of messages per second. And you have to do it with very little jitter. Our customers do not like oscillations in response time. They want them to be perfectly flat so you get low variance and low response rate with high transaction volume—it has to be very secure, very reliable, and, of course, cost-effective. You put all these things together and it makes for an interesting technical platform.

Yourdon: So performance is part of the problem. It reminds me of the '60s and '70s when their hardware was less technical and more limited than ours, and we were starting to be so much more relaxed about that long list of criteria. And now it is back again. I hadn't thought of that. That is very interesting.

Rubinow: We have two new data centers that we completed last year. One in New Jersey and one outside of London. Most of the space in the data centers is not for us; it is for our customers. Mostly because they want to reduce the limis of the speed of light in the problem. You'll appreciate this when you walk a customer into the data center, and they see where our trading engines are. They see where their equipment is placed and they'll see some other equipment and sometimes they'll say, "Well, what is that over there?"

"It's for another customer and that is all you need to know."

OK. And that is a few feet closer from where I am. And I'll say, "OK, let's review this. Rule of thumb, the speed of light is about a one foot a nanosecond (in a vacuum). So let's see what a few feet means… that is a couple of nanoseconds. Yes that's a difference but I don't know that you can take advantage of a couple of nanoseconds today. Maybe next year, maybe ten years. I don't know…but it is not something I would make a big deal about because I really don't think it should be important to you. If that changes, we will take a look at it."

But in thinking about this, we thought about how does one mitigate that? Well, one is, if we go back to something many people would remember—depends how old they are—go back to the design of the computer like the Cray, which was built in a circular architecture to make all the processors equidistant from the core. So the trading engines are the core and all the customers could be in the perimeter of the circle. So that is one way; we are not doing that, but that is one way. The other way some people have done is that they modify the length of the cable. The further away you are, the shorter the cable; the closer you are, the more slack in the cable. You would think it is crazy, but this is what some people have done to create the schematic to make everyone exactly the same to the smallest conceivable increment of time, as everybody else and that a nanosecond difference is unacceptable. That's a bit extreme—but these are the sensitivities of the industry.

Yourdon: I was completely unaware of these issues until I got involved as an expert witness in a lawsuit related to high-frequency trading. There are some staggering numbers, and I'm now paying closer attention to things I have been unaware of. Last question I have in the section is to ask your perspective of what IT is doing to retire old legacy systems and prepare for what we cannot do today.

Rubinow: The thing is, we keep pushing the technology envelope in the trading business. We constantly strive to improve. I have calculated, and I am sure my peers in other companies have calculated, what is the fastest speed you can possibly achieve by integrating the most advanced technology and at what point is it a limitation of processors that are not fast enough or memory that isn't fast enough, etc.

And we do have other considerations we can't get around. And so we are trying to be on the edge of technology and do whatever is possible. Having said that in the technology business, we address the needs of what we refer to as the capital markets community. We are constantly white boarding new products and services that we think the industry would want and may know to come to us or may not even know they need yet, but it makes perfect sense. And so we are trying to come up with all kinds of things like that.

Yourdon: So you have the "aha" opportunity to introduce something down the road?

Rubinow: Yes, it's one of these things where that's so true in so many other industries. If you ask a customer what they would want—for example, the iPod—if you went to people and said, "Describe to me what kind of iPod-like device you would like," before it existed, they wouldn't know what to say. But then Apple built one, and people said, "Oh yeah, I always wanted one of those, I just didn't know it until now."

Yourdon: It is funny you should mention it. There was an article in the *New York Times* today that said just exactly that. It is not the customer's job to figure out what he or she wants. It's the job of the company, perhaps with focus groups for customers.

Rubinow: I probably have done that so many times. You see someone and say, "Technology would enable the following things." They would say, "Gee, I never knew that was possible. I never thought of that, but now that you've described it to me, it sounds like a fantastic idea." But it just wasn't in their gestalt to think about such things and they use it like a little blast from left field to remind them.

Yourdon: I don't want to go too far off on a tangent, but there is another aspect to this as I am sure you heard of. When you first introduce a new technology to some people, their immediate instinct is to continue doing old, familiar things—maybe a little faster or cheaper—instead of looking to complete new applications. And this is true of all kinds of things that go back to hundreds of years. When Alexander Graham Bell invented the telephone, he himself told people what they could do was stay home in the comfort of their own living room and listen to a live performance of an artist playing in a concert hall. Is that something you run into in your business as well?

Rubinow: We do run into it because the financial services industry is full of really smart people, but in many cases they are smart people who are in a particular valley or rut mentally, and sometimes when you help break them out of it, they are smart enough to know it, but they never spent the time to do it, because they didn't have the stimulus or catalyst to make them see things in a different light or from a new perspective.

That is why I am a big promoter of people that have worked in different industries coming together. Only half of my group has spent their whole career in financial services while the other half are newer to financial services, and bring a different perspective than people who have worked their whole life in financial services. We just recently hired a head of global development. When we were doing the search, I wanted to look in other industries, so I brought this fellow in who came from Silicon Valley. He was an accomplished software guy and when he interviewed here, several people said he had never worked in our industry.

But I said, "Well, OK, he'll learn. He is not stupid, he'll learn. It is not rocket science." Second thing, he had never worked in a regulated industry. "No problem. He'll learn that too. He'll understand the rules." The third thing is the most telling. They said because he had never worked in our industry, he has never worked with difficult people." I said, "Oh man, take your blinders off. We haven't cornered the market for difficult people." So it is nice to get other people with different perspectives.

Yourdon: I am wondering if I will see that there is a pattern. I have already interviewed the CIO of Microsoft who ultimately got into the Silicon Valley kind of world, but who started off in a totally different career. I am wondering how to differentiate between the ones who are really interesting and the ones that are not interesting.

Rubinow: Well you know, with my biochemist background, hybridization often yields a stronger product, and I believe that is true even with a CIO as well.

Yourdon: There is another aspect of this that I thought you would be able to comment about: the generational phenomenon. The fact that we have the younger kids without all the preconceptions.

Rubinow: We will take advantage of it, and I will say, in my limited experience I read and hear all about that. You know, for years and years prominent scientists said that their most creative discoveries were in their twenties, but they didn't think the big discoveries were as likely as they got older.

I can tell you that I think all the time about the younger generation, meaning people in their twenties working here. They grew up with video games. They are used to very visual interfaces. They are certainly not strangers to technology. They have certain expectations for what their workplace should be like.

In my immediate work environment, I find that someone in their forties may frequent and be as adept at Facebook, Twitter, and LinkedIn as someone in their twenties. Maybe a 20-year-old is better at video games. I don't know if such distinctions help us that much in what we do, but maybe the examples haven't jumped out at me. Maybe there are subtle differences around, but I just haven't noticed them. I don't see a profound difference. I have found smart people in every generation. I find different people in every generation.

Yourdon: Well, it's a profound change to go from a world where we have limited resources that are very expensive that are controlled and regulated and doled out very carefully to a place where many of these are pervasive and free and therefore ought not to be controlled, yet they are.

Rubinow: Yes, and that is one of the positive aspects of technology we have today, and if I heard it once, I have heard it a thousand times. When I was a developer I used to ignore performance in software—because the assumption was, oh well, buy a bigger server. We don't have that luxury here because, first of all, we are very cost-conscious, but second of all, the idea is not to rely solely on hardware because the software has to be hyper efficient too, otherwise you are not competitive. And you can be sure that the competitor down the street is thinking the same way.

So anybody who comes in and says, "I'm a software guy. I don't have to worry; just buy more memory, or buy more processors." It is not as simple as that. You actually have to think about a lot of things, but we have a niche that not everybody plays in. So we do think about those things.

Someone observed the other day that they were looking for a typewriter ribbon and they used the Internet to find a typewriter ribbon. So it is kind of ironic that you would do that. It is a cultural thing. One guy here, in his thirties, made a comment about using a Rolodex to look something up. I said, "Let me stop you for a second. Do you think someone ten years younger than you would understand what a Rolodex is?" And he said, "You know, they probably wouldn't." Well that's a term that we take for granted but it doesn't make any sense anymore

Yourdon: The other aspect of this generational thing that I heard a lot about from financial services industry is that the difficulty of reaching out to the consumer marketplace. They're asking themselves, "How do we make our stuff more relevant to kids in college, who would only find things out through Facebook or Twitter?" It's a pretty big culture shock. This is probably not so relevant in your realm, because you are not marketing to college kids.

Rubinow: You're right. Our direct customers are traders and they're not so focused on it. In fact, in most of what is built, they help guide the development of the interface. We are just the technology supplier, and so they can leverage whatever pleases them. But we do have a website and we do sell our data on the website and a few other things. And we want to make it appear contemporary and create an innovative impression. Regardless of the industry we look at, we want to let people know that we are the leaders of the twenty-first century. And that helps to create that impression.

We haven't gotten into general mobile applications in a big way because few traders would do anything mobile (other than in the special instance of using wireless devices on the floor of the exchange) because of response times and security, among other reasons. And we want to create an impression that we are out there. We look around the country and see a lot of iPads around. Our use of them is symbolic of us trying to show that we are where the innovative people go. You bring the iPads to me and maybe there are applications that would be informational, so we are exploring all of these things.

Yourdon: I would think iPads would be interesting to trade from.

Rubinow: Well, it takes us down another avenue of discussion in terms of collaborative technology. Our technology group is spread out to many cities in the world. Four throughout the U.S. and three in Europe, and we are trying to find ways to make it feel like, whether it be with an iPad, video, or collaboration tools and knowledge sharing, we are exploring all those things to try and bring the community closer together. This also includes customers, vendors, and academics, so that anyone who wants to be part of our network is properly segregated, working confidentially, but they all participate in helping us to become smarter and do things better.

Yourdon: That's interesting because that has become one aspect of a whole collection of issues, when you want to do things behind the firewall, but also cross the firewall, and communicate with outsiders like former employees and customers and so on.

Ironically the best examples I have found so far are in the pharmaceutical industry. They have an enormously long product development cycle— from ten to fifteen years to bring a newly discovered drug to market. Eli Lilly and Pfizer are examples of companies with collaboration involving people outside their firm, and these are very conservative companies. So it's very exciting to hear you talk about this, all the more so in a regulated industry like yours.

Rubinow: As a matter of fact, just this morning there was an Internet radio show called CIO Talk Radio. I was on that program talking about what they were terming "collective intelligence" and we touched upon this very subject.

Yourdon: This generational phenomenon is one that people seem to react to very differently, especially when it comes to tools, and I would imagine that must be relevant to developers. For example, I ran into someone who said the average college kid today has never seen Microsoft Outlook, and would be horrified if he *did* see it—not just because of the user interface, but because of the overall perspective on how he spends his day.

In my case, I get up in the morning and think: what do I have to *do* today? I look at my e-mail to see which clients are complaining, which clients have new tasks and deadlines, and so on. But a college-age kid is likely to get up in the morning and ask, "Where are my friends? What are they doing? How far away are they?" I see that kind of thing on Facebook with my nieces and nephews. In fact the whole world revolves around that.

Rubinow: Well, I understand that perspective, but I am sure there are other reasons Microsoft thought of that interface when they developed Outlook. A better solution to that is being put into Windows 8 on the desktop. With the limited number of people I have talked to that have a Windows 7 phone, they like that aspect—that they have a Facebook tile and whatever else they use often that they run continuously and they are literally one click away.

I just want to bring up one other generational issue. People sometimes say to me, "We have to offer our new younger employee a computer device, and nine times out of ten, they will choose a Mac. If we don't offer them a Mac, they will not work here."

My response is: the Mac is primarily a tool. Whether they get to use a particular tool or they don't, is that the most important thing to them? Maybe— I am not really sure if that should be their primary motive, or maybe they view it as symbolic of the rest of the work environment. I am not sure, but I don't know anyone who comes to us and turns down the job because we said, "No, you can't have an Apple, you have to use a PC." You often hear that, you have to ... "X" or otherwise they will not work for you.

Yourdon: Well, I think it is more symbolic with Mac users. I think it is representative of a larger phenomenon. It may be Mac vs. PC, but it is usually smaller, newer devices versus old, and where I see the battle particularly being played out is in the mobile device. I think it is 3M or one of the Fortune 500 companies that has made a big splash in the enterprise when their hire new university graduates and tell them, "Bring whatever device you want. We are not going to force you to have a BlackBerry. We will figure out your iPhone or whatever you've got."

Rubinow: We have talked about that here as well; in one sense it would be a great relief to say, "Here is a list of devices that are in the realm of possibilities. Pick your favorite one—go buy it and we, in combination with the vendor, will support it." There is a certain appeal to that, but on the other hand, we are a little different from a lot of companies, from a regulatory and security standpoint. We would not be as freewheeling as, say, a non-regulated company that is not under potential attack by a lot of people from around the world trying to break in. But we have talked about it, what it would take to do that, though we have not come to the point where we say, "Go ahead." The iPad is one that runs through the conversation often. People go and buy one, and it is cheap enough—and now that they have it, they want to be able to use it in the corporate environment. And we make it work, and so we have a taste of what it is like for people to bring in a device to the party and make it work.

Yourdon: It's interesting that the iPad app environment is somewhat controlled by Apple, as opposed to the Android world that's open, and that may turn out to be very scary. Well we have touched on "futures" here, and I started off by asking what are some of the new trends influencing industry? Mobile, obviously, and generational issues. Are there any other key technology trends that you see?

Rubinow: Well, I am very quick to say that "cloud computing" as a concept is not something new, but something that other people remember from the sixties as time sharing. One of the main enabling cloud technologies, virtual machines, dates from that era as well.

Having said that, we would like to provide cloud computing, or whatever technology would comprise it to our customers. A private cloud where our customers would include almost any software and infrastructure—whatever service they are looking for, we would provide it for them. It would be the most efficient, and that resonates for our customers, they are all looking for a better solution.

Everyone needs similar infrastructure, so why have your own "server department"? They all do the same thing and instead of them all doing it separately, where there is no real competitive advantage, why don't they have a firm like us do it for them in a cloud, where we are set up and they get all the advantages of the scale that we operate and maybe some of the analytical services that we do for them today as well? So that is a big opportunity for us in our position.

The other thing that we talked about is social networks and multimedia. We talked about how we collaborate with the larger world—we get ideas when we communicate with people. From the technical standpoint, I don't know if there is anything unique, we are particularly pushing the envelope—faster processors, bigger networks, more efficient storage—and in some cases we are impressed and in other areas we are disappointed in the speed of the technology. I don't know if there is anything here that I would say is the "next generation" yet.

Yourdon: Virtualization is right in there with cloud.

Rubinow: There are two categories of applications in our world. One that lends itself to virtualization quite nicely, but it is just an extra millisecond here or there of acceptable overhead. We virtualize a lot of our environment in that respect. But the trading world operates in microseconds now, so it's important to eliminate unnecessary overhead. And so we virtualize what we can and don't virtualize what we can't.

Yourdon: The next thing I had on my list is interesting because with all this thinking about the future, we can all look back there on a bit of history—even if it is only 50 years for the whole industry, it is a lifetime for some of us. What do you think are the most significant IT discoveries in your career—the "defining moments"?

Rubinow: Well, things like the advent of the Internet and the Web, more powerful interfaces. I think that has changed a lot of things. In terms of knowledge versus what people ever had before, I think, there are a lot of things that we are still relatively primitive on. In terms of software development, I don't think we've moved light years ahead. We have different languages, different methodologies, but I don't know that we are all that better off for them. They are different flavors and people might have more bulletproof software as opposed to "pretty good," and I don't know that a lot has happened in that regard, too.

I will tell you in terms of history, there was one of our developers in Europe who wanted to throw out one of our software tools and replace it with a newer one. And I said "What was your primary reason?"

The response was, "Well, the one we use was developed in the '90s so it is old technology."

And I said with my typical sense of sarcasm, "Okay, now let me follow this thread. You would like to replace the technology because it was old."

I said, "Do you know many of the languages and tools we use to write most of our software were developed a long time before the '90s, so those systems are also based on 'old' technology? So I guess you should throw those away too. Clearly, they could not possibly be any good."

So I think we are always looking at the new stuff and then the old stuff, some of it is robust enough that we sometime don't appreciate the technology that has been around for a long time and has advanced over time. But in terms of dramatic changes, I think that it is really the Internet along with more powerful interfaces, but I can't think of anything else that is dramatic.

Yourdon: You brought up a good point. You are probably familiar with Howard Rubin. He often makes a point that in terms of development, some of the organizations are a hell of a lot better than they were 20 or 30 years ago, but the average productivity level hasn't changed all that much. It's a little depressing that conference organizations calling people like me to give talks to the current generation, about software development—and they just want updated versions of the talk about things I used to talk about in the '70s.

Rubinow: There is something else that is kind of a "back to the future perspective." As you know, processor speeds are not growing at the same rate they were, and to make up for that, one of the things we talk about all the time is in order to keep the ball moving at a reasonable rate in terms of performance and speed, we should have better parallel programming models.

We don't have a lot of these models. We ask where has this occurred before, and then we can use the language that was designed to attack a similar problem 20 years ago (as in the telecom industry) and it wouldn't be necessary to start all over again.

But if we focus on that kind of thinking and teach programmers how to do things in parallel, as opposed to primarily letting the operating system do its best, we could take advantage of all the multi-processing options that are available to us. That is something that a lot of people in our industry talk about and I don't know how soon we will be able to accomplish that.

Yourdon: You have actually touched on something important there. My colleagues have written a lot of books suggesting that we look for the specific solutions rather than general solutions.

Rubinow: Yes, you have touched on something that I think about a lot lately—the way we are thinking, and I can tell you now that I think I am an example of that. Because of rapid changes in information presentation technology, I jump around from one hyperlink to another. We see less and less of the desire to sit and think deeply about a problem and research it to a high degree. Once upon a time I used to think like that, but I think like that less now than before because of the information environment in which we work.

Some people will argue that it helps you to think more quickly versus the argument that is there are times you need to think deeply about a problem and spend a long time on it. When I was in high school, I was a chess nut. I was very competitive and I could sit at a chess board for hours. I would lose all track of time. I cannot do that anymore. My mind won't readily support the same single activity for hours, and I regret that.

Yourdon: Some of that, of course, is age.

Rubinow: Ha, you have to remind me.

Yourdon: It is definitely because I used to watch my sons play competitive chess and the younger boy placed second in a national championship. But I don't think it is typically an advantage, especially when we have so many other urgent problems to solve.

Rubinow: You may have heard about the software that you put on your desktop that shuts off your e-mail. It forces you not to have e-mail, so you cannot be distracted. Wow—I would have never thought of that, but I understand the value in someone telling OK you have enough e-mail, I'm going to shut it off for a while so you can focus.

Yourdon: Yeah, that is intriguing. Let's see, what next on my list? What about problems and issues that you worry about?

Rubinow: We are always trying to be more cost-effective. It is always a big issue for us, especially because of the nature of our business—there is a lot of focus on efficiency here. And then the other thing is that because we are an icon of capitalism around the world, we are particularly attractive to people that have bad intentions. So security is a big issue for us.

Another concern: how do we find the best and the brightest, and how do we keep them? How do we motivate them? How do we get peak productivity? From an economic standpoint, our business is correlated to volatility in the world because that's when people trade more.

Yourdon: Actually you have just reminded me of a question. When I was looking through your file, I saw that you guys are out there in public forums quite a lot, whether it is CIO Radio or keynoting in any number of conferences, and so on. And clearly you are not talking to your immediate subordinates or peers. It is not like here in the office, but people outside. Do you see a growing role for CIOs in general, as a public spokesman for some aspect of your business?

Rubinow: Yes, I certainly do in this company. Certain people in the world know that there is this place on Wall Street and they see the big American flag, they see activity on the floor there, and they don't realize how significant we really are.

When I tell people what we do, with sophisticated people and sophisticated technology, they say, "That is really amazing, we never knew that."

So part of my job is to remind people of that—our customers, our employees, and our potential employees, those people who would say, "Why would I ever work here?" Many of the things we are doing are cool, so I am a PR person for the company. I do that a lot.

Also, another customer base that we haven't talked about: the customers that are listed here, we get revenue from that. I don't talk to every company but I do talk to a lot of technology firms, and I explain to them why their technology might be used here, what their affiliation with us means to them, and the interesting things we can talk about together and that we can work on together. And in some cases they weren't aware of it and, it might be an obvious partnership for us and then again it might not be. So for all these reasons, I find myself talking about these things.

Also, in some regard, we try and help push the industry forward. Here is an example: when IEEE was talking about networking standards, the next one they wanted to go to was the 40Gb standard. We said, it is going out of style—we'll surpass 40Gb in no time, why don't you guys think about 100Gb? We tried to advocate our need for technology, so people would do things for us that we need them to do.

Yourdon: I was thinking simultaneously that where you have historically assumed that the spokesman for the company would be the founder or the CEO, you would not tend to think of the CIO as the technology spokesman—but, of course, those were the more classic companies and now there is a much larger set of "classic companies" that rely entirely on information.

Rubinow: You are absolutely right though; let's use Apple as an example: I don't know Steve Jobs, I'm sure he is a very capable guy, but he is not solely responsible for the iPhone or the iPod. Apple has all sorts of products, and he does a really good job of promoting Apple but it takes others as well. From my perspective, many of the things we do are the products and services that all of our customers will become familiar with one day—and so I can probably talk to them better than many other people in the company, so I have a very useful prospective that someone on the business side may not have.

Yourdon: Well, the CIO of Microsoft said something interesting to me—he said, "A lot of our customers come to us and say 'You're a big company and presumably you know stuff about IT. How do you discover it and how do you do this or that?'" And so his role, from that perspective, is to be a spokesman or the champion of technology.

Rubinow: The CIO is becoming more prominent in the highest levels of the corporation. So many industries have an information technology emphasis and some CIOs are so prominent that he or she is going to be the spokesperson for one of the most important growing parts of the business. They focus more on communicating then they ever did before. And that sort of resonated with me, too.

Yourdon: My wife suggested an interesting example to me: So many of the problems and recalls we've been hearing about lately in the auto industry seem to involve software. And so you often wonder, how would that be handled in different IT organizations, with different CIOs?

First of all, how would that problem have been created in the first place? And second of all, who found the problem? And thirdly, how was the whole thing handled by the CIO? Whatever that story is, it's probably different at Toyota than it would be at Ford or Honda. So it points out that the CIO not only has to explain to the media the good things that are done, and why your company is so successful, but also how you screwed up with its use of IT in its products or services.

Rubinow: This is my philosophy. We talk about two things that I like to get people focused on. One is communication skills, and I always point this out to people. People ask who had the greatest influence on my career. I say the first thing that pops into my head is my father, primarily because he told me, no matter what your job is, you are always a salesman. You are always trying to sell something to someone.

It is not enough to sit back and say "I am brilliant" and everyone will recognize you're brilliant. You've got to make it happen. So I thought about communication skills since a really young age, and I encourage people to do that too and to take advantage of as many communication opportunities as they can.

The other thing is that you never get too far away from your technology, it is critical for me to keep on top of it. But many CIOs, too often, were a developer at one time and now they're an administrator.

I know one CIO from another firm and when I talked to him, I asked him his opinion about technology. And he said, without hesitation, "I don't have to think about it anymore, I have people who think about those things for me." And I said, "Wow, we all know that technology can be very challenging and you have to have a seat at the table. Otherwise, what they are going to end up doing is that everyone around you will be smart and give you conflicting recommendations and ideas and all types of things."

I often find myself with two smart people; one says we should go right and one says we should go left, and if I don't have an appreciation for what they are trying to decide and help them come to some conclusion, then I just have to say, well you know, he is usually right, so I will go with him.

So I try not to get too far from technology either. I try to stay close to the work going on. I am a voracious reader and I think in order to be an effective CIO you really have to comprehend a lot of technology. It doesn't mean that you can always tell what qualifies one project as a success and the other as a false start, although I can do that with some things. That is the culture of things we are talking about.

Yourdon: Would you emphasize the whole multi-disciplinary approach? That seems to be consistent with your career and what you have seen elsewhere.

Rubinow: Yes, I would do that too. I think that there are many computer specialties, and there are many different aspects of a business. Technology is always important. And I would go further: I don't want to say that someone that has been at the same company for decades is limited, but in the earlier part of my career, I got my degree in chemistry, but I always used computers as an essential tool.

I wanted to develop more and understand things better, so I started taking classes in computer science. Because I knew the direction I was headed, I would probably never write an operating system, or write a network protocol on the job. But I wanted to make sure I was more well-rounded and on top of that, an even better technologist—but I also wanted to understand what business was all about. I tried to get myself exposed to as many situations as possible.

It worked for me and I think I would encourage people to have as many different perspectives as you can have because it also helps to bring fresh ideas to things that need freshening up. I always liked the idea, and like people who have done a bunch of different things as an augmented background, because they make contributions to people that are more useful as well.

Yourdon: On the other hand, you said something fascinating that will be true for every student today, but that was not true in generations before: in every university, a significant part of your arsenal of intellectual pursuits from high school onward involves computers. And obviously that was not true for me when I was in high school in the 1950s. There is a period of time that you can either get involved with computers or not.

Rubinow: Today, you can take it for granted. I remember my very first programming class was when I was in eighth grade, and I had to go across the city to a university computer room to use the technology—which was the mainframe—and I had a terminal. And it was nice to have a personal computer at home where I would program ever since then. I was an outlier then, as to what was expected.

Yourdon: Well, actually, you don't have to worry about being an outlier. My youngest son originally intended to study physics in college, but ended up with a degree in philosophy from the University of Chicago. And then, about five years later, he went back to Columbia to earn a bachelor's degree in physics and then on to Toronto to get a master's as well. I envy the broad background he got along the way.

Rubinow: And I respect that as well. People come up and say to me, clearly you don't use this chemistry you studied. On the contrary, I developed disciplined problem solving based on the scientific method. It applies to the sciences, but is also applies to so many different things in my job and so, no, it is useful every day.

Yourdon: Yes, scientific method problems solving.

Rubinow: And you know the processes—the logic, philosophies, analytics—are valuable.

Yourdon: Let me turn that around and ask you, is there one common piece of advice for people who want a career path to the CIO?

Rubinow: People that come to me and say, "I want to do what you do," focus too much on technology. If they're really technically smart, then it is a logical progression, and then I tell them there is this whole other thing called management and leadership. You can't find it in a book, it is really hard to take a course and say now you are an effective leader.

I don't often know the prescribed path that people take to become good at those skills. It's acquired through experience, coaching, and mentoring, or being mentored, and all those sorts of things. I impress upon people, those "soft skills" differentiate CIOs from wannabe CIOs. They need those skills to work effectively in a company.

I'm often asked, well what class do I need to take to become certified, say, in Microsoft skills? And I say it goes well beyond certifications. And by the way, I don't always have the answer to that. You may not have the oratory skills of President Obama no matter how hard you try. Similarly, not everyone can be a really good leader.

Yourdon: To go off in a different area, how do you have conversations with your peers in the business units about the crazy ideas they bring to you?

Rubinow: You know, I think that there is an assessment you can do with numbers and that's the easiest tool. Then there are the people who become "believers," or intuitively they feel something is right. And you sometimes have to dissuade them from it if the facts don't support it.

My decision ability is good, so when they recommend something to you, you may know it doesn't make any sense. It is not just a difference of opinion; it just doesn't make any sense. You go to them and say, for the following reasons, "I don't think this will work."

And they say to you, "But why?"

I'm pretty good at making decisions and if my intuition is telling me it is a pretty bad idea, you have to work extra hard to find ways to tell people that I don't think that is going to work. And then again you can be wrong too, but…

We have had some examples of that in the last few days. People come up with ideas here, and I immediately get ten examples or changes in priority to accommodate them, and somehow they feel it has more value than it really does. And that is the way it is and you have to find ways to persuade people with leadership and management because these are other people over whom you have no authority and you can't order them to do what you want.

I learned this more than any other place when I worked at Fidelity Investments. A new job was created, and I interviewed for it, and they hired me for it, and my job was to integrate things—to develop an information architecture integrating all the relevant information of 40 divisions.

And I said "I am not naive about these things, not everyone is going to report to me. How do I get them to do go along with it? How am I going to do this?"

And they said, "Oh don't worry about it: the chairman wants it done."

I said OK. So I go to Boston, and I go to the first meeting and present a report on another technology.

And they said, "Why would we do that?

And I said, "Well, apparently the chairman wants it."

They replied, "Well, can we give you a list of all the things the chairman asked for? Join the club."

So I said to myself, that is not going to work—so how do I get all these guys to do what I want them to do when I can't order them to do it? And I found many different ways. I found persuasion, escalation, politics, barter, forcefulness. I found there were many different ways, and I got cooperation from people, not always on my schedule, but I got people to do what I wanted them to do. The practice of influence management was a very valuable lesson from this. Good communications skills, good listening skills—that is a very important skill and I notice that among people who work for me.

When they get frustrated and complain to me, when they want that guy to do something and he just won't do it. I tell them, you just try it a different way. Here are some of the ways you might approach that. And that's a good educational lesson, too.

Yourdon: There is an aspect of that I would like to explore a little further. In a way it has to do with this global issue of the CIO getting an equal seat at the table with other C-level officers. You mentioned earlier that in many businesses, there are people who are now up at that level who have been very successful on their way up at doing something, which is usually instrumental to the success of the company. Now they may have been the best automobile engineer and as a result, they often feel that that defines the company's success. How in general do you think the CIO is going to be able to get the kind of influence and respect that they need to be able to operate as an equal?

Rubinow: Well, sometimes I think that every technology department in almost every company should have their own PR function or internally rely on skilled people to make contributions in the best possible marketing way, as if they were selling toothpaste or another consumer product.

We do remind people. And just a couple of weeks ago for our management committee, we did a report of what we've done over the last three years. It is mind boggling, the things we have accomplished. In terms of cost reduction, in terms of output, in terms of innovations, and we put it together because we are conscious of it every single day. But our management team has other things to worry about, and they're not focused on, how great has IT been in the last year?

But when we brought them the report, it reminded them and they were unanimous. They said, "Yes, we were aware of this, but when you put it all together, it is a great record." But we have to keep reminding people of our contributions, and our impact—and relying on other people to take an active role is not a good strategy.

Yourdon: Well, in fact, it seems more often that you don't even have the option—you are more or less thrown out. Howard Rubin used to make that point a lot, there is an enormous amount of money being spent on stuff the senior executives couldn't touch or feel, it is very intangible. And yet if you package the story properly, you often could say, "By the way, this is really what we have done."

Rubinow: I remember one of the managers I worked for at Fidelity on the business side, said to me, "Show me what you've accomplished every month."

And I said, "Like what? A total redesign of our network?"

"No," he said, "that activity is invisible to me. You might think about the amount of money you saved the company."

And I said, "How about quarterly?"

"No," he said. "Every month …do something."

We found things to do. We know that certain managers are skeptical, and we've got to find a way through our activities to remind them of the value we provide.

Yourdon: That is a big part of the future as well. First, recognizing the need that can be addressed with IT— and then being able to pull it off.

Rubinow: Well, everyone wants to see progress. When people have the confidence that you are doing good stuff, the outcome becomes more predictable as a result. So you have to think long term.

Yourdon: Here's a different question: what attributes do you look for in the direct reports who are going to be part of your "CIO team"?

Rubinow: I remember reading something a long time ago about a study on football teams. You can have a really great football team where none of the players like each other, but technically they are very competent. But if you can, a football team that is technically good and where they also really like each other, you're going to have much better results. And I think that is what we have here. We tend to enjoy working with each other and understand each other; we know what the expectations are.

People know what to expect from them. They know when to ask questions and they are on the same wave length. That is an extremely important thing. And by the way, when working long hours, you want to do it with people that you like. You don't want to spend 12+ hours a day trying to solve a problem with people you can hardly stand, or need to get away from. There are some people here that I have gone on hiking trips in the mountains with, because we really get along well. And so that is an important characteristic.

Then again, technical competence and all those kinds of things have a big role in making good decisions and making the right calls. Also risk taking, perspective—otherwise, you will not be able to advance as you want.

There are several things I ask of people when they work for me. One is that you can see a lot more than your immediate job—see the bigger picture. Second, if you make a decision and it turns out poorly, I ask myself and others if another skilled practitioner would have made the same decision at the same time given the same information. If the answer is yes, then even if we're not happy with the outcome, it's hard to fault the decision maker by using hindsight. On the other hand, if you made a decision to go left when other people in your position would have said go right, then I think there is a bit of a problem. Thirdly, let's not make the same mistake over and over again. Let us learn from our experience. And I think people understand that.

So I think there is a sense of loyalty here. And equal commitment to each other. I know that they have my back and they know that I have their back. When times are tough, I am not going to distance myself and say, hey, there's a problem, I didn't know what was going on. We know we can count on each other. And that, combined with the other points makes a really great team.

Yourdon: You mentioned in that effort, you would be working 12 hours a day. Do you see this job as a 12-hour-per-day job?

Rubinow: I am a self-admitted workaholic. However, I don't try to impose that on others. But having said that, there are things here, especially during the day, the trading day, where you know that something is pending, involving a lot of money.

We're global and so we need to talk to each other all hours of the night. People know that I read my e-mail at two o'clock in the morning. I don't tell everyone, but they know I am going to be that way. Most of the people here work a standard work week on the job, but they are really available seven days a week. And it is rare for someone to say, you know it is a weekend, I'm on holiday or I'm on vacation, don't contact me.

I don't want to ruin anyone's family life but if you don't mind it, because you're part of the team, you have professional pride. And that is just the nature of what we do here. You will find people that work here, even off site, who work really long days. Work is part of what we do. And they enjoy the personal satisfaction of accomplishment and being part of the team.

Yourdon: Do you think that's true of CIOs across the board?

Rubinow: I think people are not hiring, so people are working longer hours, doing more jobs. I do see that, until times get better. People do want to have some time at home, and the hiring will start to peak again. And I'll tell you—in 1998 when I went to work at a start-up in Silicon Valley, I had this image that I was going to work day and night, that I was going to sleep in the office at night, and that I would survive on a diet of Diet Coke and Oreos. These are all the visions I had. And when I got there, I did find a lot of hard-working people, but I found I was one of the hardest-working, so I asked some of my younger colleagues about this. They said they didn't work late nights just because someone thinks they're supposed to work 12 hours a day. It's also generational—they also realize that there is a life outside of work. Dedicating yourself to the company is not a life that they need to or want to emulate. I understand that and I respect that. It is not a choice that I make, but I understand.

Yourdon: I remember after I first visited some of the companies out in Silicon Valley, a lot of them had the motto, "Live hard and play hard."

Rubinow: I think younger people are even more so that way, than maybe people who have grown up in a different generation—for whom work really dominated their lives. I was thinking, though, that some people understand how important work is and are far too passionate about their jobs. In some countries, labor laws have prevented people from working too much and they are realizing the benefits of that.

Yourdon: I remember hearing that in Germany, they would literally lock the office doors at five o'clock—and if the server crashed, you could not get into the building. I was stunned.

Rubinow: And that is the lifestyle they want. It's very successful.

Yourdon: That leads into my last question, not about that technical but about the social aspect. One of the philosophies of the "agile" approach to development is that of a "sustainable" work schedule. You're not running a sprint, you are running a marathon. And you got to be a little more careful to pace yourself. If you go at top speed all the time, you are going to burn out. I'm curious from your prospective what do you think about this whole movement in general.

Rubinow: Agile development—I like it. I like the outcome, like the fact that I know what we are going to do in the timeframe of a single sprint. Everyone knows what they are supposed to do and I like the productivity. For the right application, it really has a good impact on programming, too.

Yourdon: On programming?

Rubinow: Yeah, wherever it makes sense to use it. Sometimes we use it for entire projects. Sometimes we use it for individual tasks. So I am an advocate for all these things.

Yourdon: I've been amazed by the growth of agile—I went to the last big Agile conference last year, and there was somewhere near 1,200 people in attendance. They are coming up on the tenth anniversary of the Agile Manifesto. And there are some very interesting surveys and statistics about making it work with multi-national projects, making it work in regulated industries. It definitely works in certain environments—especially when it's already in place and the project is all inside one organization. If you have arms-length, contractual relationships between vendors and customers, and you have developers all over the world and it is more than 100 people, then it can be more problematic.

Rubinow: We are a little more careful with that but then again we use it where it makes sense.

Yourdon: Okay, I think this is probably a good point for us to wrap things up, and bring the discussion for a close. I'd really like to thank you for taking the time to talk with me today.

Rubinow: Thanks.

Lewis Temares

CIO Emeritus, University of Miami

Dr. M. Lewis Temares is VP/CIO Emeritus for Information Technology and Dean Emeritus of the College of Engineering at the University of Miami. For the majority of his career, he led a staff of 300 employees and was responsible for all aspects of computing and telecommunications, operating with a $40 million budget. Dr. Temares joined the University of Miami in 1980 and later became the first officially designated Chief Information Officer in higher education in the United States, while simultaneously serving as Dean of the College of Engineering from 1994–2007. Selected as one of the "Premiere 100 IT Leaders in the World," he led the University of Miami IT Department to place in the top ten of Computerworld's "Best Places to Work" for eight consecutive years, a distinction only the University of Miami can claim.

A frequent keynote speaker, author, and presenter at academic, business and information technology conferences, Dr. Temares has consulted with governmental agencies, private companies, and multinational organizations alike. He is often cited in national publications and is a senior member of IEEE, a Fellow in the American Marketing Society, and a member of multiple executive councils and advisory boards, including the Dell Platinum Council and Microsoft Higher Education Advisory Group.

Dr. Temares: Let me make this comment first so that we get everything straight and straightforward. I am no longer the CIO for the University of Miami, because I retired in August.

Ed Yourdon: Right, yes, I do know that.

Temares: So I'll put everything with the caveat, "as of August," because the new person coming in should have a new perspective and obviously have different goals.

Yourdon: Yeah. Let's start with something specific: one of the things I'm obviously seeing—as I've kind of expected—is that all of the CIOs have some fairly universal tasks of keeping the lights on, worrying about security, and so on. But I'm curious from your perspective: what is different about the CIO role in the university or academic institution than you would expect to see somewhere out there in the Fortune 500 commercial land?

Temares: Well, there are a couple of things that make you unique. First of all, my customer is the student. A student coming in has this unique role of being my customer and probably the gentleman or the woman who is most likely to raise a breach of security. You know, when I was dean and a student came in with a 1600 on his SAT, we said, "Yes, he could have gone on to Carnegie-Mellon, could have gone on to MIT, he's at the University of Miami." And the VP side of me, the VP/CIO side of me says, very succinctly to himself, "Oh, damn, I think I have somebody coming in that's going to be way ahead of my own people and he's going to break into my system." So, you know, my customer is also one of my most dangerous security risks, just being an 18-year-old student.

The sad thing which happens, which is very unique, is that we recruit faculty members who are all very smart and doctors who are all very smart—and they have individual entrepreneurial characteristics. They have tenure, they can do anything they want with regards to setting up a network; they have funding, they have research, they have everything, and they can make the same decisions as the person who does research in the field of medicine. We have a bunch of people who are actually very independent entrepreneurs, and yet I've got to bring them all together to share in the network and share in the mission so hopefully everything that they all do will meet standards. So that is a very unique characteristic that we have in education, especially in higher education.

Yourdon: Interesting. Now, when you were doing this role, did you have to act as a champion, so to speak, for using more computers and technology in the classroom itself—which I can imagine some faculty would resist?

Temares: Well some people are, because of the generation gap, the older faculty, are resistors. I thought of bringing computers into the classroom for a long time and I can give an instance of something that happened. I looked in [a classroom] door and [noticed a faculty member] writing on the whiteboard from yellow notepaper. … I said to him afterwards, "I've got a couple of questions here. One, did you notice those devices that were with the students? Those are called computers. You could have sent them notes in the mail. And they could have had them available and learning for the first time in front of you. And, secondly, is that paper yellow from age or is that new paper?" And I didn't score many points, but I made my point. I think it really didn't help because, as a senior faculty member, you cannot tell them how to teach. If they want to use technology, fine.

And yet I have a young faculty member who was teaching English and teaching how to do research and immediately went to the computer and showed them how to use the Web and showed the students that they can't trust the Web. It has to be totally accurate 'cause the stuff on there is not reviewed and not verified. So you can verify something or not verify something—just between an encyclopedia and Wikipedia, that kind of thing. So, it depends on the faculty member. Some grasp it immediately. Some don't. The same thing happened with the doctors putting in an electronic hospital record right now. There's one third of your doctors who are really excited, one third of your doctors who are indifferent, and one third of your doctors who are opposed. And the big thing is keeping the one third "indifferent" away from the one third "opposed" so you can get it in.

Yourdon: Interesting, interesting. Now you raised an issue that was my second question for you, and it is kind of an obvious one. Obviously, a university like yours is likely to see, and is going to be forced to deal with, a much denser population of these New-Age, technology-savvy kids—so my question is, what advice do you have for the CIOs of various other companies that are likely to be hiring them as soon as they get out of your university?

Temares: Well, one of the things that's good about these kinds of students is that they teach you what's the next step in technology. I mean, I knew enough about mobile technology and the need to have wireless for my campus long before people knew about having to have wireless computers for their workplace—mainly because I'm dealing with students there on the leading edge. See, you're dealing with a bunch of people that truly grew up with computers that are attached to them, and now you're learning from them—and social media is another example.

Using social media, which they do, they think that we have to communicate differently with homework. You see, we're not a corporation that has to communicate something it wants to get out to its customers. So the new recruit that comes in has to work towards it and is expecting things that are not necessarily available at the firm that they're coming into. They're expecting to be able to use the social media. You know, this whole generation, it's a non-secretive generation. We've always told people, "You've got to be transparent if you want to be trusted." You've got to tell people to communicate. Well, this generation, this is TMI [too much information]. There is too much information about this generation. They feel nothing about exposing themselves on Facebook, on Twitter—I say "exposing themselves," because they communicate what we (the previous generation) used to consider private information. This generation just talks and talks about people freely, and that's a whole different environment for us in the computer field, and in the security of computers. This generation will expose things to the school and forward it and not think twice about it. It's a totally different culture.

Yourdon: Very interesting. Yeah, I certainly agree with you, having watched some of this myself. Well, that kind of leads me into the next area: what are some of the key technology trends that you see shaping the next few years? I mean, obviously, social media is now in front of us, but do you see other things coming along that we should be watching?

Temares: Mobility. Mobility is a big one. Everybody's going to want video mobile, I mean, you know, your RIM [Blackberry] device, your Apple device. I used to say the students coming in had a six-second attention span. They're down to three seconds. And one thing that occupies them is the picture. So they want more and more video entertainment. And so if you want to get to your customer, or you want to get information out, you've got to use a mobile video device.

Yourdon: Yeah, I was just reading some details about a speech the CIO of Delta gave at some computer conference, and she was saying similar things, saying that, you know, "One of the things we want to do at Delta is to be with the customer 24 hours a day. You know, whatever they're doing with our mobile phone apps, and so on," and so I think that's how business has got to look at it. Aside from mobile, what else?

Temares: It's very simple. The life of a CIO, getting into the corporate world, getting into the executive suite, it's a different kind of lifestyle. More and more it's going to be a checklist of how you're going to use the technology. More and more, it's going to be a marketing effort of trying to explain to people in your corporation how information technology can better sell the product or can better reduce the less cost of a product.

Yourdon: You know, it's interesting: earlier this week, I was interviewing the CIO of the New York Stock Exchange, who was saying that maybe the

CIO of the future has got to be the Chief Media Officer also—explaining all of this stuff.

Temares: There's no question about it. I agree completely. I think if anyone does not understand or become fluent in media, the whole relationship between voice/data integration, they can forget about it. I agree completely; and don't forget about the advantages of voice. It's been overlooked, and people forget that the phone conversation is a valuable tool as well. And it's a lot quicker in a lot of ways than detail work.

Yourdon: Absolutely. Well, all of this had to do with looking forward. What about looking back? You've been in the field probably almost as long as I have. Throughout your career, what would you say have been the most significant changes or developments that you've seen in the field?

Temares: Oh, there's no question that life changed with the personal computer. The second time life changed was with the Internet. Even being in the educational field, I was on e-mail in the early seventies, because we had ARPANET and the Internet and things of that nature for the research networks. But the fact that the personal computer became so commercial, was a major, major change. The second thing is the Internet, and the third thing is mobility.

Yourdon: Yeah, I think I would agree with all of those—although something I'm coming to appreciate just in terms of the pervasiveness, particularly with students, is the Google phenomenon. The fact that any question that occurs to you about anything at all—which you would often have shrugged and ignored in the past—you now Google it.

Temares: Absolutely. And I'll add to that, not only can you answer any question, but you can also do it anywhere, at any time, because of the mobility of a wireless device. You don't have to go to a library to look it up. In the old days, even when you had computers, when you first had computers, you had to get to computers and then do it on your own.

Yourdon: Yeah, that's a good point. Wherever you are, even if you're out on the street.

Temares: Absolutely, wherever you are, and you add to that the GPS technology that's everywhere you are. There's no getting lost anymore if you have an intelligent phone.

Yourdon: There's a related issue that has occurred to me a lot: one of the things that old timers like you and I would have seen is that back in the '60s, there were a lot of technologies that were very expensive and very scarce, and, therefore, very restricted and very controlled. For example, think about mainframe computers. And now we've got a lot of stuff that is essentially free and ubiquitous and pervasive, everywhere, and yet we still live in social institutions that are trying desperately to control these things. Mobile phones are a good example of this phenomenon. Do you see any more things of that nature coming along, things that are going to become universal and free?

Temares: Well, I'll tell you, one of the things that I've been involved in is telemedicine. And the most difficult part of telemedicine is the cost of telecommunications for processing data from Latin America—because it's all government-controlled and their prices are absolutely ludicrous compared to what it is in various other parts of the world. So, eventually, I think the economy is going to break that down, the same way it has broken down barriers in terms of dealing with China, trading with China. It's going to break down the telecommunication barriers also because we're going to have to communicate to be in business, and if that's the case, if it's too expensive, it won't get done. And Skype is in business; you're doing this on Skype. Skype is in business because they found a way to get business done and in a cheaper way.

Yourdon: Good point, good point.

Temares: And economics kills everything.

Yourdon: Yeah.

Temares: And it changes things.

Yourdon: Let me move on to another category. You hear a lot of talk these days about IT being a strategic weapon to enhance the business. Would you say that's true for universities, too?

Temares: Oh yeah, there's no question that the only reason for IT's existence is to support the business unit. For example, IT supported the admissions applications: you need to have a great Web presence, for a quick response and getting information out to people who are inquiring. We now do a lot of things, for example, in terms of inquiries. It used to be we lost the inquiries. You know, they'd inquire but we'd be so busy about applicants that we didn't have time for inquiries.

Now, with technology, anybody that inquires, we start to send things to them—because they're a tentative, they're a possible, they're a future maybe. So now we can go after different people; whereas we were only dealing with the admissions applications, we're now dealing with anybody who asks about the university, sending them promotional information, because we can do that over the Web. We've got their e-mail address, they're coming through the Web, we give them back the information through the Web.

The other thing is the cost. Obviously it reduces the cost to support the information technology, to have the infrastructure to reduce the cost of delivering the classroom information. But most important of all is the way it's changed our whole medical side. Being an academic medical center, you need the high-performance computing to do your genomic research, you need your high-performance computing to do other kinds of research, engineering research, architectural stuff, so the whole of information technology is networking. We have to keep the network up 24 x 7, 365, no question about it—so in addition to the network that supports the faculty members doing their individual intelligence and research and work, we also have to have the support in terms of the applications systems that will allow them to keep performing their administrative duties as well.

Yourdon: I would imagine also, as a recruiting tool, you've got to have up-to-date and leading-edge technology to attract the best researchers and the best professors.

Temares: There was no question when it first came to my attention. I think we were the fifth school that had all our campuses wireless. We have five campuses, but three major ones that are ten miles apart; each is like ten miles away from the other one, almost like an equilateral triangle. The medical school, the marine school and oceanographic sciences, and the main campus, which is basically the undergraduate and graduate school. And all three campuses had to be interconnected, all three campuses had to have wireless, because no matter where you go, from campus to campus, you had to have the connectivity that you needed to do your job. So a faculty member may be teaching on the marine campus when in fact, he's a biology instructor, so he has to have that ability to be in both places at the same time. And that's what's happening. I like it. You know, you used to say, "You can't be in two places at one time," but now we can, now, because of the mobility. We *can* be in two places at one time.

Yourdon: That's a good point. Well, as I'm sure you know, this has been a very frustrating area for CIOs in normal companies because they have kids coming in applying for a job who will say to them, "I've got better computing equipment at home than the crap you want me to use in the office."

Temares: [laughter] That's true. That's very true. We find that all the time. All of a sudden they're saying, "What do you mean you don't have split screens? You only have one screen for me to do my applications on? You know, I'm used to working with two or three screens at one time so that I can have multiple applications open at one time. And I move one from the other." I mean, the things they come up with … you know, instead of criticizing them, you've got to listen to them. That's one of the most important things, I think, that has changed in the CIO role. The CIO role is more of a listener now and asking the problem of what's going on and listening to what's going on than the guy who's promoting what he thinks is the future rather than watching the future appear in front of his eyes.

Yourdon: Interesting. I certainly would agree with you. I had one other question in that category, and that is whether IT is expected to enable entirely new things which the university simply cannot do today?

Well, let me give you somewhat of an off-the-wall example: both MIT and Berkeley are the two examples that come to mind. They have essentially put all of their lectures online. Well, Berkeley has put everything onto YouTube, which in a sense changes the essence of a university as being a place where you have to go there for the most part to get your degree. Now, aside from laboratories and the experience of interacting with other students, you can get a lot of your education through YouTube. I mean, that kind of changes the nature of the business, doesn't it?

Temares: Well, that goes along with the whole idea of having online, to the resident having the experience of being in the classroom. There are a couple of things that go wrong as far as I can tell. First of all, part of the differentiation is the faculty member. The reason that private schools charge a different amount of money is not only the support they get from the government but often there's the quality of the researcher or the instructor that they're talking to. You want to deal with the guy who writes the book rather than the guy who reads the book. The guy who writes the book is someone you can deal with, and he's a decent faculty member, too—you get a huge interaction that you can't get if you were doing it online. And the interaction of students, in terms of the student's interactions with another student, is immeasurable. So there's something to be said about the environment that's worth working on.

We've almost gotten to the question of: can you have all telecommuting workers? When you want to do a project, you want to get together for something that requires bigger than individual effort, how difficult it is to get there through telecommunications? It's not the same when you can't watch the body language, you can't watch the facial motions, you can't watch the whole combination of what is the human interaction.

For a big psychology class, which normally has 350 students in a lecture hall, what does it matter? Fine. If you're talking about a graduate course, or where you're doing something with the sciences, I think it does matter. Stanford turned their lecture-hall engineering degree all online, and they found a very, very difficult time, because they were paying a bunch of graduate students to be available if a student had a question, because you couldn't move forward unless you had an answer to the question.

They ran into some very big difficulties, because they were charging the same for the online degree, the same as the in-person degree.

Yourdon: Well, it will be an interesting area to watch, I think, as time goes on.

Temares: Oh yes. And, again, one of the nice things about IT is that you can predict a little bit of the future, but it's virtually *days* that you predict. You can't predict more of the future, because the things that come out are just overwhelmingly incredible, even when they're advancements over existing things. Who would have thought everybody would want all this information out there on Facebook? Or some idiot walks around and has, you know, five million followers on Twitter? I mean, this is nuts!

Yourdon: [laughing] That's right. Let me switch to a different topic area, of problems and concerns and issues. What would you say are the main problems or threats that concern your kind of IT industry and the academic environment over the next couple of years?

Temares: If my number-one concern wasn't cyber security, I think I'd be asleep in the closet. The answer is security, security, security—and especially with the new generation, who doesn't view security in the same way until they get burned. Until their identity is stolen or something else happens to them, because they really are just too open and they don't appreciate the level of security that's necessary to survive in our domain. So I really think it's a combination of you need security because more and more of the information will be available. If you're going to have your wallet somewhere on your RIM [Blackberry] device, you'll have a real problem if somebody breaks in because it's like stealing your wallet and stealing your life away. So I think the biggest, my biggest, concern is always the security protection of the individual and the individual's data.

Yourdon: Okay. Well, a related question is how do you communicate that kind of concern to the university people around you, your peers and superiors, as well as the customers right outside—which would be your students—and then the people outside the university firewall?

Temares: It's really like a losing campaign, it's part of the marketing. You know, faculty members are the same way. Don't forget individual faculty members are used to publishing their research and sharing everything they do. You know, we live in a crazy world in higher education. Think about this: we send people to conferences to deliver papers on all these unique things they learned, they've accomplished. After somebody outside sees these unique things they've accomplished, they offer more salary and hire them away from us. So we literally pay for our faculty members to leave us.

Think about it. It's a crazy environment. But we do! So we want to publish, because it's a great reputation builder. You know, your Stanfords, your MITs, they get their reputation because of the good research everybody knows they do and the exciting things that come out of them. But guess what? A guy who's got exciting things at MIT will get a job offer from Carnegie-Mellon that will probably give a 30 percent pay raise or a 40 percent pay raise because of the uniqueness … they wanted to bring him. And offer him graduate assistants or whatever. And by the way, once you have tenure in an institution of any prestige, the next institution you go to automatically gives you tenure. It's virtually a given.

Yourdon: Interesting.

Temares: You give the person the opportunity to advance himself, show his knowledge, make the world know you, and then he can go out and get another job somewhere else for more.

Yourdon: [laughter] That certainly is true. Well, given that state of affairs, then, how do you go about communicating the need for more security and maybe a little more privacy?

Temares: You try to educate them by publicizing leaks, publicizing when you have meetings—it goes along with all my other desires to publicize what IT can do and can't do. So I meet with academic deans and counselors, or I'll meet with the various people of the faculty senate, I'll meet with the people in terms of the research council. The idea is that the CIO has to get out of his ivory tower and [get] on the road. And "on the road" means selling IT and selling the points he wants to accomplish with IT. A lot of times people don't even know what IT can provide them. They'll give you an awesome look like, "Really? We can do *that*?" I have to say to them, "If you have a problem with your systems or your mobility or anything of this sort, just give it to us. That's what we're here for, we're the pros. We'll deal with them." And people don't even realize that this thing exists.

Yourdon: Well, I think you're right. So a lot of it is marketing and, as you say, getting out on the road. Certainly, one of the things I've noticed now that I've been looking more closely at CIOs is how often they are out on the road, speaking at conferences and public gatherings and so forth—much more than I would have guessed.

Temares: And, by the way, there are two things that I have to do. You have to be aware of what other CIOs are running into, which means going to the conferences and talking privately with other CIOs and what problems they're confronting, even if they're in another industry. It doesn't matter because the things in their industry will move to your industry one day, so, if they have problems in the financial industry or the higher education industry, they will have the problems eventually in the retail industry and in other industries. There are twin towers, you know; it happens.

The second thing that you've got to do is market yourself and your department and your abilities internally to your organization. You can't just say, "Okay, I'm there when they need me." No, no, no, no. You create the need, you let them know what's going on, you let them know what's available so they can make use of it. And ask them, go out and ask, "Would it be helpful if? Can I do this? Can I help with that?" and so on, and that's the way you learn things.

Yourdon: And that's how you stay on the radar screen also, if you're seen as a contributor rather than just a pain-in-the-ass cost center, which I think is important.

Temares: [laughter] Exactly. Oh no, you said it better than me. You're absolutely right. What makes you a revenue producer rather than a cost center? If somebody says, "Hey, Lew Temares of the IT team was just over here and they really gave me something of benefit," and you know, your boss and the rest of the guys will be looking at you in a different way. Rather than just saying, you know, "I need more hardware, I need more software, or I need, I need, I need, I need."

Yourdon: Yeah, I agree.

Temares: And there's nothing the matter with saying, "I need," because, generally speaking, you *do* need. At such-and-such a cost-per-item. I mean, you can't live with five-year-old technology, whether it's servers or whether it's hardware or software. Everything has an age. You know, one of these days they're going to come up with something that will replace ERP. You know, we always are adding new systems, we're always adding philanthropism, we always had COBOL. Then came ERP in the '90s. That's 20 years ago—the '90s—or 15 years ago since the '90s. How come we don't have anything better than ERP now? It's going to be there, but then in five years we're going to have something that's no longer going to be called ERP. It's going to be called something else and it's going to be better.

Now, a good example of that is cloud computing. I have this mania about cloud computing, because really, what it is, it's host computing. We've had host computing since the '70s. IBM used to have data centers, if you remember, and you're going to have your data and get your result on your console in your office. These existed way back then.

Yourdon: Fundamentally, you're right. Well, that raises an interesting question that kind of gets us back to this generational issue. How do you communicate to the younger generation that there are a lot of things that were done before, that there are a lot of lessons that can be learned without having to repeat the same mistakes and failure all over again?

Temares: Are you a parent? [laughter] How do you convey adages to a younger generation?

Yourdon: [laughter] Oh, okay.

Temares: It's no different than being a parent. You hope that when you say what you say you're not spitting into the wind, but really some of it … actually, you throw it and it actually sticks to the person. Don't know how much sticks and how much not, even including the new worker that comes in. The hope is that they are bright enough to be as open as you are open to them, that they will be open to you rather than just saying, "Oh, you're just old-fashioned, you're an idiot."

Yourdon: Well, of course, it's a lot easier for them to have that attitude in our field because the technology is a million times faster than it was when you and I were young kids.

Temares: Well, they sort of understand that. They really do. You know, you tell them: what's the difference between a "client" and the end of the terminal? I mean, there's *no* difference between a client and a terminal basically, and we're going more and more towards a terminal concept if you think about it. I mean, the, the new RIM device that's going to be coming out is as close to a terminal as a tablet, basically. It's going to be as close to a terminal as you'll find, but yet at the same time we'll have the ability because of the RIM device to do everything through the Internet.

Yourdon: Yeah.

Temares: It's going to have very little storage. You're going to have to buy storage from a vendor so I try to tell that to the younger generation, I tell them funny things. One of the things you can use as an example is a camera. When you want to take and keep and store pictures, you used to be able to do 12 pictures, 15 pictures, and then they went to 27 pictures on an entire roll of film and you thought it was incredible, then 36 pictures. Now all of a sudden, you've got this little thing in it and it's got 2 gigabytes, 4 gigabytes, 8 gigabytes, 16 gigabytes, and you can hold hundreds of thousands of pictures. But the principle is the same: it's a camera and it's got a modem, you've got this little digital device.

It's the same principle. You just got better technology. But the same thing is happening to computers. It's the same principle, better technology, which makes things happen more conveniently, faster, and sometimes, and a lot of times, just nicer. I mean, the quality is better.

Yourdon: That certainly is true.

Temares: And they always relate to the camera. It's crazy, when you relate to the simple thing, you relate to the throw away camera compared to what you do when you buy a camera and you put your memory in it and they can see, "Oh yeah, I guess that's similar."

Yourdon: And you can give one to every single guest at a wedding reception. That's where I've seen it a lot. Tell everybody to take pictures, hundreds of pictures, and maybe one or two of them will be good, and then we can throw everything away at the end and that encourages behavior that simply was not allowed, let alone encouraged, a generation ago.

Temares: Listen, every firm, every business has old computers that they get rid of on a regular basis. I mean, everybody has a cycle now, their economic budgeting. It's what your cycle of your computers, what's your cycle of your servers, what's your cycle of your *everything*, every piece of equipment. What's the cycle? You've got to put in your budget plan for the next five years what the cycle is for that replacement.

Yourdon: Absolutely. I've got one more generational question, and that is related to, say, the young graduating student who sees a possible career that will lead up to your role. He says, "Some day I want to be just like Dr. Temares. I want to be a CIO." What advice would you give such a person to prepare?

Temares: I always, I always tell that person to try and get as much education as they can when they're young, because it's so tough to go back when they want to go back.

Yourdon: Ahh.

Temares: So perhaps you can get a master's afterwards. I also promote, if they possibly can, to get a combination of degrees. For example, if you're going to get a bachelor's in business administration, get a law degree or get something else other than a master's in business afterwards. If you've got an engineering degree, go get an MBA unless you're going to go into pure engineering. If you want to come into the technical field, into the business world, you have to have business background. You have to have some business courses. You can't just fit in there unless you have the MBA, unless you have the BBA, or you have to have some criteria that gets you in there so you can understand accounting, economics, because it's not just technical. There's a cost factor and one gets weighed against the other, and you have to know, you have to know the difference between an income and a balance sheet.

You have to understand the business. Otherwise, you can't talk to the people in the business, and you're going to be viewed as just a techie and you're going to go nowhere. Now, you can become chief technical officer, that's what some of them want to be—but even the chief technical officer has to talk to the boardroom sometimes, has to talk to the senior management sometimes, and has to market their ideas. I tell students, engineering students, that they have to know how to market themselves and market their ideas. Think of the greatest invention in the world, and unless they know how to market it, it's a waste.

Yourdon: I certainly agree with you.

Temares: Whoever's going to make the money is the guy who knows how to market it.

Yourdon: One of the things that has impressed me with the interviews I've done so far is just the enormous breadth of backgrounds that these people have. The guy I interviewed earlier this week had a PhD in chemistry. The woman who's the CIO at Delta is a concert violinist. The CIO at Microsoft started off in the Parks and Recreation Department. It's just, it's amazing. So this idea of the breadth of the education and exposure to things is great.

Temares: Somewhere in the background are communicating skills and business skills, somewhere, because they can't get where they are and they can't stay where they are unless they have communication and business skills. And that's the other thing I tried to explain to them—that you have to learn how to communicate. You know, Twitter is one form of communication. It's not the all, the end-all. You have to learn to talk and present and deliver. And, you know, that's why we have a speech class at the university. My new pitch is in project management. People nowadays, when they do project management tend to underestimate the cost and the time. They are really bad estimators, and, of course, if you estimate low and you come in high, you're looking for your next job. If you estimate correctly, you look like a hero. But, you know, the idea is not to hit it on the exact date and budget, the idea is to always come in lower than you estimate. So you don't do yourself or your company a favor by saying, "Oh, I'll have this up in three months for $2 million," and you actually get it up in five months and it cost you two and a half million dollars. One day late means you missed the timeframe. One dollar more means you missed your budget. One dollar fewer means you came in under budget. And that's the way you can deliver it. So it's all in the marketing.

Yourdon: Interesting. Well, I certainly would agree with you. Let me move on to another category. One of the things I've been trying to figure out is the typical responsibilities and duties that a CIO has, and, I get the impression that a lot of it is pretty basic in the universal—keeping the machines on, keeping the lights on.

Temares: Sure, sure.

Yourdon: So from your perspective in the university, what are the key responsibilities of a CIO? Or maybe you've already covered it in a sense.

Temares: Well, I'll say it again. I have a diverse population, having faculty members and researchers, grad students, and doctors. So having them being able to perform their tasks, some of it life and death, it's truly —you know, I often use the phrase on the administrative side, to the provost: this is not rocket science, this is not life and death, and the shuttle will go up, whether I make this happen or not. It's not like something that would be disastrous if we are one day late or some disorder just happens. However, when you are dealing with doctors, it is life and death. When you are dealing with faculty members who are only here a given amount of time, they are only in that classroom for that hour. It's a little different in terms of the operations in an academic medical center than it is in a normal business. I hate to say it's only money, because, of course, money is important, but it really is on the administrative side, only money. This is a lot more significant.

Yourdon: Interesting. One of the other things I've found in the interviews I've had so far is that CIOs do not act alone; they're not solitary actors. They all have a team. And so my question is: if you are assessing various candidates that might be a part of your team, what kind of qualities and strengths do you look for in a candidate?

Temares: Ahh, well, one of the strengths that is very, very important is that I try to interview to see if they fit. Let me give you an example. Two years ago I was looking for an assistant associate vice president for applications of equipment. But really what I was looking for was that person had to have the characteristics that possibly could assume my role, 'cause I knew I was going to retire. So when I was looking at the person, I was assessing them in terms of their communication skills, their presentation skills, but also to whether they could handle the day-to-day administration of the applications systems and how they communicate and deal with people. So the attributes of the person basically have to do with [whether] they fit in with the team.

You know, I would say that an all-star team of the best player in every position will lose to a team that plays together regularly because as a team they play better rather than an individual effort. So while I need a superstar maybe in terms of a tech-math, in terms of the network, I need somebody that's really good at security. Overall, if I'm looking at the meld of where they can go and what they do, above all else, I want people that know their specialty but also display keen knowledge of their specialty by explaining their specialty and being part of the team.

Yourdon: It's interesting that you should mention that because I've now heard that theme a couple of times, particularly in the private sector—where a lot of these CIOs are saying that they themselves are putting in 12-hour days, as is everybody on their team. And you don't want to work 12 hours a day with people you fundamentally dislike, so it's very important.

Temares: I'll say. That's very true, very true.

Yourdon: That's amazing. One last question for this area. Are there priorities for a CIO that you consider essential that other key executives, like the provost or some of the other people in the academic environment, might misunderstand and feel differently about?

Temares: Yeah, you have to have a passion. Our business is education and your passion in IT really becomes a passion of providing a service as best you can. It runs into conflict because to provide the best services very often is beyond the economic means of the institution, so the adaptability is that you have to provide "good enough" for the person and yet to have the trust of the provost and have the trust of the chief financial officer, who may feel that it isn't good enough because of economic reasons, not because you think it's acceptable to be good enough.

Yourdon: Okay.

Temares: It's a very difficult line to walk, you know what I mean?

Yourdon: Yeah, sure. I've been hearing from some of the other CIOs that they find themselves surrounded by other key business leaders in their company who rose to their position because they had not only good talents, but very strong opinions about the right way to do things for their business

—and they often don't like to hear the CIO telling them their ideas or requests are unreasonable or impractical.

Temares: I've got 3,000 of those. Every faculty member and doctor thinks that they know the business better. You know the only difference between a doctor and God is that God knows he's not a doctor?

Yourdon: [laughter] I think I've heard variations on that one before.

Temares: Yeah, right. So they all think they know the business better. I can't tell you how difficult it is with all these paper records the docs have, to tell them, "We can scan this stuff in and then when you have a file of this stuff. See, you still have it but you don't need your file cabinet. It's called document management. It's been used for years and years. You're not the first to do it."

"Oh no. I want to see that paper; I want to be able to read it."

"You can still read it. You can read it online instead of reading it on a piece of paper."

I'm telling you, I swear to you, this is a conversation I've had innumerable times, including with faculty members. Oh no, I mean, that's way back to the TRS-80s. Remember the TRS-80s?

Yourdon: Oh, yeah.

Temares: The TRS-80 was very big with faculty members because they could buy it at a local store and do their own thing, and I was telling them that they've got to do stuff because that's the digital policy, they had to buy IBM, or they had to buy from a real company that was in the business of this type of computer. And, you know, they wanted to do their TRS-80s. It's been there forever, it stays. Whatever they used in graduate school they think they can use when they come into your environment, and I've got to make sure it works on my network. And all sorts of diverse things are on my network. It's anything—a university is different than a real corporation in that they're allowed to buy and do whatever they want because they get free money. They have government research money.

Yourdon: Right.

Temares: Government research money doesn't tell you, "You have to use a Hewlett-Packard piece." It doesn't tell you, "You have to buy a Dell piece." You see? It doesn't tell you anything of that nature. It says you can do whatever you want.

Yourdon: Very interesting. I thought I'd finish up by just asking a couple questions about your background. I've read your bio.

Temares: Sure.

Yourdon: Is there anything about your background and rise to the CIO position that you feel are really unusual or unique that, you know, we ought to tell people about?

Temares: My father owned a grocery store.

Yourdon: Really?

Temares: And I grew up in the grocery store. And after school and for the first 14 years of my life, what you did was you worked in the grocery store. When I came back home, I went to the grocery store. In the grocery store you learn a lot about customer service. First, the customer's always right, and you get a variety of people with a variety of intellectual levels and a variety of economic levels.

So one of the great experiences I had was dealing with retail and dealing with a variety of people face-to-face and learning you had to communicate and had to be proper and respectful, but yet in a convincing way. I had to convince somebody to buy Bumblebee tuna when they want Starkist because Bumblebee was more expensive. It's a real knack, it's a real challenge. You learn a lot by dealing with that kind of environment. So if I had anything to say, I'd say that the experience of dealing with part-time jobs, you can't have enough internships, you can't have enough part-time jobs, you can get various experience in dealing with people. You have to use the knowledge that you gain by dealing with people in your later life by getting people to work together as a team, by convincing them that you are transparent, convincing them that you are honest. Never, never, never lie.

Yourdon: Ahh.

Temares: Because you always get caught. And I have to say, if it's not good enough to tell them the truth about it, it's not good enough to do. You have to have a good reason to do something, and if you can't tell them the right reason, then you did something wrong.

Yourdon: Interesting. Well, with that background, how did you make the transition into IT?

Temares: I came from the academic side in a sense because I was working at the university and I needed a computer to do my research. So I started on a 1620. I was a statistician. My major was statistics.

Yourdon: Oh, okay. Yeah, I saw that.

Temares: So I got into right away the SPSS programs, the SAS programs. I needed all that stuff to do my research, in terms of my field and then eventually what I did was I became a teacher, a part-time teacher, and then I became an administrator.

Yourdon: Oh, okay, interesting. All right, one last question for you and I think it's perfect for you given where you are in your life right now—and that is, what's next? You know, what comes after being a CIO?

Temares: Listen to this idea, Ed, how's this? You know, it's sort of like a Facebook mentality, but it's a little different. I just got a site called matchmakerexecs.com. Matchmakerexecs.com really is my company. I'm going to do a company, I said. And what I'm going to do is what I have: the greatest attribute somebody has left is his former contacts. Or his current contacts.

Yourdon: That's true.

Temares: And one of the things we do is we give away that information for free. All my contacts—you say, "Do you know somebody that's a candidate for CIO?" Since I'm not in the position of being a headhunter, I'll say, "You know, maybe Sam Jones is available. Let me give him a call and I'll get back to you. I'll give it to you." But I don't ask for any money for that.

Yourdon: Sure. Well, that's what LinkedIn is all about.

Temares: Yeah, that's what it's all about. And so what I'm going to do is I'm going to, let's see. I've got rainmaker.com, matchmaker.com; what I want to do is I want to be a rainmaker.

Yourdon: Oh, okay.

Temares: I want to do things to bring people together to get things done. I do that well, I know a lot of people, and those people know people. So what I want to do is if somebody wants to do something, they need a bunch of people to get involved, to develop something. I want to work with them to get the people involved developing, especially in the IT industry.

Yourdon: Seems to me that that's something that a lot of CIOs could think about, for exactly the same reasons. They've got a lot of contacts and a lot of ideas about what skills might fit certain situations. Interesting.

Temares: Since I've retired, the most that people have … asked me is, "You know somebody in the industry? You know somebody from Cisco? You know somebody from Dell? You know somebody from … wherever? Is there any possibility you can introduce me to them? Because I've got this great invention, I've got this great idea, I've got this great project, and I need some help."

Yourdon: Well, certainly among CIOs, I can get a sense that it's a very clubby environment. You know, everybody knows everybody.

Temares: Yeah. That's right.

Yourdon: Probably because they've got a lot of common problems to deal with and grapple with and it's almost kind of a game of musical chairs also. People are obviously moving from one place to another because the shelf life of a CIO is only a couple of years long I think.

Temares: I'll let you know in a year. Ten years ago, I would have said, "Give me three to five years and we'll know whether we'll do it." Now if it ain't made it in a year, we are unsuccessful.

Yourdon: I think that's true. You know, that is one of the advantages of today's environment. You can fail more quickly or at least get an idea if you're going to succeed.

Temares: You're right. It is whether you can know if you failed quickly or you are not. Now you know it very quickly.

Yourdon: And you can do it at almost no cost. That's the other thing. You don't have to go to a venture capitalist, which is huge.

Temares: You're absolutely right.

Yourdon: That's a big change, I think, from the '70s and '80s. The whole Web 2.0 industry has that characteristic. People are now financing it off their Mastercard, cash advances, and so on.

Temares: Yeah, you know, I agree with you. We're talking about thousands rather than hundreds of thousands or more.

Yourdon: Exactly, exactly. So, all right, I agree. Listen, this has been fascinating. I could go on for hours and hours, but I want to keep us within our time limit

Temares: Well, I appreciate it, Ed.

Yourdon: Well, I appreciate your taking the time and it was very generous of you.

Mark Mooney

Senior Vice President and CIO, McGraw-Hill Education

Mark Mooney is the Senior Vice President and Chief Information Officer for McGraw-Hill Education, where he is responsible for developing strategy and implementation capabilities for new digital products and technical infrastructure within the $2.7 billion company. He manages a multi-disciplinary team of approximately 400 personnel to provide a number of revenue-generating, customer-facing applications within the education market, including educational gaming (GradeGuru), simulation gaming, data-driven classroom prototyping (State of Indiana), Connect (connect.mcgraw-hill.com), Create (create.mcgraw-hill.com), and Acuity (formative assessment). He is also a mentor and adjunct professor for Columbia University's Executive Masters of Science in Technology Management program.

Dr. Mooney left McGraw-Hill early this year to form two endeavors. The first is MyEdulife, a company that provides data governance and a life-long learning portal. VeraMea, the second, creates new realities through the production of unprecedented results. It provides strategy and the execution for difference-making and bold initiatives. It also focuses on short-term results and the execution for long-term sustainability.

Prior to his position at McGraw-Hill, Mr. Mooney was the Chief Information Officer and Vice President at Reed Elsevier. There he strategically repositioned the publisher through a transformational infrastructure that enabled the use of a distribution portal and content management system, which allowed content providers to upload and manage their own content. Mr. Mooney was also the Chief Technology

Officer and Vice President at Houghton Mifflin and Vivendi Universal, where he served as the first CTO in a newly structured organization with the mission to provide governance, technical strategy, and execution across the enterprise.

Ed Yourdon: There is a starting question that I've asked several CIOs now, which is, basically, what was your career path leading up to the CIO position? You obviously weren't born with that title.

Mark Mooney: Well, it was interesting. I grew up in Ohio, Irish and first-generation Italian immigrant, and actually went to the Naval Academy in Annapolis, Maryland, and was an engineering undergrad. After I graduated from the Academy, I went into the Marine Corps rather than the Navy because I didn't like going to sea and thought it was much more glamorous going into the Marine Corps … which I don't know if it was or not.

But they actually started the program in the Navy and the Marine Corps—now this would have been the late '70s—where they had two master's programs out at the Naval Postgraduate School, which is out in Monterey, California, one being in computer science and one being in information systems. And I thought, you know, this just sounds like a neat thing to do. … I think from an intuitive standpoint it made sense. So I started my master's at the Naval Postgraduate School in information systems. It took about 18 months. So that was the first start, and then I came back to do some work mostly in black box, NSA/CIA software development space in the military and then came out from there. I then left the military to work for General Electric.

Yourdon: Aha. Well, I'm surprised you were able to leave the Naval Postgraduate School. I've been there, and it's a gorgeous, gorgeous part of the country.

Mooney: Oh, my wife loved it. I, of course, I had to study while I was there…

Yourdon: Aha! [laughter] I guess that changes one's attitude. But, then after your government work, as I recall, you went into the aerospace field, didn't you?

Mooney: Well, I was hired by General Electric. It was right when Jack Welch was starting to take over. He had already taken over GE, but I was in Washington, DC, and we were part of Space Systems, which was out of Valley Forge. Our group was relatively small, with the overall Valley Forge organization having about three to five thousand employees. And we did work for primarily NSA around the Washington Beltway, developing software. It also included AI or artificial intelligence capabilities. And we lived in

Annapolis, Maryland, and then commuted into Washington and actually bounced around, as you probably know well, too, we did a lot of "skiff" work. So you went to places where you couldn't talk about what you were doing, you flew in unmarked planes, and all that kind of stuff, which sounds a lot more exciting than it really is.

But that was really the exposure to the hard-core systems information technology, and it was right about the time that Digital [Equipment Corporation] had a large presence in Washington. The ARPANET[1] had just started to take off. Obviously it was somewhat archaic at the time, but they started to pick up on it. So there was a large opportunity to really, really take advantage of a field that was brand new.

Now, what happened was, I realized that as good as an engineer I was, I really enjoyed working with organizations and people, so what I did—I call it the Bermuda Triangle—I started going to graduate school at Johns Hopkins up in Baltimore, so I lived in Annapolis, drove to work in Washington, and then drove up to Baltimore to go to school either in the evenings or on the weekends. And actually, the work that I did there was more in applied behavior science, specifically about how technology affects organizations, how you measure it. I don't think there was much being done at the time. I developed an acquaintance—I don't know if you remember Paul Strassmann.

Yourdon: Oh yeah. He's one of the people I've interviewed for this book.

Mooney: Unbelievable. Well, Paul and I developed a relationship when I started my dissertation at Hopkins. I was a Fellow at Johns Hopkins while working on my doctorate and he was doing a lot of work and actually had a database, which I think is part of the source of some of the work he's done post-CIO with his consulting firm. And even then there was little work being done about how you measure the impact of technology on organizations. So I spent the next six years working on that and did some work with a small company called Pacesetter Software out of Princeton that did a lot of work with AT&T. So I'd pull a lot of the data, and what I found, which is rather common sense, is that you need to align the deployment of technology and technology budget with the production of customer-facing and digital products—not that the back office isn't important, but more so on the customer-facing and product development. And that would have been back in the '80s, so that was before the Internet had this huge effect on what we're doing. So that was real exciting and it was

---

[1] Advanced Research Projects Agency Network, considered the precursor to the Internet.

really the foundation for the rest of the work that I was going to do as a CIO.

Yourdon: Interesting. Well, then, why don't we move into what you've been doing as a CIO? I've interviewed about a dozen people and they all have slightly different stories. They all are involved in just keeping the lights on, for lack of a better phrase, just running the internal IT engine. But beyond that, they all have different stories. So what would you say are the key responsibilities and activities that you have found yourself doing as a CIO?

Mooney: Well, I've been at four publishing firms. I was at the Bureau of National Affairs (BNA)[2], which is still an employee-owned legal publisher. It competes with Westlaw and LexisNexis. And then I went to Houghton Mifflin, and we were acquired by Vivendi, and then Harcourt and Reed Elsevier—and each of these is sort of a little case study—and then obviously McGraw-Hill. So you're going back almost probably 15, 18 years. Because of what was happening in publishing and media, in particular, the desire to have the back office keep the lights on and run the data centers was absolutely critical. But because of the huge paradigm shift—and even more so now at McGraw-Hill, I'll be very candid—most of the CEOs, the presidents, the business leaders don't really care, but assume that the systems will run on time and with a certain level of quality. They want that done, they expect us to have a dial tone much like the phone company, or the electric company, electricity at the wall.

And the biggest challenge and where we're spending most of our time now is more in customer space and product development around the digital world of education, specifically in the publishing and media, moving from print to digital. Now sometimes technology is a necessary evil. In particular, what the struggle has been, at least within the existing budget, is that we've been bypassed for the traditional back-office legacy—and so what we've tried to do is increase efficiency, which is huge. About eight years ago, the IT cost of implementing an ERP system was under $200 million. It was only supposed to cost $80 million, but the cost was significantly more, with the idea that we drive efficiency through using that and then take that spend, that technology spend, and reallocate it to the front office. And so that's the good news.

The bad news is usually what happens is when there's a budget crunch. And the last three years as we've gone through the recession, when you tend to cut, since a lot of your back-office legacy are fixed allocations or costs, they

---

[2] Now known as the National Institute of Standards and Technology.

tend to stay and instead you cut the product and the new development and the proof of concept and those types of things.

Yourdon: Aha.

Mooney: So the big challenge and struggle and leadership requirements for me have been as a change agent, moving into that new customer-facing product space, around the digital arena, and really, really forcing it, enabling it, influencing it.

I've done that in several ways. It's everything from a strategic standpoint, having a roadmap that shows where you need to be in year three. I would suggest that beyond three is unrealistic because things are changing so much now. And then we're going on a road campaign of convincing the businesses, at least in the media space that I'm in, of what we're trying to do and why it's important. Sort of forecasting what's happening in the industry. And then lastly, rolling up your sleeves and actually starting to do more and more hands-on development work. We started doing it in the last two years, really developing an innovation center around the agile development of proof of concept. And currently we have probably about 9 to 12 proof of concepts going on now.

Yourdon: Interesting. You know, having been an author myself for 30-odd years, there are two areas where I've seen a lot of change where I could imagine a CIO getting very deeply involved. One is rather mundane, and that's just the production side of creating a book. You know, the very first book that I wrote took two years for the publisher to turn my manuscript into a book. And now everything's done online, with the author doing a lot of the work that used to be done by typesetters and editors and all kinds of production people. So there's a lot of technology I would assume that you've been involved in, bringing in to help speed things up.

Mooney: Well, the other interesting thing about that is that there's the technology and then there's the whole organizational change, there's the whole effect that it has on people's roles and responsibilities and viewpoint and it may have a significant impact on the organization. Obviously we have hundreds, if not thousands of editors, and their role traditionally was to ac- tually produce the manuscript. And what we've started to do, with every- thing from publishing systems to learning management systems . . . for ex- ample, I was on a call yesterday. We're talking about learning development systems for schools. The requirements for tagging content became an issue, so the editor now is responsible for the digital tagging so that you can mi- grate from the print to the digital or electronic media.

Yourdon: Ahh. I see.

Mooney: So that technology obviously is evolving dramatically, as are a lot of these systems. So what happens is, we would go out to the editors and publishers—at least in the education field, we've been doing this for 20, 30 years at times—and we would say, "Oh, by the way, in addition to that, we want you to do this mundane thing of tagging HTML." And they would say, "Well, wait a second. That's not my pay grade." And I think you had a percent of people who said, "Okay, I understand this," but that was relatively small. Number one, just because it was change. Number two, it was intimidating, because it was more related to the technology and coding. So there was that dynamic that continues to still go on.

Now the good news is that throughout the media there are new companies—and everybody is really jumping into the media space and particularly education right now because they see that there's this chaos, there's this void of tools to enable people like yourself as authors, editors to actually publish quickly and create something now not only for print, but obviously for the Web. I was actually again on the phone in the last couple of days with two small companies. And what they're doing is basically taking existing content, you can repurpose it and customize it, and you can do it with little to no overhead in a template format online that makes it a heck of a lot easier.

Yourdon: Interesting.

Mooney: I would say, we're not done yet. I mean, that whole shift is still ongoing and the struggle for us is the large organizations, so educational publishers, some of the media group. You know, it started in music. We saw what happened with the music, and if you use Apple ... what's happened with iTunes ... and then you shift into any of the media spaces, in particular educational publishing. The shift—because of the recession, I'm convinced—higher ed, college started it because they tend to be somewhat more progressive as far as the use of technology, plus they have more funding traditionally. For our assessments business, that started because it just made a heck of a lot of sense. And it wasn't until two to two and a half years ago during the recession that the K–12, because of the lack of funding for textbooks, has really had a huge, dramatic, passionate shift in moving to using online technology, iPads, and all that kind of technology and capability.

Yourdon: That's an interesting area that you've mentioned, because obviously not only has technology changed that authors, like me, and editors publish and produce a book, but it's completely transformed the marketplace in terms of the consumers and customers and their expectations of how they're going to get the content. And even more than that, you probably have seen some of the material that Nicholas Carr has written—he's got a book called *The Shallows*[3], which basically argues that because of the Internet he would never be able to read *War and Peace* today because he just can't maintain that attention span. And I assume that that has got to have an enormous impact on publishers, too.

Mooney: Well, we also have a "professional," basically it's a type of buyer that borders on—I was going to say "Borders," but I'm not sure Borders is going to be around. I think what's happening is the Internet, but it's also—I wouldn't say generational, but it's more…

I have three children. Two are in grad school and one's in undergrad at the University of Florida. He's a senior. First of all—one's in business school, one's in law school, and the youngest is in business, he's a business major at the University of Florida—hardly any of them buy textbooks. Now the professors require that they do or there are supplemental products. In addition to that, I would say that my son who's at the University of Florida, probably about 60 to 70 percent of his courses were online. So I feel that the shift is happening, and I don't know where the cutoff is, and I don't think it necessarily has to do with age.

But to your point there's a medium, with the iPad and all the different devices that we have now where people that are coming up are feeling much more comfortable with the type of technology. As an example, you can see the shift and transition taking place on planes. I take the train around New York quite a bit and you see, especially the trains going out to New Jersey, where people are actually using the Kindle and those types of devices. And I'm also an adjunct professor at Columbia University and was at George Washington University—and the students today—well, they're not kids, but they'd be in their late 20s or early 30s—do not think anything of using a device and/or a mobile device to actually transact stuff, but to also read.

And so I think that print will always be here. We've always said that. I think the percent is going to go down. We're always going to have libraries, but obviously not as a library exists today. It's changing within schools and other public libraries and the world of people that are there. And what we're seeing in particular is, if you were to say, "Where should we be and what should we be dedicating to spend our time and energy?" It's really around mobile computing. And in particular, what we're doing is providing educational content and reference content. On the professional side and

---

[3] W. W. Norton & Company, 2011.

our career side we provide medical reference material to doctors on hand-held devices, so that has transpired or started to transpire.

The other area is the whole social media space. [I'll] tell a story: [there] was a trivia contest, it was a product that still exists from McGraw-Hill. It started on the international side in the UK called "GradeGuru." And it was for children K through 12, and you could actually go in and provide home-work. And then other students could come in and provide homework and/or evaluations, and they got points. And through the points you could actually get rewarded in our system. Well, I remember taking it, the con-cept, to one of our higher ed, college sales meetings. And there were two separate reactions. One was, it was good stuff. Most of those were genera-tionally a little bit younger. I call them the media gurus or digital divas of our organization that are comfortable—we have several people who have come from the BBC, and the BBC has done some significant work in Europe around the whole digital idea of educational product. And so they would say, "Okay, how are you going to make money on this? … We don't have to sell the product, but we'll do advertising." You go to the opposite side of the room, and they said, "Well, first of all, we've got to charge. We're not sure of the business model, so there's that whole element of change. How do you pay for these digital products? Second of all, we *never* advertise on our products. We're not going to do it even if it's appropriate for kids."

So it was fascinating to watch this. You had a bunch of things, you had the mobile issue, you had the whole media issue, you had the whole issue about organization, advertising, the whole business model of how to get paid. That's an example which is occurring periodically and now it's occurring constantly with everything that we do.

Yourdon: Absolutely. Since you've raised this generational issue—it's on my agenda, but we might as well talk about it a little bit more now. You know, the CIO is typically the person who's in charge of deciding what kind of technology's going to be used throughout an organization, and now you've got this younger generation coming in, not only into the IT Department, but all through the organization, in every conceivable job role. What other changes or differences have you seen in terms of the expectations or assumptions of the younger generation and how they view technology?

Mooney: Well, it is rather dramatic, and I would suggest that any CIO or anybody who stays in the old paradigm is "dead meat." That's what my sons tell me. And part of what I do when I do presentations is I try to tell them that organizations and CIOs have got to change dramatically. You know, as an adjunct professor I get exposed to a lot of things, and I think that they help in that process. The things that I see differently [are], obviously, it's the stuff that you read about, but there isn't loyalty to an organization. In the case of what we're in, people are very loyal to publishing, and creating good educational products.

Then if you take the culture within a lot of the "digital divas" that we have, which tend to be people that either came out of computer science and/or they're coming out of some of the nontraditional curriculums. And what they end up doing is they like to see results quickly and with speed to delivery. You know, we have really moved away from a traditional waterfall way of doing software development unless it's some of the back office. Then it's appropriate. They're much more agile. That's another technique or way of agile development, something I call "soft discipline guidelines." The new "digital divas" don't like hard structured ways of developing software, putting things together. What has enabled us to keep their attention and to satisfy some of those changes are these proofs of concepts, and the reason is you don't have a large amount to spend. You don't have a huge amount of time for the actual development phases that enable them to create something.

Now that's the good news. The bad news is while we'll create something that at the time is rather sexy, exciting, that satisfies the existing requirements, from a scalability and from a long-term production system—we do not provide a system that scales for the pikes of usage. And that skill set, I would suggest, is in the testing, the QA, V&V[4] area. It's different, you'll see a lot of times. And so what we've struggled with is how do you get from those proof of concepts to startup dealing with the people that like to create things quickly, but at the same time developing an industrial-strength product?

I'll give you an example. We had an online system—it's still running now, really good, called Connect—that will allow teachers and professors at a university to come in and customize their curriculum. They put it out online to the students. They can do a form of assessment on a Monday morning. So, all good stuff. So what happens is, you build it. You figure, based upon the forecast that you can handle maybe a thousand or two thousand students. And the first quarter or two, that's good. But then what happens is, you've got these great salespeople that are out there selling this, and on a Sunday evening, at about midnight, when all the college students are trying to get their homework done or practice for this form of test on Monday morning with the professor, it goes from the initial load of 2,000 to 5,000 to actually 30 to 35,000 students. And it crashes. And so that's just an example.

---

[4] Quality assurance, Verification and Validation

And by the way, there's a whole dynamic of hearing back from the professors and the students. There's a whole dynamic of ensuring that at least within the media space, where there hasn't been a lot of background experience in these types of transactional systems to ensure that you provide a level of quality, how do you shore that up, make sure that there's a life cycle process that ensures that you produce products that are worthy of the quality that you want them to be?

Yourdon: Okay. Very interesting.. One of the things that I'm hearing from a lot of the CIOs is that they finally have accepted the fact that they can't really control what kind of technology today's young workers bring into the office because, in fact, it's *their* technology, it's their smartphone or whatever. What they *can* protect is the network and the data and the infrastructure and that that seems to be where they're drawing the line between things you control and things that you are much more flexible about. Is that generally true in publishing companies too?

Mooney: Well, publishing companies tend to be somewhat conservative. Having said that, what we have done both with handheld devices and hardware servers, and also the use of cloud… [I]nstead of saying that there's one device or there's one tool that you have, what we try to do is give either two or three alternatives and then let them work within that framework. The reason we do that is, number one, it gives them flexibility. I'm convinced too that it allows them to explore, which is good for the organization. Having said that, what we don't enable is having 20 devices, 30 vendors—which we've had in the past, where everybody's got their own thing using their own tool using different open-source capabilities in one area but not in the other.

And so, by doing the soft discipline and having the option of maybe two or three capabilities, it allows them to play, create, and also satisfy the requirements and at the same time, from a corporate standpoint, provide some level of standardization. And a good example of that is we were traditionally a BlackBerry shop. Obviously, in the state that we're in, when the iPhone came out, it made—and this is even before the iPad, a couple of years ago—it made a heck of a lot of sense for us to just transition to the iPhone. Most of the students in the K–12, let alone the college space, were using them. We had big internal battles about how to do that. So again, going back to this proof-of-concept theme that I seem to continue to be on, we had a higher ed, college sales meeting. Traditionally we have about 800 sales reps, and honestly they tend to be not technical in nature. There's probably a cluster that are.

And so what we did is we actually bought 100 iPhones and we enabled the e-mail capability—which doesn't sound like a big deal, but when you're "breaking a standard," it was. Two, what we did is we were using salesforce.com. They had just started. We gave the capability for them to actually do transactions using salesforce.com. Third, we have an Oracle supply management system—that's the ERP that I made a reference to and is the foundation now of our orders, and they can actually take orders and place orders and look up pricing and catalog and product information, all on the iPhone. It was the most I've been liked as a CIO, I think in my whole career.

Yourdon: [laughter]

Mooney: You know, we're giving them a device, we paid for them, and it was basically placing them in front of a customer where, as an institution or an organization, a vertical market we were kind of conservative, but meeting the needs of our customers. And traditionally the majority of our customers were using it at the same time.

Yourdon: Very interesting. Let me circle back for just a second and ask one last question about the day-to-day job. One of the things that has become much more clear to me after about a dozen of these interviews is that no CIO operates alone. He almost always has a team of people reporting to him who handle various aspects of the overall job. And I'm curious to know what you think are the most important attributes or characteristics of people that you would have on the CIO team helping you carry out your overall mission.

Mooney: Well, something about computers, because I was on a panel about a year ago and we had a heated argument about this. Obviously, you have to have a level of technical skill set—and again, my undergrad is in engineering and I think it helps with credibility. I'm not a good engineer anymore, you know, because I've been so far removed, but I do think that there's a level of technical expertise that is absolutely required. And maybe it's 30 or 40 percent of the makeup. The other 60 to 70 percent, even more so today, is the whole issue of strategy or being able to execute strategy, the whole issue of communicating and aligning the technology goals with the business goals. The whole issue as we commonly refer to it as sitting at the table and coming across as a peer as opposed to a techie person, as somebody that people have to tolerate or somebody that they don't understand. And that is more through influence, business development, being able to communicate and present and provide competitive intelligence and knowledge about your marketplace that, back when I started or even in the last five to ten years, was necessary but not as critical as it is now.

I see nuts and bolts, too, in that all organizations have a high dependency on technology. Depending on the culture of the organization, it will depend on how they leverage that skill set and the individual that is in that role. Now we got into a little bit of a tiff on the discussion, and it's come up a couple of times even in the last month or two—I'm convinced that what's happening now is the CIOs ended up reporting into the CEOs and everybody was clapping and saying, "We finally get a seat at the table and get some influence."

And then I believe there's a dynamic going on where they're going back and they're either reporting to the COOs or chief administrative or chief of staff. And I am convinced that—and this is where we got in the heated discussion—that that is not good. People say, "Well, it has to do with who's the CFO or who's the COO," and I agree with that, but I believe that if we're not careful as far as the role of the CIO and the impact that good CIOs can have on an organization, that where they fit, how they fit, and who and when they get access to people about that is critical.

Yourdon: Interesting. But does all of this apply equally well to your immediate subordinates, that is, the team that helps the CIO do his job?

Mooney: Well, it's different. The answer's yes. As you move down through the career spectrum, if you look at the vice president level and the director level, the same attributes that are necessary with the CIO I believe are absolutely critical at that level. Now what's happened with us—I don't know about other industries—we pushed quite a bit of the hard-core technical development offshore. So we have relationships with Tata, Wipro, HCL, and that was a major push about six years ago, well, even when we did the ERP, so I would even say seven, eight years ago.

Now it was done for a myriad of reasons. One is to keep costs down. Two, if you look at the way that the offshore companies work, you've got people that have the technical skill set. The problem is we have lacked the level of technical skill set residing within the organization—where the business's knowledge, communication, and influence for technical people is absolutely critical. At the lower end of the career spectrum, the technical skill set is still absolutely critical. And what we found by pushing too much offshore—and we're actually bringing it back in—specifically around the media development and digital products development, is that we lost some of that technical skill set that was absolutely critical. And the reason is because the world's changing so fast. I mean, you take all the change and then you compress it within a short period of time...

The example I use is with Salesforce.com and those using the cloud: look at what happened to them as an organization, let alone their growth, let alone how you use Salesforce. It's an example where you need that hard-core technical skill set on-site. Secondly, I made reference to the fact that we did pretty well on some of the proofs of concepts, but what we have not done well is the testing systems integration and scalability testing. And I'm convinced that you have to have that skill set resident within the organization. Now, for the CEOs and the executive VPs, they don't really care what's happening behind the door, but they do know that they want their systems up on a Monday morning or a Sunday night and not failing.

Yourdon: Oh, absolutely. What about issues of trust and integrity and just being able to work well together? I've had several CIOs saying, "These days, in this economy, we're all working 12 hours a day, and so you've got to have a team of people who get along with each other." Do you find that important in terms of the kind of team you've built to help you run your job?

Mooney: Well, two things. You're 24/7. I do leadership conferences twice a year and it's not only for the technical people, but it's for the businesses. And part of it is to create what you're talking about, so the whole trust thing—it's common sense, but if people know one another really well beyond the day-to-day of just doing their work, they tend to be more trusting. If there's an issue, they will bring it up sooner and that kind of thing. The issue is, you're working 24/7. The "my dad is coming home at five o'clock at night" is gone. The expectation on the systems side is that people need to be available whenever. We're very good from a balancing standpoint—we try to be good from a family balancing standpoint. But the expectation from the front is that this is not a 9-to-5. So within the technical organization, we have been able to achieve the balancing act by being flexible and supportive to the needs of our employees.

The problem comes if you become too confident in yourself within the technology organization and don't bridge that to the businesses. I'm finding we have little "pockets"—especially in the media groups, if one is not careful, they become proud of what they do, and have their egos get in the way of supporting the business and ultimately the customer.

Yourdon: [laughter] Actually, that's a good point, because I've seen variations on that with just about all of the interviews I've done. And the question I've asked of the CIO is, how do you persuade your peers in these other business areas to either follow a technology path that you think is important or to avoid a technology path that you think is dangerous given that they do have big egos and they're obviously very successful in their business area and at best they are peers? You certainly cannot boss them around and give them direct orders. So how do you get them to kind of go along with your view of how technology should be used?

Mooney: Well, we've done everything—and I don't want this to sound silly and trite—in New York we have made provisions where our employees do not have to wear ties or dress formally.

So there's that. The other issue where I've had significant success is you put them in front of the senior business leaders and you let them share with them the excitement about what they're doing, not so much from a hard-core technical standpoint, but from a customer perspective. We've got one individual, he's up in New York, he looks like a model of one of these digital media people that I made reference to. And he's so passionate about what he does. The only issue is, we need to make sure that his presentations and the involvement is limited because what he does tend to do is transition into the hard-core technical—and then what happens is we lose the senior managers and the businesses because they're thinking more about, "How do you price it? This technical product, how do you actually deploy it?" and that type of thing.

The other thing is to foster innovation. We have departments within my organization, one in particular over in the UK, where I have found that I can create these innovation centers, where there just seems to be less bureaucracy. We have a small one in New York. And I let those pockets, where there's probably between ten to twenty people, dress the way they want, they can wear their headphones all day, and they basically behave differently, and there's an acknowledgment in the business that we need those innovation centers to create what we need to do.

Yourdon: Interesting. Let me switch gears at this point. I would like to talk to you about what keeps you awake at night. What are the big problems and concerns and issues that you worry about as a CIO?

Mooney: We made reference to it: I'm talking infrastructure. I'm talking everything from the data center to the existing hardware that we're using to the network. Really, for us, it's the bandwidth and ensuring that we're meeting the needs of the business. It's sort of good news because we know the digital space and product is growing. So how do you meet that demand? Because it's very, very hard to predict. And how do you do that in a way that you're not spending too much money, but at the same time you're not going to catch some problems with some failures? So I said, so that's more one of infrastructure, bandwidth, and keeping up with the existing products that we have.

It's very hard for us to forecast, that whole space, and I think we have some pretty good experts. And then the other challenge is making sure that when we do forecast that we can react quickly. So that's one in particular and that's more tactical, operational in nature. The other area … is making sure that we keep the appropriate skill sets. As a CIO I've worked very well in an organization creating an exchange of organizations, people that are proud, our retention is good. The concern I have is the people that you need, referring back to this new generation and the media divas. Making sure that we can attract them and then that we retain them and we keep them energized.

Yourdon: Interesting.

Mooney: And that is a space because McGraw-Hill is a great company, it's a super organization, but we're somewhat conservative in nature and bringing those people into that type of a culture is very difficult. You say, "Wait a second. We're all in the middle of a recession. People can't find jobs." I found that even now that finding the good and the best people is still difficult. And I would suggest that going offshore isn't necessarily the answer to that either.

Yourdon: Yeah, I would certainly agree with that.

Mooney: And so that's the second one. And then the third would be making sure that we're looking out into the future, so the innovation centers—we don't like to call them "R&D"—working with the appropriate people from the standpoint that the market is shifting so fast that we're making sure that we can meet the market's trends and needs.

I'll give another example. We can talk about the figures if you want to produce it or publish it. I have a friend who has a small company or used to have it—he just sold it. Neat guy, it's in the K–12 business. Basically, they provide infrastructures for schools for wireless. And I remember the day and we were giving him $30,000 and $40,000 contracts and he was barely getting along. Now that was five years ago. He just sold his business for $120 million.

Yourdon: Wow.

Mooney: So News Corp. is creating an educational vertical. Joel Klein, who used to be the chancellor, the head of the schools in New York, has come over and he's working for News Corp. So here's a competitor, News Corp., that was, at least as far as my perspective, never competing directly with McGraw-Hill or the educational publishers—which has made a concerted effort to go digital, to invest significantly through mergers and acquisitions—we were caught off-guard, if you will. So the other thing that concerns me is that coming from a competitive standpoint, how do you stay on top of the heap?

Yourdon: Very interesting. One last major area to chat with you about for five minutes or so. What would you say are the key technology trends that have really changed the IT industry over the last 10, 20, 30 years?

Mooney: Going way back . . . you and I talked about this back in the day when I was in the military and the government and, you know, the whole shift to the minicomputer and then you see, without telling all the stories that you well know, the shift to the laptop—oh, not the laptop, but the PC. And then what's happened of late is you take all of that and you compress it—obviously, the Internet had a significant impact. Mobile devices I think will continue to have and are having a significant impact on the evolution of technology. Cloud computing has revolutionized the tech world, both technically and from a financial perspective; and whether you believe that it's here or not, it's here. The issue is it changes the game and rules we play by on how we use data centers, those types of things.

It's fascinating, because I also have a franchise and a small business, which I'll share with you quickly ... here in a little bit. If you look at the way businesses do business as a result of the whole social networking side and if you go out and you watch *Social Network*, the movie, and then you see what's happened and then you look at the Middle East, and we're getting a little bit on sort of the political side here, and what's happened in these countries by the use of these technologies that probably didn't even exist ten years ago. Facebook has enabled the shift in political power in the Middle East. What that is, is an indication that we're compressing a type of technology such as that, that has a *huge* impact on the way, not only on the way we do business, but on the rest of the world.

So I think social networking will continue to have a continued significant draw. Now it's interesting. I've been in discussions with the people out in Silicon Valley. They say that they're concerned that if you talk gaming, mobility, social networking—those three things—that they anticipate we're starting to get into a little bit of a bubble. But those three in particular I'm seeing, at least in the education space, and if you take gaming in particular, the way people learn will continue to change dramatically.

Yourdon: That's interesting. I hadn't thought about the gaming aspect of it. There's one aspect that I would think would be enormously relevant to publishers in the education world. You know, we now live in a society where we've got the technology to support it but also the available time so that any of us individually can create intellectual content for the greater good of humanity. It's out there and free to be used, in Egypt or Libya or whatever, and we obviously didn't have that ten years ago.

Mooney: Absolutely. And to your point, sometimes we tend to think U.S., domestic, and so your point is what is happening is the impact it's having … worldwide, and it's more than just business, generating money. I mean, you're talking socially, you know, having been in the military, my son was in Iraq for a year. The impact of technology can have to help the world. I was real proud that the "one laptop per child" concept originated out of MIT Media Labs and [Nicholas] Negroponte.

Yourdon: Right.

Mooney: And you know, it's taken off but not to the level probably that we would have wished, but we actually got involved in that and started putting content on the OLPC computer. And the idea included everything from using solar energy to help generate enough electricity for the computer and those kinds of things. It was just fascinating.

Yourdon: Let's see . . . you mentioned cloud computing also as something that you think is very important. Do you see that continuing on as a major trend into the future?

Mooney: Absolutely. I think we're in the early stages, so there has to be some level of structure, and I know "structure" is probably not the right word, but capable of security and things like that. And I'll tell you why I think it's going to happen. If you look at what transpired in our industry and how we behave differently, we have large data centers, building large data centers. It enables businesses and its CIOs throughout to compress the amount of time and the amount of money that you spend on product development, which if you put that in a tool set in the CIO's bag of tricks, will be very powerful. It will enable everyone to produce proof of concepts quicker and for less of an investment. Now, they're not production-ready-type systems, but we can actually prototype them and show them to the businesses, and say, "Touch and feel this. Do you like it? Do you want to change it?" Well, obviously, it keeps the costs down. It allows you to fluctuate—I made reference to this little case study story about college students on Sundays—so you can scale up when you need to and back down and do it in a way that's cost-effective.

I'll give you another real quick story. We had the sales meeting and we were using Salesforce.com. It was out in Phoenix. There was a large Marriott. Something happened with the network coming out of the Marriott, so all these products that we had going back to the data center in Princeton, New Jersey, we couldn't have access. What we did, we were able to reroute—

well, the sales reps were able to use Salesforce.com. I mean—we all sat there and looked at ourselves, saying, "My God. The world's changing."

Yourdon: Interesting. All right. One last question, which is: where do you go from here? Now that you've been a CIO for a long time, what kind of future do you see for yourself at this point?

Mooney: I've gotten to this aspect of my life for a myriad of reasons, so I want to give back. Not that I haven't, but I mean more so. And what I mean by that is through mentoring. I want to continue to mentor. We as a family have a foundation—I'm on the board of MOUSE[5], so those things become more important to me. Number two is there's been an entrepreneur part of me that I've beaten up and hidden, probably out of my desire to create a family lifestyle. Separate from this, we started a franchise. I have another business, which does not conflict with McGraw-Hill. And I really see me starting, being an entrepreneur, being on the business side. And what I've enjoyed, having fun with the franchise in particular, we've been able, in the worst recession, to hire probably about 40 people. And independent of the fact that we're making money, what's been good for me is just being able to hire people. It's the same people that wouldn't have had jobs in the past. But again, it's mostly in education and wellness and mostly around the technology side of the business.

Yourdon: Interesting. So you intend to keep your hand in, but maybe go into more of an entrepreneurial direction.

Mooney: Absolutely.

Yourdon: Well, that's very, very interesting. All right. Well, I certainly appreciate this. You know, we could probably talk all day long about some of these things, but my time's up, so I probably should bring things to a close. I really appreciate your taking the time.

---

[5] MOUSE is a youth development organization, with locations throughout the United States, "that empowers underserved students to provide technology support and leadership in their schools, supporting their academic and career success."

CHAPTER 8

Dan Wakeman

Vice President and CIO, Educational Testing Services

Daniel Wakeman is Vice President and Chief Information Officer for Educational Testing Service (ETS), where he is responsible for all ETS information technology assets and activity. In this capacity, he also is responsible for ensuring that ETS strategy and tactics are appropriately informed and influenced by information technology. Previously, he was the CIO of the Elementary and Secondary Education Strategic Business Unit. Wakeman's first position at ETS was that of Chief Technologist Officer (CTO), where he was responsible for ensuring ETS had the needed information technologies required to be competitive and secure.

Prior to joining ETS, Wakeman was the co-founder and CTO for Elastomer-Solutions.com, a business-to-business exchange for the elastomers industry. Before that, he was the Director of e-Business for DuPont Dow Elastomers. During his career, Wakeman has held a number of information systems-related and business positions with Dow Chemical, IBM, D&N Bank, and the U.S. Air Force.

Ed Yourdon: It would be interesting to ask how you got to this position here. Now you had been a CIO previously, hadn't you?

Dan Wakeman: No. I'd been a CTO.

Yourdon: So, how did you go then from being a CTO to your current CIO position?

Wakeman: Well, I was hired as the CTO here. And, initially, what I was doing when I first came here was business development activities, like trying to take the educational research that was being developed and wrap it with IT and bring it to market.

Yourdon: Okay.

Wakeman: But I've got to tell you, those first few years here doing that, we weren't enormously successful at that, and it was because the model we were trying to use wasn't really the practical one, which we learned. At that time, the CEO was fairly new and he had brought in a lot of new people. Many of us saw this wealth of R&D that wasn't being monetized. It wasn't going to market, and they said, "Oh my gosh. Here's this wealth of opportunities to bring to market." Those of us coming from the for-profit business world didn't really understand the complexities of the education business and how it works, and that it doesn't work like a typical market.

Yourdon: Mm-hmm.

Wakeman: In Education there are many influencers and there are many different channels as well as many barriers. Whether they're government or union or schools or teachers or parents, you've got a lot of constituents who have influence over decision making and the market's enormously fragmented. So, with the exception of selling textbooks, there aren't many large sales opportunities. Textbooks and assessments are usually done at the state level . . . but there's not a lot beyond that that's done at the state level.

Yourdon: Interesting.

Wakeman: Most educational product sales are all done at the state level, district and even the school level, so it's very fragmented and we soon discovered that the only way to sell into those markets was with a huge, well connected sales force. And so we tried to build one and we found out that it's really expensive and the revenue for each sale is small. It doesn't fit the way we typically operate. Over the past 65 years, ETS has been very successful in the creation of assessments that help institutions and test takers make good decisions. Typically, this is done through RFP responses or selling to a large authorizing agency, such as the GRE Board. We discovered that the fragmented sales model we were pursuing was not a good fit with what traditionally we had done very well. So, it was a retrenchment from that to kind of a get back to the basics of what we really do. And then for the last five years, that's what we've been focused on—optimizing the business model that's been so successful here in the past and trying to really make that run as effectively as possible.

Yourdon: Right, right. So was all that part of, did it also involve or include your transition from CTO to CIO?

Wakeman: At that time, I was the CTO, but as you can see, I was not working in a typical CTO manner. My transition was driven by a need to improve the Enterprise Architecture at ETS. At that time, ETS was about five years into an infrastructure outsourcing engagement and the CIO had come to recognize that there was no formal management for enterprise architecture. He asked me to formally take on the job of CTO and create an Enterprise Architecture Origination (EAO), which I did. That organization is still in place today and has made great strides in slenderizing our infrastructure, effectively managing the life cycle of our technologies, and researching new technologies that can benefit the company.

Yourdon: That's interesting.

Wakeman: So I ran that group for a few years, then was asked to, in addition to my CTO duties, be the CIO for the K–12 business. While this started out as a part-time job, it soon became a full-time one and I relinquished my duties of CTO to a former mentor of mine, John Taylor, who was the CTO for DuPont. I thoroughly enjoyed my time as the CIO for the K–12 business, which came as somewhat of a surprise as I always viewed myself primarily as a technologist. After a few years as the CIO, I was asked by the CIO at the time, "How'd you like to be CIO for all IT?" And I said, "I'd really like to do that." And he says, "No, no. How'd you like to *be* the CIO for IT?" And I said . . . I'm looking at him and I'm going, "What is he talking about? Yeah, I just told you I would like to be." [And the CIO replied], "No, no, no. Right now!"

Yourdon: [laughter]

Wakeman: What made the transition from the very technically oriented CTO to the more business-focused CIO was how I demonstrated a willingness as well as desire to grow and learn new non-technical skills. I had demonstrated in the CIO position in the K–12 business that I could learn the business and I could be very business-oriented, and I met with a lot of customers, helped with f sales, and sought to help the K–12 business grow. I have always been good at helping the business understand how IT can help them win new business or improve operational efficiency. During this time, I really honed these skills as well as my interpersonal skills, which in a CIO role are probably more important than technical skills alone.

Yourdon: Hmm.

Wakeman: I believe that I was offered the position of CIO because I had effectively demonstrated I had the skills to work with the business, lead change, manage technical staff, and bring a technical perspective to business challenges.

Yourdon: Absolutely. But you mentioned something just a second ago that I want to elaborate on for just a moment 'cause I've heard similar things from roughly half a dozen CIOs that I've already interviewed. One of the things that several of them have said is that in this position that you're in now, it's very important to maintain a reasonable core of technical skills. And I was curious as to your opinion on that. That's sort of where you came from, but is it important to maintain?

Wakeman: You know, that's interesting, because when I was at Dow, I worked for a CIO who came from the business side. He was a sales guy, and the guy had had zero IT skills. And the problem was, as anyone who had IT skills could see, was he lacked a solid understanding of the decisions he was making. He was also fairly easily persuaded to make dubious IT decisions.

Yourdon: By vendors or just anyone?

Wakeman: By vendors or IT people, key people, who wanted to get their way and once he would build a trust with a certain person, he'd believe whatever they'd say because he had no way to evaluate that on his own. So a guy who's a very good mentor to me, John Taylor, who was the CTO at DuPont and then came to work here as a consultant for many years for us, he used to always say, "You can't buy a product if you're not an informed buyer. And to be an informed buyer means you need to understand what you're buying." And he said, "If you don't have the skills to understand that, then you'd better get somebody in with you that can be your informed buyer."

So I think, despite the fact that the whole world of IT is changing, there's no doubt about it. There are a lot of people selling services that encapsulate a lot of the complexity of the IT processes and systems and everything, right? So you can go buy a Salesforce.com and not really understand anything about how they built it or how it works. But if you do understand or at least have some understanding of it, you're going to make a better decision about picking that product versus another one because you're going to ask questions like, "Well, how am I going to integrate it with my back-end systems?" or, "How are you doing security?"

Yourdon: Right.

Wakeman: Or, "How are you doing DR [disaster recovery]?" You're going to ask questions that the uninformed buyer won't ask. They're going to be asking, "Well, does this process? Can I do this? Can I do this?" which are relevant and important questions to the business side, but they're not going to ask a lot of the back-end questions like, "Are you storing my data in Ethiopia?"

Yourdon: [laughter] Right.

Wakeman: Where is your data? They're going to look to someone else to do that, and if it's so easy to go buy those services now, they might not even bother to, and then only to find out later. What usually happens is, they'll go and get a service, and the first thing they want to do is tie it in to all the back-end systems. And then they'll start sending XML files and pretty soon they've got an unsustainable process. You can't run a business that way. It's not scalable. It works initially, but then no one in those groups wants to keep doing it. Over time, operational complexity and the lack of clear processes and costs outweigh the benefit that was originally sought.

Yourdon: Okay, well, that's good that you've confirmed that. You mentioned another thing that I want to explore just a little bit also, with the magic word "mentor." You said it was a gentleman from DuPont?

Wakeman: John Taylor.

Yourdon: Is it just one or has there been a series of mentors?

Wakeman: Well, it's been different mentors in different areas for me. If I go way back, when I was in the military, there was a guy I worked for, Steve Wegrznyek who has passed away since, he was really my first mentor. I was just a young airman, and he was a civilian, and he taught me a lot about managing and leading people, organizing and he really took an interest in helping me out quite a bit. I ended up working for him for like three years and grew a tremendous amount during this time. It was his belief in me that gave me the confidence to grow and develop. He pushed me out of my comfort zones in a way that was challenging yet rewarding. I really miss him.

Yourdon: Aha.

Wakeman: And I did quite well in the Air Force under him, so he gave me a lot of confidence in myself, just saying, "You know, you can do more. You think you can." You know, just those simple things. But it was just enough to get you going. He was a great mentor to me. And another one—this is a kind of a funny one—there was this guy that at DuPont-Dow, who was a sales guy to us. He was our CSC sales rep. And so you could call him a Friendster, a vendor—you know, Dilbert has that thing…

Yourdon: Right.

Wakeman: So I knew that, and I knew he was trying to sell us products, but he was a very insightful guy and he knew a lot about IT and the business of running IT. I learned a lot from him. I don't know if I'd call him as much a mentor as [much as] somebody who was willing to share a lot . . . we would just get together and talk, and he would just talk a lot about how his company sells its products and how they go to market, and how they win clients. And I learned an enormous amount about how vendors work from him.

Yourdon: Ahh, okay.

Wakeman: I also learned a lot about the whole IT industry from him, to be honest with you, because he had a real keen insight into the IT industry. When you're young in IT, you don't think of it that way.

Yourdon: Right.

Wakeman: It's a job. But it's really a big business in itself. And so he gave me this whole perspective that I had never had, so I learned an enormous amount from him. And then there is John Taylor, somebody I met at DuPont, and he was just a very insightful person who really has a keen awareness of IT and how to practically use it. I can remember—I don't know if I should repeat this, but—he was really not a big fan of Microsoft. And so he and I and a few others went to meet Microsoft, and we're representing DuPont, and they were trying to sell us all their products. And they just came across like they knew it all and they understood big business, and John just let them have it.

Yourdon: [laughter]

Wakeman: John remarked, "You guys don't understand a thing about how big businesses work. You don't know what you're talking about." He explained it all to them. What I learned from John was how to ask really good questions because that's one thing he really did, and how to know when you're being bamboozled.

Yourdon: Ahh, okay.

Wakeman: By asking the right questions, you could quickly determine whether the vendor, or somebody you're working with, really knew what they were talking about and whether they could deliver. That was his special skill, and one I have tried for years to emulate.

Yourdon: That's very interesting. One last question in this general area. Either before or immediately after coming into the CIO role, were you given any specific training? Did they send you back to get an MBA or anything of that sort?

Wakeman: Not anything specific to a CIO role, but I have many courses in leadership, interpersonal skills, communications skills and other soft skills. I already had an MBA, and after I became CIO, I attended the Gartner CIO Academy. knew that was available. Years before I had become CIO, I had read the book called *The New CIO Leader* by Marianne Broadbent and Ellen Kitzis, and had met these two at a Gartner conference, and I thought to myself, boy, if I ever became a CIO, this is what I'd do. So, guess what happened when I became CIO? I pulled this book out and I called Ellen up—she was the first one I called—and I got her at Gartner and I said, "Would you help me do this? I want to do what's in your book." And she said, "Sure." So she came to ETS, and she worked with us to do what's in this book. We actually implemented pretty much everything that's in here in my first couple of years here.

Yourdon: Aha.

Wakeman: Working with my leadership team at the time, we launched the initiative "Getting to Great," G2G. The plan was to take this fairly good IT organization and make it into a really great IT organization, and the way we're going to do it is by following the ten-step process that's laid out in chapters of *The New CIO Leader*. Probably the most critical thing we learned during that process that really stuck is the demand-supply model. We split IT into a supply-demand organization and built a process framework around that split. It has worked very well as a way to understand the work we are asked to do, the demand, and how we supply resources to do that work. We have discovered that the most challenging process is effectively managing demand into supply.

Yourdon: Ahh, okay.

Wakeman: Today, I have leaders that managed both the demand and supply side. On the demand side, the IT relationships managers work closely with the business units to understand the needs and requirements and convert them into demand that is captured in our Book of Work. The supply side is responsible for providing the services, whether they're through vendors or they're through our own capability. And then there's Development, whose job it is to build the IT services used by the supply side to satisfy demand. Development is a supply side function, and is also responsible for Solution Design, so Development straddles the line between Supply and Demand at times. Once the model was conceived, we went to work implementing it, which was a major change initiative in and of itself. There was a new language for everyone to learn and many new processes to be developed, taught and monitored.

Yourdon: Aha, okay.

Wakeman: The critical role on the supply side is the BTL. Are you familiar with IT account reps?

Yourdon: Yes.

Wakeman: At ETS, the Business Technology Liaison plays the role of the account representative. They work with the business to understand the needs and communicate our capabilities.

Yourdon: Oh, okay.

Wakeman: Each BTL has a small staff of business analysts to help them quantify the demand. And many of them sit right within the business teams and they work with them as part of the team. Our struggle continues to this day, though, to be the management of demand [from our business users] into supply [by our IT project teams].

Yourdon: Aha.

Wakeman: That business process is the most difficult—if there's anything I've learned, that's where the hardest process is, is getting the demand and supply, because to do it effectively you need to know your capacity and to match it against the demand. Given that this is a formidable challenge, we looked to see how others are effectively doing this. This has led us to begin implementing ITIL version 3, as our service management framework.

Yourdon: Interesting. Well, you've also said something very interesting here that I've not pursued with some of the other people I've interviewed, though I've seen examples of it elsewhere. I don't know how best to put it, but kind of creating a common mindset, in this case perhaps by getting everyone to read the book or—

Wakeman: I must have given out hundreds of copies of the book.

Yourdon: Yeah. Well, that's kind of what I was going to ask, that's occasionally happened, I'm delighted to say.

Wakeman: Everyone had this. This was everywhere.

Yourdon: That's occasionally happened with one or two of my books, which took me by surprise, but I've not heard other CIOs say that a critical thing in the development of their organization was creating shared values, shared vision—and it could be accomplished either by bringing in a consultant or a book or various other things.

Wakeman: That was the key. It was really to get people focused on, "We're going to become a great organization, and here's how we're going to do it." Because our mission as a company is to provide fair, valid and reliable assessments that advance quality and equity in education. Well, if we're going to do that, and that's critical and that's important, we've got to do it without making errors and we have to do it well. So how do we support that? And one of the things *The CIO Leader* instructs you to do is to create your business maxims. Ellen Kitzis, one of the book's authors, was hired to run three workshops composed of the senior leaders of the company. It was in these workshops we created the business maxims.

Yourdon: Okay.

Wakeman: And from the business maxims we created the IT maxims. In fact, I have a meeting coming up to revisit those and to make sure they're still relevant, which we do from time to time. To make sure the maxims we originally created are still our maxims, because they should be, right? They're supposed to be long-lived. One of the things that came out of that was, given that we were struggling with trying to say, "We're a learning company," was "We are an assessment company." And that became one of the business maxims. So we went from this kind of diffuse maxim, and reached outside of our core of assessment … and then we came back. We said, "No, first and foremost we're in assessment." And that became one of the business maxims. "We are an assessment company."

Yourdon: Okay.

Wakeman: Another one that came out of that that's still used widely today—and it got reworded a little bit—was, "Do what we do best and partner for the rest."

Yourdon: Aha.

Wakeman: Thanks to these workshops I gained some much needed credibility, because I was a brand-new CIO, to run those workshops. It demonstrated that I was really interested in first focusing on what the business wanted and how I was going to ensure that IT fully supported the business.

Yourdon: Interesting.

Wakeman: I wouldn't have done that had I not read this book. Ellen was just such a thrill to work with, so I've kept up with her over the years, just giving her updates on how we've been doing, but she was very influential in helping me work with that. And Gartner was too. I'm part of their EXP program, so I have an account rep that I talk to every couple of weeks.

Yourdon: Hmm.

Wakeman: And he helps me if I have questions or ideas. I can go get research. I can talk to other analysts. I take my team every year to Gartner's headquarters in Stanford and we pick four or five topics that we're going to focus on.

Yourdon: You've mentioned three related things in that explanation that I want to follow up on because I'm hearing a lot of common threads in my interviews. One of them was this point about being able to establish some credibility early on, and that's something I've heard in different ways from a lot of the other CIOs. Some of them have said, "Here I am doing my job within the IT empire, and I'm pretty good at it—but obviously I'm at a peer level with other business leaders in other parts of the organization who have risen to some position of authority or power because they're very good, but also because they're very strong and they have very strong ideas, including they think they know how to do my job better than I do."

And I'm curious as to whether you ran into that, or this whole question of how to establish a relationship of trust and working together with business peers, especially 'cause you came in and you were the new CIO on the block.

Wakeman: Right. There's no doubt there are very strong personalities that are here, and many of them have their own ideas about how things should be done. The interesting thing about working here than other companies I worked at—probably because the compan's roots are in academia—it's a very collaborative environment.

Yourdon: Ahh, okay.

Wakeman: And people do tend to respect people with certain skills that they're supposed to have, so you see a little bit more of that. Because of the jobs I had before here, I was known to many of them and they respected my technical skills—so when it comes to the domain of technology, I'm usually fairly credible. When it comes to the domain of business or R&D, I'm not an academic, nor do I pretend to be one.

Yourdon: Right.

Wakeman: And I'm definitely not from the R&D side of education, so I've had to be careful to respect my peers and know when their judgment or their input, combined with mine, will lead to the best answer. So that does mean there are times where we have respectful conflict We have to hash things out, but I think by building relationships with those key people first, when you get into those tense situations, you can depend on your relationships to come to the best conclusion.

Yourdon: Aha, okay.

Wakeman: That's how I've done it. I feel pretty good about my relationships with my business peers. There's one group at ETS, the vice presidents that run the functional centers where most of the operational work happens. And there's the one group above that, the senior VPs that are responsible for all the functional and business areas.

Yourdon: Well, it leads to the next kind of related question, which I again heard from almost all the CIOs. They all say, "You know, I've got a team of people who help me get the job done." It may have been, for example, the three who were in your meeting earlier or whoever. And the question is, what characteristics do you look for—what are the most important characteristics for people that you want to have on your team? What is it that you prize most?

Wakeman: That's a tough one because I definitely prize their ability to execute and [have] knowledge of their domain, but it has to be done with the ability to work with and lead people.

Yourdon: Okay.

Wakeman: So I don't know if I can say one thing. It's a combination of leadership, personal integrity and the technical—I don't know if I'd call it technical—but domain knowledge. In leadership roles I seek people primarily with strong interpersonal skills that can bring people together to get things done. Not people with an excess of persona, but people that truly care about other people and revel in the challenge of bringing out the best in those they lead.

Yourdon: Interesting.

Wakeman: So in different roles I may look for different skills, but at the same time, personal integrity is very high on my list.

Yourdon: Well, I've heard that from several people.

Wakeman: Very high.

Yourdon: One or two other characteristics I've heard and I'd be curious as to your feeling about them. A couple of people have said, "I need people who are willing to work hard because with kind of the economy we've got, we're all working 12 hours a day. And if you're going to work for 12 hours a day with a group, they have to be people that get along with each other and who I get along with."

Wakeman: Absolutely. I look for people to join the team, which is a very collaborative, highly functional team that really works well together, that I believe will contribute to the team. We have all used Gallup's Strengths Based Leadership program to better understand and appreciate each other's strengths. A small group of us worked with a coach for a whole year. The coaching focused on how to leverage each other's strengths to do more than we can as individuals. It was a fantastic personal growth experience that has had great results.

Yourdon: Interesting.

Wakeman: I've come to the conclusion that sometimes you have to work a lot of hours, it's not hours that define how much work gets done.

Yourdon: True.

Wakeman: And that's a misconception a lot of people have. I have people here who work 8-hour days, and they get far more done than some people who work 12-hour days because they're just a lot more effective and they know how to do work. They don't waste a lot of time, and they go from task to task, they get things done, and they keep their meetings just to the right length, and if they're done with that meeting they move on to the next thing. They're just very effective at managing their time and getting and prioritizing the work, and knowing what needs to be worked on and what can be not worked on. They have focus.

So I tell this to my staff all the time: "One of the critical things you're hired for is judgment. Judgment is very important in what I'm paying you to do. And by 'good judgment,' I mean judgment in how you manage your people, judgment in how you use your time, judgment in how you make decisions about what technologies and products you use. So I'm counting on your judgment. And that's what I'm evaluating you on—the decisions you make."

Yourdon: Interesting, interesting.

Wakeman: When you have a person with good integrity who has great judgment you have a star.

Yourdon: That's very interesting. Let me go into a couple of the more general questions. What would you say are the two or three top priorities that you tend to focus on? You've already said it's the balancing the supply and demand side. Is that kind of the general answer there?

Wakeman: No. I think that what I need to do is make sure that we are delivering, more than anything, the appropriate level of service to ensure that ETS can fulfill its mission. That's the most important thing I need to do.

Are the tools, the capabilities, the people, the processes and all the things we're doing here helping ETS to fulfill its mission? And can I see a direct link between what we're doing and the advancement of what the company's doing. I don't want IT to be viewed as having to align to a mission. I want IT to be *the* mission, or part of the mission. We're no different than marketing, we're no different than sales, we're no different than R&D. We are part of the company. We don't need to align with it. I want to see us as ingrained into the business as everyone else. We work together. We build products together. We explore new markets together. We advance the company together. And where we can take what we know that's special and unique, we do that, and we combine it with the other skills so that we actually get something that's "1 + 1 = 3." We're really looking for that synergy and trying to get more than just each of us working independently towards a common goal. We're working together towards a common goal.

Yourdon: And certainly, ETS as a business is very much about packaging and selling information—those assessments or whatever. Even an automobile company these days is not really just making tangible widgets. It's a whole bunch of code flying in close formation.

Wakeman: It really is.

Yourdon: But it's more obvious that within ETS, you guys are in the information business.

Wakeman: Oh yeah. When you walk around our campus, you can't find anything to describe us except people and buildings. It's all in the intellectual property. There's no factory creating tangible widgets.

Yourdon: That certainly is true. Speaking of factory, one of the phrases I've heard quite often from some of the CIOs is that at least a part of their job is just keeping the lights on in the factory. How big a part is that for you?

Wakeman: It's a huge part. Operational excellence, as you know—any mistake we make in an assessment affects a person's life and that means they might not become, for example, a teacher when they wanted to become a teacher, or they might not get in the school they wanted to get into. Whether it's GRE, TOEFL, Praxis, or the SAT. So we have to be very careful, in that what we produce has accurate, reliable, and fair scores. And that all runs through the IT engine. That's our factory.

Yourdon: Some of the numbers you gave me when I was here last time were staggering in terms of the millions of tests that you process.

Wakeman: We have to do them all, they have to be done perfectly. So our objectives are 100 percent on-time, 100 percent accurate score reports. And the only way you can get there is to continually improve by learning from mistakes and making use of great quality programs such as Six Sigma. Great process plays a critical role as well, thus the reason we are implementing the ITIL v3 process framework. We continue to train staff in quality methods, defect detection, and continual improvement techniques. And it's paying off. Defects continue to decrease and our customers are noticing.

Yourdon: Interesting.

Wakeman: We also embraced standardization in an effort to reduce complexity and reduce variation. We've reduced the number of opportunities. The standardization effort is looking not just at where can we standardize; it's focused on where can we standardize that will reduce our defect rates. From an IT perspective, one of the big areas I have to focus on is defects in code.

Yourdon: Mm-hmm.

Wakeman: I have quite a big effort under way right now. I introduced the Software Development Life Cycle (SDLC) process and the Reference Architecture over the past year. These are efforts to bring high-quality code that's defect-free to production. And by "defect-free," we mean there are no critical defects. There's no such thing as perfectly defect-free code. Our goal is to have no defects that have an impact to the business, such as a test taker getting the wrong score.

Yourdon: Right.

Wakeman: This has been an area of continuous focus for us and one in which we still have a lot of work to do. We will not yield until we have eliminated defects that can result in severity I incidents. We can settle for nothing less if we wish to serve the test takers with the level of service they expect from ETS. We have created a scorecard to ensure we are effectively measure our progress.

Yourdon: Interesting.

Wakeman: I'll send you a copy of the scorecard, and an article that was written by Gartner about it. They actually did a best practice research note on our scorecard.

Yourdon: You know, it's interesting you mentioned this now. None of the other CIOs I've spoken to so far have mentioned scorecards.

Wakeman: We worked really hard on getting a simple, one-page scorecard that defines what's most important from a business perspective of what we do. And we track it. We use Six Sigma techniques to ensure our processes are in control. There is a control chart for each process metric.

Yourdon: Interesting.

Wakeman: Being a CIO of a big organization like mine, I'm always open to competition. There are many excellent firms out there that would like to run the IT department for ETS. It is my desire to be in a position where even if such a firm gains a sympathetic ear with ETS management I can say, "Compare us to anyone. Can they reach this level of quality? And if they can, what are they going to charge you?" We must be competitive, we must be service oriented and we must know ETS better than anyone else as the business has many other sources of IT supply now.

Yourdon: Yeah.

Wakeman: I don't ever want to be in the position where it isn't clearly visible the value we add to the organization. I want to quantify the value we add, not just through quality, but also through our costs being competitive. We benchmark ourselves each year, too, from a cost perspective.

Yourdon: Well, that was going to be my next question. It's one thing to have a scorecard for internal discussion, review, and so forth, but the next obvious step is benchmarking, which everybody's aware of and lots of companies do. But I'm intrigued that that also has now been part of the conversation that I've had with other CIOs, that it hasn't been right up in the front of their radar screen.

Wakeman: We benchmark our costs each year using two firms' yearly benchmark studies. Being in a small industry, it's difficult to find good companies to benchmark against, so we look to industries that are highly information intensive, such as the financial industry. Each year we strive to become more cost competitive.

Yourdon: Okay.

Wakeman: Currently I find that our costs as a percentage of revenue are higher than other information intensive industries. So I've been trying to bring that down, and I have. I've been able to bring down IT expenditures as a percentage of revenue by four percentage points over the past five years while delivering more projects and services than we have in the past. That's one measure of value.

Yourdon: Interesting.

Wakeman: And we will continue to bring this down by standardizing our systems, processes and taking advantage of new technologies such as virtualization and cloud computing.

Yourdon: Right, right.

Wakeman: We also analyze how much of the revenue goes to innovation or new products, O&M [operations and maintenance]. Our objective is to change the split so more of our IT dollars go towards growth and less towards maintenance.

Yourdon: Interesting. Now, there's one other related thing that I had scribbled in as a question to ask you. Aside from metrics and quantitative benchmarking, one of the things that seems to be almost universal is this sense of being part of a club—the "CIO club"—so that you can ask questions, compare notes, just sort of schmooze with your CIO buddies. How important is that in your case?

Wakeman: Yes I do. I do some of it through Gartner, but I do more of it through the CIO executive board. I go to a few of their events and I get in group conference calls with them. But I also have picked up some great ideas from the Accenture CIO board.

Yourdon: Oh, I didn't know that.

Wakeman: Yes, they've had some pretty good meetings with other CIOs. I attended a few calls on consumerization, which is something we're trying to do here. Accenture hooked me up with a bunch of people who are doing it, so did Gartner. And Gartner introduced me to not only *their* CIO, but to a whole bunch of other CIOs who I got to meet and actually learn about how they're doing consumerization in their company.

There have been other examples where speaking with other CIOs has been a great benefit, such as with the Security Standards Council PCI Standards were introduced and those of us that process many credit cards were trying to figure out how to comply.

Yourdon: Well, certainly, it does emphasize this point that regardless of what industry you're in, uhh, you all share a lot of common issues.

Wakeman: We do, especially in security, where we all are facing similar threats like you are. We deal with that every day, as do many other CIOs.

Yourdon: I've got a whole section of questions here on problems and issues and so forth—of which the first one was, what are the main problems and threats that concern you? Obviously, the one that's at the top of everybody's list has been security.

Wakeman: Security is a very sensitive area for us as we must ensure the integrity of our score results and the personal identifiable data maintain for our customers. It's without a doubt one of the risks that keeps me up at night.

Yourdon: [laughter]

Wakeman: It is disconcerting to know that there are organized groups out there, very sophisticated groups, that seek to steal information or shut down a company's ability to operate on the Internet.

Yourdon: Yeah.

Wakeman: We work hard to protect the information we are entrusted with and use leading edge technologies to do so. A few years ago I created the position of Chief Information Security Officer and was fortunate enough to staff it with an outstanding security leader. He has built a great team that works every day to improve our ability to protect ETS's information assets and monitor for potential threats.

Yourdon: Right.

Wakeman: His team is constantly looking for vulnerabilities and we always take care of them. Protecting the enterprise is a balancing act between the threats we may face and the costs to protect against those threats.

Yourdon: And I assume that's something you share with your business peers. Because ultimately it is a business decision.

Wakeman: It is a business decision. Well, yeah, because they fund how big our security budget is, or how much we're spending on security.

Yourdon: Right.

Wakeman: We participated in a security benchmarking study on how much we're spending on security a few years ago and came back and found that we're under-spending. And I used that as justification with the Board of Trustees and the Office of the President to get more money to staff up, to beef up my security organization. And luckily using this information I was able to persuade the board and Office of the President that we should spend more money on security. We were able to increase staffing and we're completely redesigning our network. It's really, really amazing what we're doing, and it's going to allow us to take advantage of virtualization and cloud computing in a very secure way.

Yourdon: Interesting.

Wakeman: There's a lot of great new security technology out there.

Yourdon: Funny you should mention that. That was the very next thing on my list of questions. What are some of the new trends that you think are really going to influence your situation over the next couple of years?

Wakeman: Well, call it virtualization, call it cloud computing, call it private public, or call it infrastructure as a service. That is huge. The ability to buy infrastructure and software as services is having a tremendously disruptive impact to the IT industry.

Now, I think for my IT organization, where we outsourced our infrastructure nine years ago—we're on our tenth year of that contract—we're better prepared for that transition than others because we don't own our data center or the staff that manage it. This gives us the opportunity to more quickly adopt these new offerings as our transition will be a bit less painful than for those that are still saddled with a data center to contend with.

Yourdon: Yeah.

Wakeman: We welcome the benefit these new technologies offers us, such as being able to move away from the concept of renting servers to buying infrastructure services to run our workloads only when we need them. This increases our ability to respond quickly to business demand while simultaneously reducing costs.

Yourdon: Right.

Wakeman: So, to me, that is an enormous change for IT because it's going to change how we buy and use infrastructure. But it will not be without new risks and challenges. We will have to change the way we operate to take advantage of these new offerings.

Yourdon: Mm-hmm.

Wakeman: What really surprises me, Ed, is how fast it's happened. Really, cloud computing is really new. Didn't Amazon start this trend about five years ago?

Yourdon: At most, yeah.

Wakeman: And look where it is already!

Yourdon: Yeah.

Wakeman: Now, I know there are security concerns, I know there are other things, but you know what? You can't be stymied by those because this is so disruptive and the costs are so big, different—the storage costs, the compute costs, everything. Because if I have to buy a server and run it for a year for something, I'm going to use [it] only a portion of the year, like some of our assessment programs. I was just quoted in an article in the *Wall Street Journal* about this topic, where they were asking me, "Well, why would you even want to buy these on-demand services?" I said, "Well, because I have demand that fluctuates." I said, "We have large scale assessment programs that happen only once a year and I need a tremendous amount of computing power. You know what that computing power does the rest of the year?"

Yourdon: Just gathers dust.

Wakeman: Right, it does nothing but burn up electricity.

Yourdon: Yeah. And it's amazing how many situations there are like that. I think of the Oscars or the Olympics.

Wakeman: Super Bowl.

Yourdon: Super Bowl. Yeah. On and on and on. Christmas shopping season for most of the retail industry.

Wakeman: Mm-hmm.

Yourdon: Yeah, it is, it is amazing to think about it. In terms of futures, I've got a related kind of social question. This whole issue of the "digital nation," the Gen X or Y or Z or whatever generation it is that's grown up with computers, how do you see them impacting what you do here at ETS?

Wakeman: Well, first, I'm going to say something that's a little bit controversial. I don't believe any of that Gen-Xer stuff.

Yourdon: Ahh, okay.

Wakeman: Because—well, how old are you? And you've got an iPhone?

Yourdon: True.

Wakeman: And I've got an iPad right here and I'm not a kid. We adopt technology just as rapidly as kids. Now, granted, there are some people who don't, but there are plenty of kids who don't either.

Yourdon: That's a good point.

Wakeman: There's a whole slew of kids out there who don't know much about technology. Oh, they know how to play a video game. They know how to program the VCR. But that doesn't mean they know technology. You know, there's this sort of misconception that they're all geniuses and we're not. And I'm telling you, it's wrong, because if you look at the demographics for adoptions of Facebook, for example, the biggest group of adopters is the baby boomers.

Yourdon: [laughter] Sure. Well, I certainly agree with that. I guess the only area where I might disagree—and it may not even be significant—is the fact that in my case, it still takes a conscious mental process to say, "Oh, I should Google that," whereas it's "wired" into my kids.

Wakeman: Well, that's wired into them, but guess what won't be? What's going to come next. This isn't going to stop here.

Yourdon: Right.

Wakeman: This is just going to keep changing. And it's going to keep changing faster. So they're going to be at the same disadvantage we are in just a few short years.

Yourdon: I completely agree. But now you've got not just people coming into IT but the entire workforce coming in out of university to ETS with whatever expectations or assumptions they have.

Wakeman: Well, so, here's how we're dealing with that. And believe me, it's not just the kids: a lot of the people are just here, too. I'm getting it from people here. "I want to use a Mac. I want to have an iPhone."

Yourdon: Aha. Okay.

Wakeman: You know, it's not just the new people coming in. It's even the existing staff. Now it's not as much. I've got people here like my boss, who says, "Just give me a computer. I don't want to manage it. I don't want anything to do with it." And I've got another group who is saying, "I want to use my technology and I want it to use it to do my job the way I want to do it."

So we're introducing a consumerization program called "Computer Choice," and the idea is it's a volunteer program. We're starting with cell phones. There's a certain group with business uses for cell phones that we can work with, and smart phones, and they'll be able to go out and get one through Verizon or AT&T, put it on our network, get access to our e-mail and whatnot. You have to sign something that says we have the right to remote-wipe it and you have to have a firewall and you have to have it encrypted and—you know, there are certain rules. But the idea is, for most of them, that they're going to get a stipend to pay for it. For some we're just going to say, "You have your own phone and you want to use it, but you're not authorized for a stipend. Well, we're going to let you connect anyway, but you have to follow these rules."

Yourdon: Right.

Wakeman: There has to be some security that we can control. So luckily the iPhones and some of the others have encryption, they have the ability for remote wipe, they have the ability for password lock. So as long as they meet those minimum constraints, which seem to be almost universal across platforms, BlackBerries do, too, we can let them on the network. The next thing we'll introduce is Computer Choice on the laptop front, and that one's a little more challenging—the problem is the technology's not quite there yet.

Yourdon: Interesting. Ahh, one last question—and I think it's the perfect wrap-up question: where do you go from here? After you've been a CIO here for X number of years, do you have any thoughts, plans, dreams, hopes, aspirations?

Wakeman: Well, the one thing I look at is where is the role of the CIO going?

Yourdon: Oh, that's a good one. Okay.

Wakeman: And, it's something I read a lot about and I try to get some understanding. I've talked to other CIOs to get their perspective and, there's a lot of debate about where the role of the CIO is going. Some think it's going to disappear. The CIO Executive Board has sure made a case that it's all going back into the business, it's going to be bought as services, there's really no need for a CIO. Others have said, "Well, in a company like ours where intellectual property and IT play a big role or like a bank, there is still a need for someone who is *the* technology leader." So I foresee myself staying in a technology leadership role, but the scope may expand to more shared services, beyond just IT.

Yourdon: Ahh, okay.

Wakeman: So maybe some operations services or whatever. So the role may get a little bigger, I'd say, because so much of those other functions depend on IT to operate.

Yourdon: Sure.

Wakeman: So you can see that there's a synergy between them, and you do see some CIOs, like Dave Kepler at Dow, who I know. He eventually rose up to be vice president of all of the services— HR and operations and quality and other similar shared service areas. Do you know Martha Heller?

Yourdon: No.

Wakeman: Anyway, she's made kind of a case that the role of CIO is going to broaden out to a more service basis. It kind of makes sense. If we're really moving to a world of buying services, and you know as well as I do, the future IT organization is not going to be about running a data center. It's going to be about buying these services and packaging them in such a way that you can use them to run your business.

Yourdon: Well, and integrating them.

Wakeman: And integrating them, right.

Yourdon: But the involvement in the business leads to another possible future, and that is running the whole bloody business.

Wakeman: You could, yeah.

Yourdon: And that's up to the CEO level, which at least a couple of CIOs have done.

Wakeman: I think if you're in a very technology-centered business, if you're in a Google or something that technology plays a very big part in where you could do that. I think it would be harder for me to do it here because the CEO here really needs credibility in the education space.

Yourdon: That's right.

Wakeman: There are a lot of CIO information-intensive positions I could see myself doing, financial or something else where they still value IT as a core competency. This is why I so enjoy working for ETS. I'm not really interested in going to work for some company that doesn't value IT as a core part of their business.

Yourdon: Why would you? [laughter]

Wakeman: Right. And you're seeing that, though, in a lot of businesses where they see IT as just a service they buy from someone else, where they've outsourced everything. I believe over time many companies that do that come to regret it as they soon find that that they lost a tremendous amount in intellectual property that was locked in heads of those they dismissed. Innovation slows and it takes longer to get things done.

Yourdon: Well, I think I will hit the stop button on that one.

Lynne Ellyn

Senior Vice President and CIO, DTE Energy

Lynne Ellyn is the Senior Vice President and Chief Information Officer at DTE Energy, a Detroit-based diversified energy company involved in the development and management of energy-related businesses and services nationwide. Ellyn leads an organization of approximately 700 people who provide information technology strategy, development, and computer operations for all of the DTE Energy companies.

In 2002, Crain's Detroit Business named Ms. Ellyn as one of the 100 Most Influential Women Business Leaders in the metropolitan Detroit area. In 2003, the Association for Women in Computing named her as one of the Top Michigan Women in Computing. In August 2004, CORP! Magazine named her as one of Michigan's Top Business Women. She is a member of IBM's Board of Advisors and the DTE Energy Foundation Board of Directors, as well as an appointee to the Smart Grid Advisory Committee of the National Institute of Standards and Technology (NIST), and a fellow of the Cutter Business Technology Council.

Lynne Ellyn: Hello.

Ed Yourdon: Hi, Lynne.

Ellyn: I'm sitting outside in Ocala, Florida.

Yourdon: Aha. So you're not in Detroit. I very much appreciate your taking the time. I can start you at the beginning in terms of how you got to where you are today. Were there any early heroes or role models or mentors that shaped your career path and future?

Ellyn: Well, not formal mentors. I think particularly for women who got into the IT field when I did, there weren't very many mentors. And that may also be true for men, but I think it was particularly true for women. So no really formal mentors, but fairly early in my career, I worked at Henry Ford Hospital, and I worked for a gentleman by the name of Jim Shipley. I was too young at the time to appreciate how extraordinary he was, but as I encountered other people that I worked for, time and time again, I came back to what an outstanding boss he was, what a visionary thinker as well as a person who was just so effective with the larger system, the people system, and the organizational work. And he was just an imminently good human being. Not to say that I worked for a lot of bad human beings, but the point of all this is: I found myself over the years wanting to be the kind of boss that I felt Jim was.

Yourdon: Ahh, interesting. And your comment about mentors is something that I need to keep in mind because I'm trying to pin down the woman who's the CIO for General Electric at the moment, Charlene Begley. And I've got another one, Joan Miller, the woman who's the CIO of the entire UK Parliament. I've pinned that one down. So, I'll be curious to see whether you know, whether your experience is a common one or unique. It certainly makes sense from what you've said.

Ellyn: Well, I'm often asked to speak to women's groups. Even in China I got these questions: What's it like to be the only woman in the room? And the other is: Who were your mentors? And I have a smart-ass answer for both of them. I had four brothers, so being the only woman in the room started really early.

Yourdon: Aha.

Ellyn: And I had no sisters. And the smart-ass answer to the mentors is, and you'll chuckle about it. When I was growing up, all the grown-up women around me were mothers: my mother, my grandmother, my aunts, the neighbors. The closest thing I had as a model of a working woman was Marlo Thomas in *That Girl*.

Yourdon: Ah, interesting.

Ellyn: And people crack up because, of course, she was a comedienne. She was always in some kind of ridiculous situation. Umm, they never really let you know what kind of work she did, but she was independent in the sense that she had her own apartment in New York City and, you know, she seemed to be having a lot of fun and she was really cute. So, it's a joke, but the truth is, not only were there not any women in IT, I mean, I heard early about Grace Hopper, but I never met her, and there were no professional women, certainly not somebody with a title like a senior vice president that I ever met. And for probably the first two thirds of my career, umm, I didn't know very many women executives, and if I did, they were at a very large distance, so there was no model.

Yourdon: Now that is very interesting. Now you spent an early part of your career out in Silicon Valley, didn't you?

Ellyn: I did, I did.

Yourdon: And there were no women out there?

Ellyn: Just to recap, the first five years were in hospitals, and I did a lot of medical computing.

Yourdon: Right.

Ellyn: The next ten were at Chrysler Corporation.

Yourdon: Oh right.

Ellyn: Where I was in advanced technology software planning and managed the artificial intelligence group. Then I went to Xerox and from Xerox went to Netscape.

Yourdon: Ahh, okay. What about out in Silicon Valley? Was there also an absence of female, you know, really strong IT managers?

Ellyn: Absolutely. There were . . . like at Netscape, the chief counsel was a woman, the head of HR, which isn't too uncommon, was a woman. There were a couple, umm, more senior-ish product development managers who were women at Netscape, but only a few compared to the number of men and certainly at Xerox there were women. As a matter of fact, Anne Mulcahey was the head of HR when I was there and Ursula Burns—I didn't know her, but I had met Anne a number of times—but Ursula Burns I think was in a product division, but certainly was not an executive. The CIO at Xerox was Pat Wallington, so she was, but Xerox was the first place where I encountered women with the senior kind of titles. To this day it remains the organization I worked for where there were the most executive women.

Yourdon: Well, that's a nice segue into my next question area, which is basically, how you got your current CIO position? I mean, without going through your whole career, how did you begin moving into more and more senior executive positions that led to a CIO title?

Ellyn: The opportunities always came to me. I can't say that it was my intention to be a CIO. It was always my intention to do really good, really energizing, interesting work. And whatever I was doing, that's what I was focused on, and the next opportunity just sort of showed up. I will say that lots of opportunities showed up that I said no to because they weren't interesting. They weren't going to be motivating. They looked like a grind.

And I let them pass. So this idea that, you know, every opportunity that comes along, you better jump on it or it's never coming back, I think it's totally wrong.

Yourdon: Did you get any kind of specific training along the way to be a CIO? Did you go back to school to get an MBA or anything like that?

Ellyn: Yes, Chrysler sent me to an executive MBA program with Michigan State when I was managing the advanced technology group.

Yourdon: Okay. So that was just part of a general training provided to people, executive people once you got to a certain level?

Ellyn: No, no, no. They only sent a few people a year and you had to be recommended. Obviously, you had to be admitted to the program.

Yourdon: Right.

Ellyn: And they had to have a good reason to do that. You had to have a pretty strong advocate. And I was nominated twice before I was accepted. The senior executive review selected me. So the year that I went, which was when Chrysler was doing pretty well, in the '90s, they sent five people from the company.

Yourdon: Oh, okay. Well, that leads into the next general area of questions, which is basically what you're doing now. You know, if you had to divide your day or your general kind of work activity into three or four categories, what would they be? I assume one is just sort of keeping an eye out for the operational area. You must have tens of thousands of servers and all that stuff. Are there major kinds of clumps of responsibilities that you have?

Ellyn: Yes, but let's talk about the directly IT responsibilities. You know, it's the usual. I have three large data centers, I support all of the DTE family, which is two large utilities and a number of non-regulated businesses, which operate all over the United States, including two energy trading floors, one in Ann Arbor and one in Houston. We have rail and transportation activities, power and industrial. So what I have is a diverse portfolio of companies, and they are very different in character. Energy trading is like a typical trading floor, and then I have highly regulated utilities. So my day is spent switching hats from a mentality around startup and growth to a mentality that's conservative and careful.

And I actually like that about the company, because I'm probably prone to boredom if you ask me to do something repetitive, and then I'll go cause mischief, I suppose. So the diversity of that and the operational requirements are a complicated puzzle because, obviously, if you're in trading, it's right now, it's "whatever I want; don't bother me, we're making money here" and if you are operating the status system that controls the flow of power and gas, the margin for error is zero. So, you know, those are very, very different things. See, the other responsibility that I take most seriously and is my fingerprint, is the way I manage, it is around the coaching and optimizing of the people system, finding the exact right place for a specific person so that they are not only highly productive and contributing; they are really, really glad to show up. Because I believe that you can pay people to walk in the door, but they either volunteer the best of themselves or don't. And as they say, people join companies but quit bosses.

Yourdon: Yeah.

Ellyn: So the people system, I would say, is the most important thing and unfortunate at this time, taken a while to build it; I had the best, the strongest director team I had ever known anywhere, and so now I really am a coach, working on refinement, not working on basics. They are so super-confident that they're amazing, so it's a little bit like the symphony conductor. Sometimes I think that I need to be careful that I don't mess it up.

Yourdon: [laughter] By waving your baton.

Ellyn: By stepping in when they don't need it and whatever, so that's kind of a refinement. And the last thing—and this is probably different than all the other CIOs that you're going to encounter, because of the nature of the utility industry and the moment in time where we find ourselves with all the smart grid and smart grid money and expansion of the grid and the cyber security threats—I spend a significant amount of my time actually talking to the Department of Energy, the Utilities Telecom Council, lobbyists, [and] political people, working with the other CIOs in our industry about what positions we're going to take. [I] also have a technical Congressional appointment, … I'm on the Smart Grid Advisory Committee for the next three years, so I'm spending a lot of my time on large industry issues with a lot of political overtones, and God knows, nobody would have ever accused me of being a politician.

Yourdon: [laughter] That's, fascinating. There are a couple of aspects of that that I'd like to pursue, but first I want to make sure that I understand kind of the main thrust that you're talking about. In terms of coaching people, I mean, you must have, I don't know, 1,000 or 10,000 people, you know, in your IT empire. How far down the hierarchy do you go in terms of practicing your coaching work or carrying it out?

Ellyn: Well, pretty far down, because I'm open to taking on anyone who wants coaching, so I do end up coaching some people. In addition to that, I'm actually pursuing certification through the International Coaching Federation, so I'm building my coaching hours.

Yourdon: Ahh, okay.

Ellyn: Which is something else that I'm working on, so I'm actually coaching some women in the company who aren't in IT. They're in other departments and I've been asked to coach them through our mentoring program. So I do a fair amount of coaching, but directly in my organization what I'm trying to build into my directors, my managers, and my supervisors is their ability to coach others.

Yourdon: Right, right, right. Now, the directors or whoever they might be who essentially report right to you: I've heard several of the CIOs talking about that, that whole area, you know, their team, the team that really on a day-to-day basis helps them get their job done. In order for people to get onto that part of your team, what skills or characteristics were you really looking for?

Ellyn: Well, obviously, they have to be technically competent. That goes without saying.

Yourdon: Sure.

Ellyn: That's ... part of the issue. And for me, technical competence comes from actually having practiced in our industry, so I'm a little at odds with the idea that you take the guy who was great with the spreadsheets and has great business relationships and then you put him in charge of some type of IT. So, personally, I don't subscribe to that. Maybe that's my background.

You know, I actually programmed, designed databases, programmed in a ton of different languages, so it could be a bias, but for me, you got to be the real deal. But you can't just be the real deal. You also have to have great people skills, strong character, and the ability to live in the gray zone, with a ton of paradoxes, and find a good answer when you're in the middle of competing priorities and seeming conflicts of interest.

Being in IT, you're the crossroads for everything and getting over-identified with your business constituents, or over-identified with the IT interests, or over-identified with technology. Any of those are deadly, and one of the things I just love about my director team, and I think makes for a really strong organization of any kind, is not one of my directors would ever allow one of their peers to fail at anything.

Yourdon: Ahh, okay.

Ellyn: If someone was in trouble, they would—and we call it "swarming"— they would swarm the problem and pull their peer out of issues because they understand that any problem anywhere in IT is everyone in IT's problem.

Yourdon: Hmm, okay.

Ellyn: And that orientation, I think, is unusual because competition, showing up the guy next to you, has for a long time been the way that people have got promoted.

Yourdon: That certainly is true. Yeah, you know, there's another theme I've heard from several of the CIOs I've talked to about this area of your team. And several of them have said, clearly technical competence, the competence from being a practitioner and some of these other things are obviously important, but they also want to have a team of people that can get along with each other because, in this kind of economy and business environment we've got today, a lot of them are putting in 12-hour days and you don't want to have to spend 12 hours a day working with people you fundamentally don't like. Has that been a big issue for, for your team?

Ellyn: It has not, but I'd go a step further. Of course, they have to get along, but I think it's more than being able to get along. It's again back to the idea that we are IT. And helping, assisting, even doing the job for your peer that's necessary in order to keep the group together, to keep it performing, that's what you're going to do. Not that that should ever happen or happen frequently, but the idea that you and your peers are so interdependent, and your identity with them is bound to help everyone's success. I think it's a level of sophistication you don't see in many organizations, and the organizations, whether they're IT or otherwise, that are going to really perform are able to move to that level of sophisticated community and deep identity with the success of the group.

Yourdon: Interesting. Now, you said another thing in this area of discussion that I want to pursue a little bit. When you said that you and your directors are very much at the crossroads because these days everything goes through IT, so clearly you and your team find yourselves interacting with a lot of other peer-level people in the various business areas with whom I have to assume you occasionally have some conflicts or disagreements, and you find yourselves dealing with very strong, successful leaders, who have risen up to where they are right now at least partly through the strength of their personality and convictions, and so forth, and who feel that they really know how to do their job or they probably think they know how to do your job better than you do. How do you and your team manage to get your point across or, you know, pursue the kinds of policies and strategies you think are crucial from an IT perspective?

Ellyn: Well, you're exactly right. Everybody who has ever used the Internet or done a spreadsheet knows exactly how easy this should be.

Yourdon: [laughter] Yeah, right!

Ellyn: It's as though everybody who ever drove a car would believe that they could engineer, design, build the factory, and produce cars better than the car manufacturers. It's an interesting thing that the complexity in systems is so poorly understood and yet, and you probably know this, complexity scientists say the most complex products on earth are software.

Yourdon: Right.

Ellyn: And so we have a situation where that completely eludes people. The idea that software could be more complex than the vehicle they drive or the most complex part of it is the software, you know, people don't get that. And certainly, trying to get that across to your peers is difficult. So back to how do we influence and work with them, again, back to the sense of community. When your directors, your managers, your supervisors, and the people in IT all understand that if they go native, if you will, and kind of veer outside in order to please somebody, then the whole all falls apart— that the consequences are bad. That we have to be clear in our communication, consistent in our communication, we have to always remind people that we're balancing competing priorities, and we have to continuously be educating, explaining, demonstrating, and, by the way, benchmarking with other companies and presenting the facts of how you stack up against the performance they would get elsewhere is the only survival technique I know to work. And that's a survival technique, 'cause this battle never ends.

Yourdon: Well, particularly these days, when a lot of the technology is cheap and widely available. You know, it's been true for 25 years, ever since the PC came out. You mentioned your energy traders as kind of an example of people that I would imagine are somewhat rogue technicians. You know, if they don't like the answer they're given by you, they'll go down to Radio Shack or whatever the equivalent is today, or download an app for their iPhone and say, "Screw you. We don't need you. We'll do it ourselves," until it gets out of hand and then they come begging for help.

Ellyn: Actually, I don't have that problem with them.

Yourdon: Oh, really?

Ellyn: Because they are also subject to daily scrutiny around what they've done, you know, when the trades are over at the end of the day, there has to be an audit trail, so it turns out they're very impatient and they want what they want, but they don't color outside the lines. It's actually more likely in other…in engineering areas.

Yourdon: Ah, okay.

Ellyn: And the like.

Yourdon: Yeah, yeah.

Ellyn: But to be truthful, we monitor and police our network and we manage the desktops to such a degree, it's really hard to do that.

Yourdon: Well, one of the other things you mentioned is very consistent with what I've heard from other CIOs, and in fact, one, I forget which one it was now, said that he's beginning to think of his job as being the chief media officer in terms of the effort he puts into communicating and educating and spreading the word about not only what they're doing, but as you just said, benchmarking against what … the competitors [are] doing, what the peers in our industry doing—I think that is going to become increasingly important.

Ellyn: Oh, absolutely. That is a big part of my job today and the work my staff does. Last year, we belonged to UNITE, which has 17 of the largest electric utilities. We spent a thousand hours collecting the data for our benchmark with them.

Yourdon: Wow. That's amazing. One other thing you also mentioned that kind of fits into this whole thing, that is kind of a no-brainer, and that is the importance of staying in touch with other CIOs both in your industry and really all industries, uhh, to keep track of what other people are worrying about and thinking about and planning for, and so on. How much of your time do you spend doing that sort of thing?

Ellyn: Well, I'm guessing it's like five, seven percent, which isn't such a big part of my time. But, it's a really critical part. It's absolutely essential, to get a handle on the sort of the lobbying efforts or industry positions.

Yourdon: Ahh, good point.

Ellyn: That's been hugely important. Becky Blalock from Southern Company and I collaborated to do some policy discussions with the lawyers at the Department of Energy. I have another one coming up and we strategized around those things.

Yourdon: Let me switch gears to another question area that I imagine you would enjoy talking about. What are some of the new trends that you see coming down the line that you think are going to influence the IT industry in your world of utilities in the next few years?

Ellyn: Well, the big one, of course, is the "smart grid." The problem with that title is that it implies that there is a stupid grid.

Yourdon: [laughter]

Ellyn: The grid is highly automated now. This is a re-automation of the grid. For example, at one time (this predates me) Detroit Edison had 140 engineers that just operated it. Today it's done with just a dozen or fewer. As we go into more grid automation and smart meters and we can debate how smart they are, but meters to the extent that homeowners adopt a lot of home automation, and that remains to be seen, but there are a lot of people who are juiced about it. And we start to bring on a fair amount of electrical cars; electric vehicles; and the automation, billing, and management that is going to be in here. It's a big deal for our industry, a big deal. Great opportunities. I don't believe the opportunities are where the popular press or Silicon Valley want them to be, but there are great opportunities to improve the manageability of the electrical distribution grid. At the same time, we have been railroaded into doing that as an IT-based network.

Yourdon: Hmm.

Ellyn: So if you go back to 1995 and '96, '97, and '98, when I was out in Silicon Valley and we were IP-ing everything, none of us, none of us anticipated the volume of security issues that we would face in the future and how that volume would ever be increasing in diversity and sophistication.

And so back in those days, we had a few security tools. You know, every company is now running, what, 20 different security tools, spending 5 to 10 percent of their IT budget on security issues, just managing the IT networks we know well. So now we're getting to IP electrical grids. So, in one column are all of these amazing possible things that we will be able to do, some of which benefit the consumer by reducing the cost, improving the reliability, allowing for better management, some of which may help the consumer if you believe all of the venture capitalists (VCs) who are funding all of this stuff out in Silicon Valley, in giving them iPod applications and smart phone applications that allow them to turn their lights off and on and cycle their pool filters and whatever if we believe that, if we believe that's what people are going to do.

And by the way, I don't believe that that's going to be anytime soon, because every experiment with that has shown that people play with it for a couple of months and then they've got better things to do, but we'll see if over time… So we have this, you know, bright, shiny future that we are in this process of creating. And we always have as an asterisk attached to it: "Oh, by the way, it ought to be secure."

Yourdon: Mm-hmm. Right.

Ellyn: Well, what do we know about IT now? They are not secure. We, we get a new security tool, a new security patch constantly. We have a "patch Tuesday" to fix problems that have already been exploited.

Yourdon: Right.

Ellyn: So logic tells me that the future for these IT networks can't be hugely different. So I see great and exciting things. I see deeply worrying and troubling things. And trying to enable without overly enabling potential problems is [like] walking a tightrope right now. And the IT industry is being hugely out-lobbied in Washington by the tech industry, because this is a lot of money for them.

Yourdon: I want to get to the problems and gists and so forth in a second, but let me just finish off this area we've been talking about. How much of an impact on your world do some of the other hot buzz words have that we're all seeing in the press these days, just like cloud computing and virtualization and so forth? Are those just sort of things that you use, or are they going to fundamentally change the way that you guys do business?

Ellyn: Well, about seven years ago, I was faced with huge capital investments to knock the walls out and make the data centers bigger. I said, "You know, we can't do this. We've got to find a better way." So it's pretty early in the virtualization game.

Yourdon: Oh, okay. Really, I thought so.

Ellyn: But we moved very strongly to virtualize our data centers. And today, I have so much white space in all three data centers, it's not even funny. So, we moved very strongly ahead of the game on virtualization. We got rid of the mainframe after we implemented a new enterprise business system based on SAP and some other technology. And we've moved along the virtualization path very strongly. So the few times we've looked at "cloud computing"—if I could set aside my concerns about security, which I absolutely cannot, you know, I'm so highly virtualized—there's not much money in it for them.

Yourdon: Ahh, okay, interesting.

Ellyn: So my point of view on virtualization is very similar to the outsourcing discussion 10 to 15 years ago: Get your house in order before you ask somebody else to do it. Because otherwise all you're going to get is your mess for less.

Yourdon: And your mess is farther away that you can't even see.

Ellyn: And the point of view

Yourdon: Yeah, right, I agree.

Ellyn: So . . . and then, you know, depending on your industry, and again, if you're a fast startup, you don't have any data centers. You're more at risk of running out of cash than you are if somebody is stealing your secrets, well, of course you'd go to a cloud. But when you're a 150-year-old utility company, you are the target of terrorists, criminals, and mischief makers, you've got a different set of considerations.

Yourdon: Interesting.

Ellyn: So, you know, if I was in another company, I'd view it differently.

Yourdon: Sure.

Ellyn: But for us, virtualization—absolutely three stars, four stars. Cloud computing—a big question mark. And if I was going to do any cloud computing, I sure wouldn't do it with the likes of Amazon or Google. So for us, that's probably not a big deal, but of course, we watch it. All of the consumer device stuff, the edge devices, big deal. We're in the process of moving to a point of view where we're going to enable a bunch of these, but we're going to view them as consumer devices; we're not going to provision them.

Yourdon: Ahh, okay.

Ellyn: So, you know, everybody's budget is cut. This year iPads were hot. Five years ago BlackBerries were hot. Three years from now it will be something else. I think our role is to keep up with the technology where we can deliver the corporate connection to you, the corporate mail to you, possibly some of the corporate applications. But it's your choice what you want to bring to work.

Yourdon: Hmm, okay. Well, that leads into, I guess, the final part of my questions in this area, and that has to do with the social media, which may or may not be brought to work by whomever. Twitter, Facebook, and related things, do you see those having a significant impact on the world that you live in, in the next few years?

Ellyn: Well, we have two points of view about that. We're on Facebook, we're on Twitter, but that's really only for corporate communications and the service part of our business, customer interface. We are not enabling our workforce to be spending time on these things because, frankly, we view it as a productivity hit.

At the same time, we are rolling out and deploying social media tools inside the firewall, so that we can have our own Wikipedia-like locations, we can have collaboration going on, we can have chat rooms about problems, you know, two people working on a problem in different power plants being able to use internal social media to show each other what's going on, what part is failing, and draw on other people.

I think [it] is a real win and a real enabler. Expanding that across the firewall boundary, we haven't seen a business reason for us to do that. The most important thing we do is keep the lights and power on. If I were a marketing company or a consumer products company, I'd probably view this differently. So my context is the company I'm currently in.

Yourdon: Sure, well, what about, you had mentioned consumer service? What about using things like Twitter so that citizens out there on the streets of Detroit can communicate back to you guys about the problems they're seeing or questions they have?

Ellyn: We do have that.

Ellyn: But, again, it's only open in the business context to those people who would be responding to that corporate communications customer service.

Yourdon: Right, right.

Ellyn: Not, not open to power plant personnel, IT personnel, whatever, because we're not responding to that.

Yourdon: Sure. That makes sense. Now, in the whole area of problems and concerns you certainly mentioned security, and that's something that I hear from everybody as being if not the central ingredient, certainly one of the biggest problems of all to worry about. Are there any other big risks and problems and so on that you're worried about over the next few years?

Ellyn: A moderate concern for my company, but a big concern across our industry, is under-investment in IT infrastructure, tools and technology, training, [and] recruiting. You know, most IT budgets have been viciously constrained, that we're not building the farm club for the future and we aren't across the industry making the kind of investments. And part of this I lay at the feet of the vendor community because the durability of their products over time is an issue. You know, I have an enterprise business systems policy that includes SAP, Maximo, Advantac, a bunch of other products, sitting on IBM hardware with a million tentacles into other systems. Well, you know how this is. There's a new release of the operating system as soon as you are up and you have to go to it, because otherwise you lose support. As soon as you make that change, then you have to upgrade another product. And if you upgrade that product, then you have to upgrade a third product.

Yourdon: Right.

Ellyn: We spend such a significant part of our budget just in life support for these large systems that doing the new thing becomes very, very difficult from a budget perspective. And that's problematic. That is very problematic. You know, back when we all embraced the idea of component-based architecture, object-oriented programming and whatever, and the idea that Java was going to be multi-platform-portable, we thought we were going to get to a point where there was enough level of abstraction between components and enough granularity that you wouldn't have to change everything in order to change one thing. We have not gotten there. And this is a serious problem for expansion, growth, agility, flexibility, and responsiveness.

Yourdon: That's a good point, and I don't see that changing in the next few years either.

Ellyn: Not until somebody says, "Enough is enough. I'm going to fund a very different kind of company that is not going to be dependent on support revenues to keep my focus and product market." You know, in the utility industry, we have an 11 percent limit by law. That's the best we can do. We have to deal with the likes of Oracle and Cisco, with huge profit margins. So they can out-lobby us, they can demand that level of increase in order to just keep running what we already paid for.

Yourdon: Right.

Ellyn: We have to maybe tax it. It's a problem and it requires radical change. You know, I wish I were young and had less to risk. I'd want to take this problem on, but I hope somebody . . . but I think you might have to be old to see the problem. [laughter]

Yourdon: That's true.

Ellyn: But I'm hoping one day it will change.

Yourdon: I have two relatively small question areas left for you. One is the whole generational issue. Do you see significant differences in the behaviors and attitudes of the new generation of workers that you're hiring out of university today as compared to, I don't know, five or ten years ago?

Ellyn: Yes. However, because I've always been at the edge of advanced technologies and the new, new things, even back in my Chrysler days, I had the fresh-out-of-the-university rotational. Everybody wanted to be in the advanced technology group for at least one rotation.

Yourdon: Right.

Ellyn: When I was in Silicon Valley, the two times I was there, obviously, I was doing the adult supervision thing. I think, there are some characteristics about being young, not being jaded, having your whole life in front of you that are kind of durable. Whether that was your state of being in 1970, 1980, 1990, 2000, or 2010, and then the whole context around you kind of colors in that outline. So yes, there are differences. I keep hearing about all of this conflict in the workplace based on those differences. Maybe we just don't have enough difference for me to have experienced that. But my observation is, there is a norming sort of pressure whenever you work in an industry or company that over time you are going to be more like them or you are going to leave. And so, I'm just optimistic. With young people comes a lot of energy, a lot of naiveté, a lot of "just do it," and you'd like to preserve some of that. At the same time, you'd like them to start building judgment. And I think it's a great process, I like it, so I don't know. I'm not concerned about it.

Yourdon: What about the fact that they now bring with them a whole lifetime, literally since birth, of familiarity and maybe some degree of competence with, I hate to say IT, but the computerized toys and gadgets that they've had access to?

Ellyn: Well, when I get people who think that because they drive a car they know everything about designing and engineering them...

Yourdon: [laughter] Yeah, yeah, okay.

Ellyn: I usually try to give them a tour of the data centers.

Yourdon: Ahh.

Ellyn: The systems operations center where we're managing the flow of power. Get them on the energy trading floor. Get them a visit to a nuclear plant.

Yourdon: Ahh, okay.

Ellyn: And knock some of the stardust right out of their eyes, and they start to realize that an edge device doesn't tell you much about what goes on in the center and smart people get it. I mean, they get it.

Yourdon: Oh, okay. That's very interesting. Well, one last question in that area which kind of goes back to the very beginning of your comments. What about differences, generational differences in terms of female IT people? You know, the young women coming out of engineering schools, are there more of them or fewer of them? Are they smarter or whatever than they were, you know, when you first came out of university?

Ellyn: Well, there are fewer of them. You know that statistically.

Yourdon: Sure.

Ellyn: That women signing up for engineering and science programs and IT are fewer and fewer. One, they believe all the jobs did go somewhere else. Two, there are now much wider opportunities to choose from, so they have opportunities that I would have never even thought of. Three, I think there are some, and my daughter would be an example of this. She always said, "Mommy, you work too hard."

Yourdon: [laughter]

Ellyn: She's a very talented designer. She's done museum design and whatever, and she kind of balances between periods of working and periods of raising her kids, so she was able to make a choice that I can't think of any opportunity I had like that. And I don't know what I would have done. But they have choices we didn't have. So having said that, though, the young women who are in IT today and I meet a lot of them, I'm an advisor to the Michigan Council of Women in Technology. They have over 600 members. They are far more ambitious, aggressive, technically educated and savvy in so many ways, so the ones I do meet are pretty awesome, and I hope we can attract more to the field like that. Now, instead of being systems analysts, we have women who are computer architects. You know, we didn't have that back then.

Yourdon: Hmm, yeah, yeah. That's encouraging. Well, one last question, I guess it's kind of appropriate for the end of a discussion like this, and that is, what's next for you? You know, do you hope to be a CIO for the rest of your life? Where do you go from here?

Ellyn: Well, remember I told you all the opportunities always showed up?

Yourdon: [laughter] Oh, okay.

Ellyn: Rather than me finding them. So I have faith there is something else. It's going to show up. Now, having said that, I think it's likely that I will finish out as a CIO, but I'm expanding right now in two directions. One is this coaching thing, because I'd like to help other CIOs, would-be CIOs in organizations work on how do you get appropriate synergy between computer systems and technical systems and the big human system? I think that's where all the opportunities are. The second thing I'm doing I start next month. I'm pursuing a postgraduate certificate in the neuroscience leadership from Middlesex University in London, and this kind of harkens back to my science and roots. I'm very interested in cognitive science.

Yourdon: Hmm.

Ellyn: How we apply that to . . . we now know so much more about the role the brain plays, the structure, the chemistry of the brain, and how successful you are, how you relate to people, how deficits in one area of the brain do . . . I'm passionate about how that relates to building really effective organizations, but also in how that relates to building really effective systems. So I don't know where it's going other than I'm going to spend ten months studying my brains out.

Yourdon: [laughter]

Ellyn: But, you know, something will happen from here.

Yourdon: Sure.

Ellyn: I've been tracking challenges on our remote access capacity because of the number of people who are out, so...

Yourdon: I can imagine.

Ellyn: You should be glad you're where you're at and I'm certainly glad I was able to get out of Dodge.

Yourdon: [laughter] I'm sure. All right, well, we'll, I'm sure we'll schedule for sometime later in the spring, and I look forward to seeing you in person then. So, thanks again.

Ellyn: Great. You take care.

Yourdon: Thanks a lot, Lynne. Bye-bye now.

Ellyn: Okay, bye.

Becky Blalock

Senior Vice President and CIO, Southern Company, Atlanta

Becky Blalock is Senior Vice President and Chief Information Officer of Atlanta-based Southern Company, where she directs the electric service provider's IT strategy and operations across nine subsidiaries and 120,000 square miles. She leads more than 1,100 employees in a company that has been consistently recognized as one of the 100 Most Innovative Companies by CIO magazine and one of the 100 Best Places to Work in IT by Computerworld.

Since beginning her career at Georgia Power in 1978, Ms. Blalock has provided broad leadership in many positions, including accounting, finance, marketing, corporate communication, external affairs, the office of the CEO, and customer service. She serves on the CIO advisory board for Sierra Ventures, as well as the Customer Advisory Boards of Oracle and AT&T. She is listed among the Who's Who in Science and Engineering, and in 2006, she was inducted as one of Computerworld's Premier 100 IT leaders.

Ed Yourdon: One of the things that I find that people are very interested in is to get a sense of how you got started and particularly whether there were any mentors or guiding lights that pointed the way when you were just getting started in the field.

Becky Blalock: I believe my background growing up influenced where I ended up. I'm an Air Force brat. When I was growing up, we moved a lot. I went to four high schools, three junior high schools, and eight elementary schools. I don't think I realized it then, but one of the things that all the moving around taught me was to be very adaptable and unafraid to go into new environments. A lot of people fear change and going into new environments because they grew up in the same town, went to the same schools, know the same people. I came into the corporate world and wasn't afraid to do things that I really had no background in because I'd been doing new things all my life.

Yourdon: That's very interesting. I mean, it hits close to home. I'm not an Air Force brat per se, but my dad worked for a defense contractor and we were stationed just outside Air Force bases, so I went to 17 different schools, but only one high school as it turned out, but every year we moved to a new town, and my parents said, you know, "The school is down the street. Go check yourself in," and so I can relate to what you're saying. [laughter]

Blalock: You're the only person I've ever talked to that's been to more schools than me, 'cause I went to 15.

Yourdon: Well, I was lucky that I ended up in just one high school, but I understand what you're saying. To be able to adapt to completely unexpected circumstances must be a very valuable skill?

Blalock: When you go into a new environment, it's all about how you adapt and how you fit in with people. I think my background taught me a lot of adaptability. I don't think I put all those pieces together until later, because I hated moving around in middle school and high school. Loved it when I was young because you're the new kid in the class, but when you get to high school and middle school, it's tough.

Yourdon: Oh yeah. Absolutely.

Blalock: And I got my undergraduate degree in marketing and then moved into finance inside the company. I went back to school at night to get an MBA in finance later in my career. I ended up in IT was through my stint as assistant to our then-CEO at Georgia Power. He had me working on an initiative to get better information and better metrics for how we could manage the business. He wanted an executive information dashboard and he was having a really difficult time trying to get that data out of our financial organization. At that time, our systems weren't designed to pull information in those formats, but we did make some progress when I reported to him.

At that same time, IT was going through a big reorganization. They were pulling IT out of our operating companies and centralizing it. They created regional CIO jobs, and the Georgia Power Management Council decided I would be good in this role. So the CEO walked into my office and said, "You know, we're creating these regional CIO jobs, and I want you to go do that." And I said, "You've got to be kidding me!"

You know, I had no background in IT other than the fact that I did some systems development work early in my career, but I really didn't even know any of the people in the organization.

My CEO said to me, and I have really carried this with me throughout my tenure in IT, "It's a job about information ... You know that I am struggling because I do not have the information and the metrics I need to run this business." And he said, "Help me get the information that I need to more effectively run this business."

You know, when the CEO asks you to do something, you don't really have a choice about it!

Yourdon: Yeah. True.

Blalock: As a regional CIO, I had responsibility for Georgia Power, for our telecommunications company, and then system-wide, across Southern Company, I had responsibility for marketing and customer service. It was a fabulous time to be there because we were going through a major transformation. We had to downsize, which was tough, as I'd never been through anything like that.

And the mindset that I took into IT is the mindset that I got from Allen Franklin, who was [the] CEO at the time. He said, "Let's not be so enamored with the technology. Let's think about how we use the information to more effectively run our business."

I was in the regional CIO job for nine months when the job of running corporate communication at Georgia Power opened up. The company decided we were going to be an Olympic sponsor, so what a great opportunity to run PR for a company that's going to be an Olympic sponsor. So I left IT after those nine months and ran our corporate communication group and then had an opportunity to run our business and economic development group. I was named the Vice President for Community and Economic Development and had been out of IT about six years when the CIO job opened up again.

It was the third time it had opened up. There had been a lot of churn, a lot of turnover in the position, and there was not a good, clear, strong candidate for the job. And I was fortunate that I had some brief experience there. I had a lot of success on the business side and did many things in the business and then got the opportunity to come here and lead this group for the past nine years.

Yourdon: Wow. Well, would you consider the CEO who got you started on this path to be a mentor in the traditional sense? Any others?

Blalock: Absolutely. He was not a mentor in the sense that he knew a lot about IT, but he was a great mentor in terms of staying focused on what really drives business success. One of the things he said to me, and I share this a lot when I mentor others, is, "Normally, when somebody comes into a role like this, I tell them to think about the three most important things you want to leave as your legacy when you walk away from the job. Normally, I'll write those three things down for people and tell them what they are." And he said, "I don't know what to tell you when they are in IT."

He said, "I want you to think about what those three things should be, then come back and let's meet again." So I did. I went off and I interviewed employees. I interviewed the people we support inside the company. I interviewed our vendors and took all that information into consideration.

And I told him, "I think I figured out what my three things need to be. Number one, you've got some of the smartest people in the company working in IT. But they grow up and they stay in IT. They really don't get the opportunity to go out into the business and take that knowledge. There's a huge opportunity to grow future leaders for Southern Company and this needs to be a big part of my focus, grooming and growing that workforce. Also IT changes so much that it's important for the people we have to stay very current on what's happening."

The second focus should be the opportunity to brand Southern Company as an innovative company, through the way we were using technology. We were doing incredible things. We were way ahead of anybody in the industry, but we weren't telling that story. We needed to be more proactive in making people aware of how Southern Company was a leader in the way we applied technology.

And then the third focus would be to look back—at the end of my career—and show that we rolled out incredible technology, which delivered significant business value and drove our business to be a leader. I didn't know what these technologies would be, but that to me, I'd like to look back and know we did some things that were significant in terms of the way we applied technology.

And he said, "Okay, I think those are the right three things. Now, write those down on a sheet of paper and every Friday, you pull that sheet of paper out and say, 'Is this where I spent my time?'"

He said, "With these jobs, these very senior-level jobs, there's all kinds of minutiae that people are going to want to pull you off to do and distract you from this focus. It's very important that you always keep these three things in front of you because it will keep you focused on the most important things you need to do for Southern Company. If you can look back each week and say, 'This is where I spent my time,' you know your time was well spent."

And really, I have used that as a guiding principle to keep me focused and to say no to things that did not fit this focus.

Yourdon: Well, it's a good one. It's kind of the first-things-first maxims that you hear in a lot of other places and it leads into the next area of questions that I had for you, which is basically what you're doing and what you have been doing as a CIO to make your company more successful? And it sounds like those three things you just mentioned, I would assume, continue to be at the top of your list today.

Blalock: Well, they are. We have focused a lot on our workforce. IT was—I think it was a demoralized organization. We were viewed only as a cost center. I think we've turned the corner now. Some of the feedback I got from the executives we support is, "I don't need a bunch of order-takers. I want people to show me what's possible."

Yourdon: Aha.

Blalock: We've turned the corner in a couple of ways. First, we focused on making sure our people got recognized for things. We had no intellectual property patents nine years ago, so we started an intellectual property program and made sure that our people got financially and otherwise recognized for their creative ideas. Today we have 56 items that have cleared the hurdle to go in the pipeline for patents. We only have eight that have actually cleared because it takes a while to get there, but we actually got our first three last year.

Yourdon: Hmm.

Blalock: An employee who received one of these patents asked me to come to his office. He said, "I've been in the company 34 years, and I want you to know this is the thing I'm most proud of in my career." And we had given him a plaque and $1,500, and I thought, "A 34-year employee and this is the most important thing," and it was really so little of an effort on our part.

Second, we started winning awards. We started getting picked by *CIO* magazine as one of the most innovative companies for IT. We started being on the *InformationWeek*'s 500 list of the most creative. A number of people on our senior team have been picked as one of the 100 top leaders in IT by *Computerworld*. In fact, this year, Dave Coker, our VP of Computer and Networking Services, got that recognition. Aline Ward and Marie Mouchet, who are regional CIOs, have gotten that recognition in the past, and I've gotten that recognition in the past. But it's not just us. We have people across our organization who are getting recognition for phenomenal achievements. In fact, one of our employees was named Engineer of the Year by Georgia Power last year.

Yourdon: Wow.

Blalock: We try to make sure our successes get highlighted and celebrated. *Computerworld* magazine has a survey of the 100 best places to work in IT in America.

Yourdon: Right. They do that every year.

Blalock: And we have been honored for the last five consecutive years with that recognition. This year we received our best ranking—#18! I take a lot of pride in this ranking because it is based on a survey our employees complete.

Yourdon: Ahh.

Blalock: It's not just the programs you have. It's not just what you say about yourself. They are surveying our own employees. Morale has improved dramatically in the organization, and we have a lot of folks in our organization who get opportunities to go into other parts of the business now. In fact, our new CEO was the CIO when I was regional CIO. It's the first time we've had a CEO who used to be a CIO.

Yourdon: Interesting. Yeah, I don't think I've run into that in the various other interviews I've done. That is very interesting.

Blalock: Yes, so we are very excited about that.

Yourdon: You know, I can't resist the temptation to ask a question that normally comes up more toward the end of this conversation, having to do with the new generation—the digital natives—the young kids who are coming out of college right now. How do you view them in the context of what you've just been talking about, as potential leaders and so on? Are you optimistic, pessimistic? Do you see them as being any different than the generation that came out 10 or 20 years ago?

Blalock: I think they're going to make life very exciting for us. In the past, IT was trying to push technology out, trying to get people to embrace it and use it. These people are coming out of college and they're pushing us.

Yourdon: Right.

Blalock: IT needs to embrace them. Gone are the days when corporations are going to be deciding what PCs employees use. I think you're going to come to work and bring your own PC, just like you do with your phone. We're a ways away from that yet, but we're headed in that direction. If you don't embrace technology and really allow people to use the tools they're comfortable with, they're going to go work somewhere else where things are more open and flexible.

Yourdon: Well, that's one area where I've gotten a pretty consistent response from everybody, very much the way you've just said it. And I'm sure if I had asked that question five years ago, I would have gotten a very different answer, because people were still pushing technology down the throats of all the new employees.

Blalock: Well, in knowledge today, it's not so much about what you know, but what you know about where to get the knowledge. And I'll give you an example, it was just this weekend. I was at the lake with a bunch of my relatives and my niece was there. And she said, "I need to call my brother." I said, "What's his number?" She said, "Well, I don't know what his number is. I have to go get my cell phone to tell you that." You know, they don't even know phone numbers anymore, but they know where to go get them.

Yourdon: Yep.

Blalock: So much of what it's going to take in the future to be successful is knowing where to find information. No one person can know it all, and they have the Internet at their fingertips. Young people know how to really leverage these tools, and they've grown up with them.

Yourdon: Well, you're certainly right about people—and it's not only that they know where to get the information; they don't even have a conscious pause. It's just wired in, whereas in my case, it requires a conscious recognition that, "Oh, I can go to Google and get that information." Or "Oh, that phone number is already on my speed dial list." So the younger generation has got a split-second jump on me usually in terms of getting that, but I think that phenomenon is true everywhere. On the other hand, does it give you any concern that the younger generation can afford to operate in a more superficial fashion, for lack of a better phrase, because the stuff is right at their fingertips? They don't have to do any deep thinking.

Blalock: No. I still think you've got to be smart enough to know what you need to look for. I still think you've got to have some thought leadership. The research might be easier. It might be easier to find the information, but you've still got to be researching the right things.

Yourdon: And you've got to know what you can trust and what you can't trust.

Blalock: Right, and also, I think it's 24/7. Work is. You used to have to be in your office between 8 and 5 and wait for the phone to ring. People can work from anywhere now and they work all the time.

Yourdon: Well, you know, another thing I've heard from almost every CIO, and I assume it's going to be true for you as well, is the notion that even if their business is ostensibly a local business, everybody's business these days is global, so that you're going to get a phone call at 3 in the morning saying, "There's a revolution in Egypt. What are we doing about it?" And, I'd be curious to know how that plays itself out for the Southern Company. For example, when there was the earthquake in Japan, did your phone start ringing?

Blalock: Our phone did ring because we are building the first new nuclear unit in 30 years in this country. I can assure you that it was a very busy time for us.

It was a very busy time for us now because there are a lot of tornadoes touching down, and they don't touch down just in the middle of the day. They touch down in the middle of the night. Our systems have to be working, so that our crews know where those outages have occurred and know where to go and restore power. We are definitely a 24/7 business and IT, of course, is 24/7, too. And there are events around the world that impact us.

Yourdon: Well, I think that's the thing for everybody. It doesn't matter what kind of business you have these days, IT is central to everything. And as a result, we are not only 24/7, but global, no matter what we think we might be doing with our business, and so that's a good confirmation. I'm glad to hear that.

I've gotten a lot of feedback that the next generation of workers do not have the same passion for work or the work ethic of our generation. What do you think?

Blalock: I think we're going to be just fine with the next generation. They embrace change. They are not nearly as bureaucratic as my generation. We're going to need them to be flexible and adaptable because there's going to be fewer of them having to do a whole lot more work. Their innovation and their creativity are going to be very, very badly needed. That's really what sets the U.S. apart, but they're going to be competing against all the people around the world.

Yourdon: I hadn't thought of it that way.

Blalock: And these kids are bright. You know, they adapt so much better than my generation did. They're so much more open to new things, and I think so much about success is being willing to take some risks. If there's one thing that we've got to be cautious about, it is that they're too open to risk. Some things that they may think are okay to do, like downloading copyrighted movies—you can't do that in the corporate world.

Yourdon: Well, you're even more straightforward; they may think it's okay to run an app that they got on their iPad in a safety-critical part of your business that you just can't afford to do. So, I hear what you're saying.

Blalock: Communication and education will be essential, because it is a little different in the corporate world than it is in working for an entrepreneur or when you're in college.

Yourdon: That's true. I want to ask you about another area that you mentioned on this list of the top three priorities that you have. One of them was—I think it was the third one—was rolling out technology to enhance the business now.

Blalock: Yeah.

Yourdon: Speaking of people, how does a CIO create a successful team?

Blalock: As CIOs, our success is most directly tied to who we surround ourselves with. You cannot be successful as a CIO if you don't have a good team of people around you, and those people need to be very different. You may need to have someone who knows a lot about finance if you don't know a lot about finance. Or you may need to have someone who knows a lot about marketing because no one person can know it all, and the beauty of IT is that you get to see the whole company. It touches everything, but that's also the challenge in it.

Yourdon: What are the key criteria or characteristics you look for on the part of the people that are your team, the direct reports? And your point about having a wide variety of skills is interesting. The two other more interesting responses I've got are a deep sense of integrity. That everybody's got everybody else's back.

Blalock: Absolutely. When I got this job, one of the things I heard was that it was not a team and that people didn't like each other; they didn't support each other, and that the first thing I had to do was fix the team. It's like the book, *Good to Great*[1], but you've got to get the right people on the bus. The first thing we did was focus on building a much stronger team. Today, I think the IT team at Southern Company is probably one of the stronger senior teams anywhere in the company.

My senior team—there are 14 people on the senior leadership team—we actually complete a teamwork survey twice a year. We rate how effective we think we're working together as a team. And the first time we did that, I think we rated ourselves a 5.4 on a 10-[point] scale. The last time we did it, everybody gave us a 9. We have some people who are never going to rate everybody a 10, but we rated ourselves a 9 as a team. As part of the survey they also rate each other individually, to remind the team that no one of us can do what we need to for this company. We have to do it together.

This survey keeps the focus on teamwork. We don't really need to continue doing the survey, but we do it because it's affirmation that we need to continue to look out for each other. You are really under such scrutiny from the business that you support. The survey pulls you together cohesively as a team in IT, and it's only together that we can be successful in doing what you need to for this company. We have each other's back. I can't reiterate that enough, how important it is to have a team that pulls together. Generally it doesn't take more than one person to mess up a team. You have to just nip that in the bud if it's going on.

---

[1] By Jim Collins [HarperCollins, 2001].

Yourdon: Well, that's a good reinforcement of what I've heard from others. I want to ask you about another area that you mentioned on this list of the top three priorities that you have. One of them was—I think it was the third one—was rolling out technology to enhance the business now. To some extent that's something every CIO would say he feels responsible for doing, helping the business become more competitive or more successful. In your case, are you and your IT people expected to come up with completely new things that the business has not even thought of doing, but have become possible with new technology—or just enhancing the efficiency of what's already going on?

Blalock: I said earlier that when I got this job and interviewed people in the business, they said, "We don't need a bunch of order-takers. You're here inside our business. You understand our business, and you should be helping us figure out what's the next great thing that's coming in, in the way of technology." We have embraced that, and we have two processes in place at Southern Company that I think have really helped us with that. We have teams that are made up of people from IT and people from the business called Technology Leadership Teams (TLTs). There are 14 of those teams. Some of them meet once a quarter, some meet every month.

For example, one of the TLTs is in the distribution organization, the wire side of our business, the folks that actually distribute electricity to the homes. They're one of the most active teams that we have. They meet every month, people from the business and people from IT. IT will discuss some emerging technologies that are becoming available in the market. We will work with the distribution team members to determine if we can pull together a business case to evaluate doing this in our business.

Sometimes, people in the business will go to a conference and talk to a vendor, and they'll bring back an idea to IT and say, "Here is what a vendor says they can do." And then IT will get involved and we'll say, "Well, that's vaporware."

Or we'll say, "Hey, that's a really good idea." And then we work together to prioritize the money that's in the budget and make the decisions about how we proceed. IT has absolutely got to be aligned with the business. IT should never push technology that doesn't drive value to the business. And these TLTs work very well for us. Engaging the business in the decisions that we make helps them take more ownership and helps them not to see us as a cost center but as a partner who's truly driving value and success to the company. This process has helped us deliver tremendous value from the projects that we roll out, which is critical because we have about 100 active projects under way at any point in time in IT.

The second thing that we did is develop a technology lab where vendors would give us the beta version of a product and we would test it, because you need to have these products ahead of time so that you can then build the infrastructure to support them. We have since evolved that lab into a showcase where we can bring our employees in and show them what's coming in the way of technology. We also use it as a place where we can brainstorm about how we should apply some of these technologies to move the business forward.

And it has been a huge success. Incredible ideas have surfaced in that center.

Yourdon: I'm sure you have.

Blalock: We live in a world where the consumer market leads the business world. Look at what's going on with sensor technology. That really came about in the consumer market, and there are huge opportunities to take that technology and develop a business case for saving money and applying it inside the corporate world. But sometimes it's very hard for people to visualize that unless you get into a brainstorming session with them.

Yourdon: Ahh, interesting.

Blalock: And this facility, actually, it was showcased in our 2008 annual report. It talked about how we're bringing in lots of innovative ideas in terms of how we drive this business forward. We really empower our employees to use technology to be more efficient. We're doing things that help the company apply technology, because most of the customer-touch in our company today is not through people, it's through technology.

Most of the people who call the Customer Care Center talk to the voice-response unit, our unit that's computerized, or they go online and do self-help, and never talk to a person. You think about the banking industry: most people go to the ATM when they want to get cash.

Yourdon: Sure, yeah.

Blalock: They don't communicate. And so how do we in IT play a role in enhancing that experience? That is an important question, because one of the most important strategic things we focus on as a company is making sure we provide world-class customer service to the people we serve. And we want to make sure we are looking at the technologies that are out there and utilizing them in the most efficient way and in the way that our customers will embrace in terms of how we serve them. It also saves us money when we use technology. On average, it costs $3 per call to have a customer service representative handle a request. And to the extent we can apply technology, we not only enhance the customer's experience, we also save money.

Yourdon: Well, that leads me into the next obvious question—which is what interesting technologies do you see coming down the road in the next few years that you expect you'll be able to take advantage of?

Blalock: Mobility is exploding everywhere. As a company, we have to think about is how do we better serve our customers on mobile devices. Not everybody's going to have them, so you've got to have some traditional ways of reaching people, but there's a new generation of people coming and they want their information in a different fashion. So I think how we provide mobile solutions to our customers and how we put mobility out there in the way of dashboards, so that our employees always know what the state is of the things that are going on inside the company.

One example I'll give you is when there's an outage. To be able to give every employee in the company information about how many customers are out and where they're out is helpful. When the power goes out in my neighborhood, who do you think people call wanting to know when it's coming back on?

You can imagine, as an employee, if I have that information at my fingertips, I'm a lot better equipped to answer those questions. One of the things we've started doing is tweeting what the status is on our outages. And a certain portion of our customer base really likes getting information that way, so I think there's a great opportunity in that mobility space, especially to engage our customers in more two-way communication.

The second area where there's a huge opportunity for us is on data analytics. Business intelligence is going to be huge because we have so many sensors out on our network now that we can better predict when an outage will occur. We'll never be able to predict them all because you don't know where lightning's going to hit. You don't know when somebody's going to run into a pole in their car. But there are sensors that allow us to look at our equipment and better tell if you've got a transformer that's getting ready to blow. Predict it, so that you replace the transformer before that happens, and the customer's power is never out.

Also, analytics allow us to perform better service. when somebody does hit a pole, instead of it taking down electricity to 200 homes, there's enough intelligence in the network that it only takes down power to, say, five homes.

Yourdon: Wow. Okay.

Blalock: In many cases, the system is self-healing and can automatically switch the flow of power to keep some customers from going out. Instead of 200, like I said, it would only take a few homes down until you can get a truck to the location. And the trucks are equipped with analytics, as well. They receive information about the exact location of the outage to save time. In addition, the analytics can be shared with out call center. The customers don't even have to call us. We can call them and say, "A pole in your area has been damaged. Crews are on site and repair should be complete soon."

All of that is coming in the very near future. And the other thing is that in the future there will be a lot more distributed generation. For example, there may be customers that are generating their own power through solar panels. We're putting smart meters on everyone's home so we can tell them—in the future—how much electricity they're using at different times of the day. If customers want to be more efficient, these smart meters have the intelligence to tell them when they're using a lot and determine what it is that's driving usage up.

Yourdon: I assume that's just one small part of the overall buzzword of the "smart grid" that you folks in your industry are looking forward to over the next 10 or 20 years?

Blalock: Absolutely. There is lots of transformation coming in that area, and we will be leaders in helping move in that direction. I could talk forever about the things that we see coming, but I do think mobility and business analytics are going to be huge. I think the smart meters and the electric vehicles are two technologies, not necessarily in IT that are going to revolutionize our business in the way people are going to use electricity.

Yourdon: It certainly makes a lot of sense. You know, there's one kind of mundane answer that I was expecting everybody to give me that I haven't really heard, and that is the response from people who say, "We're depending on Moore's Law to continue for another decade"—you know, the fundamental law that says computing power doubles in price performance every 18 months. I've been around since that started, and there were all these predictions it was going to stop after ten years, that we were going to run out of ideas for continuing to improve technology. And the latest I've heard from Intel is that it's going to keep going 'til at least the year 2026, beyond which I won't really care, but that's very reassuring.

Blalock: And I don't see any of this slowing down. If anything, we're going to continue to reinvent.

Nobody really even thought about virtualization—that was a buzzword five years ago, and now it's commonplace. Cloud computing—most large enterprise groups were saying, "Not in my lifetime." Well, guess what? We're figuring out how to do cloud computing. Maybe not everything, but we're taking higher chunks of it to the cloud, so it's coming.

Yourdon: I would certainly agree with that.

Blalock: And these leapfrog innovations that will continue to surface because the amount of data is … it's mind-boggling how much data we're going to have. We think we've been growing at about 35 percent a year at Southern Company, which is I think pretty much on par with what we've seen traditionally in the world. It's already starting to double every year. We haven't seen that yet, but we're bracing ourselves for the fact that we're going to have a lot more data in the future.

Yourdon: Yeah. I've heard one or two people, CIOs that I've interviewed focus on the same thing, the importance of the data analytics in this new world, but I don't think there's quite enough appreciation for it yet. You know, there's one last thing I'd be curious about in terms of futures to see if you think it's important.

There's a buzzword that was introduced by a futurist named Clay Shirky called "cognitive surplus." He argues that we are at a point now in society, for the first time, where we have enough spare time supported by technology that mankind can contribute its surplus cognitive energy, and do things that have never been done before—the classic example of which is Wikipedia. You know, we now have a society that can give back in thousands of different ways. And I'm curious whether that's something that's meaningful to a utility company.

Blalock: Absolutely. This can actually go back to the history of mankind because mankind used to have to spend all their time growing food, just to survive. Then, farming technology progressed enough, so that today, you don't worry about food. You go to the grocery store and there is a ton of anything you want. In the developed world, we're even growing stuff out in the middle of the desert now. And genetics has allowed food to get even more progressive.

I do believe more cognitive time has been freed up, but I also think there's a lot of stuff consuming our time.

Yourdon: Okay.

Blalock: The Internet has changed the way we live and think. And it has turned us into a global society, more so than anything ever has, and I think we're continuing on that evolution. And that you're going to continue to see big changes in medicine. And you'll see big changes in energy and the way energy gets produced and consumed, and it's all because of all this knowledge-sharing that's going on. I don't think it's so much that you've got free time. It's the collaboration and the fact that we're bringing all of this brainpower together so that you can problem-solve in ways that we couldn't have done.

You wouldn't have had somebody from China and someone from the U.S. collaborating 20 years ago, solving a problem.

Yourdon: Yep, yep. That's true.

Blalock: The power of that combined thinking is what I think is driving innovation. It's not that people have more free time. They have more time and better tools to collaborate.

Yourdon: That makes sense. I want to make sure that I have some time to ask you about the other side of this—the dark side of the force. What are the things that give you nightmares and keep you awake at night, if there is anything?

Blalock: People ask me that question a lot, and it's really not that much to do with IT. I think the single most challenging thing you deal with as a CIO is personnel. Anytime you have a challenging personnel issue, to me, that's difficult, because it's not black and white. IT is pretty black and white. You solve the problem and you move on. Human beings are not, so those are the things that keep me up at night. I also worry about cybersecurity.

Yourdon: Mm-hmm.

Blalock: I'm not inordinately worried about it because I think that Southern Company has some of the best thought leadership in the country. We do a wonderful job managing threats, but will always have to stay on top of it. There are people who are always trying to move the company to become more and more dependent on this technology. As we become more dependent on technology, there are also people who would love to be disruptive in that world. And so I think it's a challenge to stay on top of that.

I love a challenge and I like learning new things and doing things in different ways. So I think that's one of the most exciting things about IT. The systems are getting more and more reliable. I can remember when I came to work for the company: We had a mainframe system and I was out in the field, and if this microwave tower went out, you were out of business.

Yourdon: Yeah.

Blalock: And it used to happen on a regular basis. You kept microfiche by your desk. And I knock on wood, but we rarely ever have anything go down now. And it's because we have such great intelligence and redundancy in the system, and it's only going to continue to improve. But the people aspect of it is crucial. As CIOs, we are responsible for leading all this technology, but you can't do it alone. What I do not see enough of sometimes is the leadership around the people dimension. And that's really what is so important, because you've got these really smart people who you have to keep motivated, and you've got to bring them along with you, if you want to be successful.

Yourdon: And I would imagine you've got to focus a lot also on getting the knowledge out of their heads and into some sharable form, so that when they do eventually retire, you don't lose it entirely.

Blalock: Absolutely. We've focused a lot on cross-training and IT is a key part of the solution to all that. We did a focus group meeting in one of our district offices. And we talked to some of the senior linemen and asked, "Would it be helpful to you if we took a lot of the maps and stuff that you have here and we put them on a computer and you could take them to the field with you?" And they said, "I don't need that. I built this system. I've got it all right up here in my brain."

Then we talked to some of the young engineers who were fresh out of college and asked them, and they said, "Could you do that for us?" They said, "That would be so helpful if I had those maps at my fingertips instead of having to go back to the district office and pull them out and look at them and try to reengineer the system. If I had all that knowledge right here at my fingertips, I could be so much more productive." So I think IT is the solution to all of that.

Yourdon: Interesting. Well, that's encouraging to hear. Let me wrap this up with the final question that I've asked every CIO—and that is, where do you go from here? What is life after a CIO, if there is such a thing?

Blalock: Life after a CIO? Umm, I think CIOs can go anywhere they want, because you've gotten such great knowledge about the business. I think the real challenge is when I talk to a lot of my peers, they really don't want to go anywhere else. They really love running and working in IT. Nothing else really quite compares to doing this, and the fact that you've always got to be one step ahead, in thinking about how you apply this technology and how you embrace it.

Yourdon: Well, certainly, if your company continues to grow and take on more challenges, that keeps your job from being boring.

Blalock: And like I said, our current CEO was the CIO. We're very proud of him.

Yourdon: That was very unusual.

Blalock: But it is becoming more of a trend. CIOs today have such broad knowledge of all business processes across the enterprise. The technology they provide is touching the customer in a powerful way. This knowledge is a strong foundation for the CEO of the future.

Yourdon: Hmm. Well, maybe it will continue to do so. All right, so your idea is that a lot of CIOs would probably be perfectly happy continuing to be a CIO, maybe, of a bigger and even more challenging company as time went on.

Blalock: Yeah, a lot of CIOs do move around, and they go up to bigger companies.

Yourdon: Yeah, I certainly have seen that as, you know, I've been tracking these people down everywhere. And I've also run into a lot of CIOs who are at the end of their career and who have said, "It's been a great run, but now I'm going to go out and be a university professor or do stuff in the community." But, you made the point that if one wants to, one could go on to be a CEO or any other position in the company.

Blalock: You've got to know the business to apply technology. It's interesting because I have talked to two former CIOs recently. What they have elected to do is sit on boards for small technology startup companies. And they love it. They are having fun, and they are bringing incredible knowledge to make these companies successful.

Yourdon: Yeah, I have heard that from a couple of them. Yeah, you're right.

Blalock: There are many young companies who are just starving to know how to get in, and how to sell to CIOs.

Lately, I have had some headhunters contact me about board positions. Companies are beginning to think about the fact they need somebody with IT expertise, somebody who can counsel them regarding cybersecurity, disaster recovery, and how the company should be embracing and applying technology. CIOs are certainly great at this.

Yourdon: Well, that certainly makes sense. I've been on a few boards, and there's been a huge vacuum in that area for some of them because the people they bring in have got very strong finance backgrounds or marketing or whatever, but not that IT component, so I think you're right.

I very much want to thank you for your time. We could talk all afternoon about any one of these topics, I'm sure—but hopefully, this will at least get people thinking about some new ideas and directions.

Thank you, Becky. I very much appreciate it.

11

Ken Bohlen

Vice President and CIO,
Arizona Public Service Company (APS)

Ken Bohlen is Vice President and Chief Information Officer for Arizona Public Service Company (APS), Arizona's largest electric company. Based in Phoenix, APS serves more than 1.1 million customers and is one of the fastest-growing investor-owned electric utilities in the United States. Bohlen heads APS's Information Technology department where he oversees the company's vital electronic infrastructure and manages the digital challenges faced by a major electric utility. Bohlen also leads the Lean Six Sigma improvement process for APS.

Before joining APS, Bohlen spent 10 years at Textron, Inc. where he served as Executive Vice President and Chief Innovation Officer. Prior to joining Textron, he served 25 years as an information/supply chain executive at both AlliedSignal Inc. and John Deere. Bohlen is a member of the American Production Inventory Control Society and a senior member of the Society of Manufacturing Engineers, Computer and Automated Systems Association. He was recognized with the 2005 Stevie Award for "Best MIS and Systems Executive," and is a member of IBM's board of advisors. Bohlen also was recognized by his peers as one of Computerworld's *Premier 100 Leaders for 2006.*

Ed Yourdon: I find that a lot of people in the IT industry—especially young aspiring IT professionals who think some day they're going to be a CIO—are curious how executives like you get to where you are. Is this your first

CIO position, or did you move up through the ranks to get to where you are?

Ken Bohlen: It's kind of an interesting story. I knew early on in my life, in high school, that these things emerging as computers or intelligent work environments were growing, so I looked into what they had at my high school, which was a co-op program with local companies.

Yourdon: That's common in college, but not in high school. That's interesting.

Bohlen: Yeah, I did it in high school, I wanted to find something different. My school advisor gave me the opportunity that if I could find something I liked, she'd sponsor it. So I worked for a small company that had computer processing and they made cardboard boxes.

The company was Doerfer Engineering. I worked with the old punch-card routines and the slot machines, and the wires around for sorting. I realized that, "This thing is something. I don't know where it's going to take me, but I like it." So when I went to college—I went to Iowa State—I majored in computer science. But I wasn't a geeky techie guy, so I took several minors, industrial relations, psychology, sociology. I knew that I wanted to focus my energy with computers, but I felt I needed to know how to use them in social settings as well. So I kind of visualized a plan early on. I didn't realize where it was going to take me or that I would land in manufacturing, but I've just retired out of the manufacturing industry after thirty-five years. Now I've jumped into the utility or energy industry. Completely different worlds.

Yourdon: Wow. That is interesting.

Bohlen: And it's been kind of fun, exciting. I look back at your historical basis. I was a part of PDP minicomputers, with DECnet and some of the communication activities from the CIM, the old computer integrated manufacturing.

Yourdon: Oh, right. Yeah.

Bohlen: So it was a lot of diverse backgrounds, trainings, opportunities. In my last job, I was actually the CIO with the "I" being "innovation."

Yourdon: Oh, really? Hah!

Bohlen: And Michael Tracy—I don't know if you know Mike or Clay Christensen.

Yourdon: Oh, yeah, Christensen I do know. Yeah.

Bohlen: Well, Michael Tracy wrote some of the original books on innovation. He said, "You know, Ken, you've got to be one of the first in the Fortune 100 companies with the title of Executive VP/Chief Innovation Officer." At that time I managed all of engineering, IT supply chain, worldwide ops in India, so it was an interesting way of growing, but it's because of the very beginning, diversity, branching out, knowing the computer's going to be prevalent in many areas. So my counsel to young people is never say no to an opportunity to learn something outside of your bailiwick, particularly if you're in an industry field outside of technology.

Yourdon: Well, I was going to ask a similar kind of question because I've heard this from other CIOs that a broad education is far more valuable than you might think it is, as opposed to a very narrow, geeky computer science education.

Bohlen: Well, I think it kind of depends. If you want to stay in the Internet, gaming, social media development area, then you are okay! I think that provides you an awareness in areas that are still unknown territory. I think huge riches remain to be made there. But I think that's a very small group of very talented people. If they've got that calling and that desire, God bless them, let them go.

Yourdon: [laughter] Okay, one other related question. Did you have any particularly important mentors or role models along the way?

Bohlen: You know, I've had several. There were a few at John Deere, one in particular, Jay Harmon, who was head of production control. I had to step inside of that while I managed the worldwide billing materials and interfactory buying and selling for John Deere Waterloo operations. Jay would spend time talking with me after hours and actually even come over to my home. We would talk about people, progress, and relationships. John Deere was a very family-oriented company, but we had some tough times in the '80s, and Jay spent a lot of time mentoring me on the soft skills, if you will.

Yourdon: Interesting.

Bohlen: And, again, this was outside of the IT arena, which I find reflective of the fact that many of my peers in IT at the time were growing and bumbling through the process of turning it into a legitimate profession.

Yourdon: Yeah, I think you're certainly right on that. And what you're saying here is similar to what I've heard from other people that the mentoring is far more likely to be outside of technology *per se*. I don't know about you, but when I went to college, I never took any courses on management or … you did take a broader range of things than I did, but I knew nothing about

interacting with the human race [laughter] until I started getting management positions. One last question in this area: as you rose up through the
ranks, did you go back to school or get any special training? Did you get an
MBA or anything of that sort?

Bohlen: Yes, I did. I went back and got an MBA in my early 40s. I had no
intent of ever leaving John Deere. They were really good to me, and my
family, everybody was there in Iowa—but after getting the MBA, I ran into a
person by the name of Jerry Stead. Jerry was part of the AT&T environment. Anyway, he was a traveling executive. And Jerry and I developed quite
a relationship. At the conclusion of the MBA program, where we did a lot of
case studies with Allied Signal, I told Jerry, "If I ever had a chance, I'd probably go to work for Allied Signal and leave Deere."

Yourdon: [laughter] Interesting.

Bohlen: Well, guess what? I got hired at Allied Signal after my MBA
graduation, as the director of supply chain. So I essentially got two MBAs,
a legitimate academic MBA and then an experiential learning MBA from
Larry Bossidy.

Yourdon: Interesting. There have been a few people I've spoken to who
have gone back to get an advanced degree, but it's been less common than I
might have thought. Well, I think we get a sense of what brought you to this
point. In terms of where you are now, the central thing I'm interested in
finding out is how you view IT as making a significant contribution to the
organization's strategic success in the future.

Bohlen: Well, we look at the future and the prevalence and the ambiguity
going on in hardware platforms. IT, if not prevalent in the industry group,
will have to be in the future. As I look at manufacturing, IT had a tremendous impact on processing speeds, billing cycles, cash cycles, customer relationship opportunities. All of those kinds of things, I think, were really good.
We're seeing that in the financial industry. Just the beginning. In the energy
industry, I have been a little surprised at IT's lack of credibility in many of
these organizations, as a platform from which to operate.

Yourdon: Hmm.

Bohlen: So I have a little hypothesis—and then there's what I see. In the
manufacturing arena, it's not uncommon to find the CIO—the super CIO, if
you will—in some of the annual reports and proxies. In the utility business,
it's difficult to find any CIO in the proxies of their companies. Now, that's
just one indicator, Ed, but it's an indicator that I see the IT profession losing

ground. I see many IT executives are now becoming subservient to CFOs. Some in the utility space are reporting to HR generalists.

Yourdon: Really?

Bohlen: Yes. When I first came to the utility business, I met with 19 CIOs. I told them I was underwhelmed at how many organizations and the industry looked at IT. Much to my surprise, they came back and said, "You're right." I understand you're talking with Becky Blalock [of Southern Company, interviewed in Chapter 10]. She was one that said, "You're absolutely right, Ken." I said, "You know, I don't know how to change it, but it's my opinion that, if anything, the power, the grid, the energy environment that we're operating in is just one huge infrastructure."

Yourdon: Right.

Bohlen: Who better to run that than people that have grown up managing the growth of this tremendous infrastructure called the Web in our company infrastructure? So, it's a mental note that I've made to myself. That's why APS is a new, exciting challenge for me. I have been helping improve ways to manage infrastructure, including security. I jumped back in as a way to "give back." I also find myself speaking more at conferences trying to energize potential future CIOs to get out of the techie world in the business environment, grab hold of ERM, grab hold of disaster recovery, business continuity because that's what we grew up with.

Yourdon: Interesting. So, how will you use IT to make APS more successful in the future? And it sounds like you're saying that IT has to take more responsibility for things involving the grid and the infrastructure.

Bohlen: I think that's one of the components. The other is technology. Too often in my career I've noticed these problems are loosely understood, but the solution is clear. I got to know Jim Womack really well in my last job. He has influenced me to focus first on making clear the problem we're trying to solve. And if we can't articulate it, I'm not throwing dollars at technology. Inside this arena, what I'm finding is that people really don't know what problem they're trying to solve. So you get a lot of little pilots. I've seen these pilots have different technology directions, some of which are counterproductive to each other. Overall technology direction always needs to be very clear.

Yourdon: Ahh, interesting.

Bohlen: Then, the third thing is business value. I sometimes find we already have technology that would indeed answer a problem. But you know how it goes, people see something new at a latest gizmo/whiz-bang show and suddenly the organization finds itself trying to incorporate new technologies. So one of the values that I've added is that we are not doing projects unless we understand the business value.

Yourdon: Okay. Well, that certainly makes sense.

Bohlen: You know, it's the kind of thing we all talk about. This is one of the first times I've experienced it. IT really didn't drive that before. It was the old—I call it the 1970s' management style—they would yell and scream until IT felt that they needed to come to the requestor. And I just don't do that.

Yourdon: [laughter] Now, as CIO, I assume you are also in charge of the thousands of desktops and servers with which all APS employees get their job done every day. So how big a job is that, just keeping the lights on, so to speak, for the internal IT operation?

Bohlen: If you look at my budget, over 60 percent of my budget is keeping the lights on. Which is very high from the industry group I came from, but what I'm beginning to learn is that that's not uncommon in a lot of utility spaces.

Yourdon: Hmm, interesting.

Bohlen: So, part of the reason for that is the previous discussion. "We don't know the problem we're trying to solve, but I think this nice tool will help me." So over a period of time, the organization had accumulated hundreds of different applications products.

Yourdon: Wow.

Bohlen: Well, that's an opportunity for improvement. I always like to operate from a base of facts. I hired a benchmarking company. I used them at John Deere, Allied Signal, and Textron, and now I brought them in to help us at APS. They performed a benchmark for IT, finance, and HR. And that gave me a baseline to begin directing my efforts. Otherwise, standing on a platform without data, I'd sound like a wolf crying at the bottom of a hill.

Yourdon: Right.

Bohlen: I was able to point out that we were extraordinarily high on the applications compared to peer groups of our size; however, compared to other world-class companies, we were fourth quartile. Directionally, this gave me the areas that we needed to go attack. It provided a third-party source of data our organization could refer to as we promoted the necessary changes, that it wasn't just my personal opinion or a pet project. As business people, it also showed that we've got a lot of opportunity.

Yourdon: Hmm. Fascinating.

Bohlen: So yes, we've got to support desktops, but what was really adding to the overall support cost was all these other apps. What we did was unique and different for me. IT has always been in the role of saying, "No, you can't do that. No, you can't do this." When we had green screens and then Apple came out and the Intel machines, we said, "No, we've got to test them." Then we went to distributed computing, we first said, "No," and then it took off. So what I've developed here is a program called "Just Say Yes."

Yourdon: Ahh, fascinating.

Bohlen: What we're doing is transitioning from the company buying personal-asset laptops, the iPads, the iPhones, to the employees buying them themselves. We don't care what kind of smartphone you get as long as it's within a certain family. We're using products like Citrix and GoodLink, so we have a secured venue into the device. What the person does with it outside of that controlled environment, that's their legal responsibility. What we're trying to do is get outside of the security/privacy issues in the workplace. All of that we're trying to eliminate in giving people freedom.

Yourdon: Well, I'm certainly hearing conversations of that sort from just about everybody I've spoken to, and it's fascinating to see how everyone is grappling with this, because it is an unstoppable tidal wave in many cases.

Bohlen: Yes, we've had the program in place for about four months and it's been positively accepted. We did the traditional return on investment and looked at what we needed to invest, so we are providing incentives for people to say, "You mean, you'll give me x dollars a month and I just put the package on my own home computer, and I don't have to use this other stuff?" That's exactly right. It's been very successful. We are doing it in phases so we don't tax the team as we do it, but it's been really good.

Yourdon: And it's interesting to see how this correlates with the industry that's providing the devices and apps. So I spoke to the CIO of Google, who said, "You know, in the old days we used to build things for the enterprise and hope that it would trickle down to the employees."

Bohlen: Yes, you're right.

Yourdon: Because it was very expensive and very scarce, and therefore it had to be controlled. And he said, "Now at Google and Microsoft and all these other places, like Apple, they're building things for the consumer marketplace first and foremost, and if it trickles up into the enterprise, that's wonderful—but we start with the consumer." And, of course, you're experiencing that from the other side because all these people walk in your door holding something in their hand that they bought at home and that they're bloody well determined to use, regardless of whether you say no or not, so.

Bohlen: I love it. You know, I didn't put the two together, but that's a significant paradigm shift.

Yourdon: Yeah, I think it is, and that really is the next whole area I wanted to get into is. "Paradigm shift" is a term that's overused a bit, but you've obviously been in the industry a long time, and we've all seen enormous things happening over the last 30 or 40 years. But I'm curious to let you speculate on what kinds of paradigm shifts or major things we should look forward to in the future, over the next few years?

Bohlen: That's a tough one. What we're seeing more and more in this cloud computing environment is an opportunity to have storage of our company data in diverse locations. I think we're going to see a huge move—now this could be "what you are now" is "where you were back when." So being an older person, seeing some cycles, I'm beginning to wonder about what is going to happen. For instance, is all it's going to take is one security breach of a significant magnitude that's going to spin companies into a tailspin and they're going to bring their data back to a resident location?

Yourdon: Ahh, interesting. Okay.

Bohlen: It's more an issue in the hard-line manufacturing/R&D companies, but also in the energy/utility spaces—but all it takes is one, and you're going to have legislation. So one of my desires is to try to understand what's happening with government legislation. And that can change so rapidly and change everything that's going on. Some of the ITAR[1] relationships that we have in the DoD[2] world are cumbersome, but very important and critical. And I think those are the kinds of things that I think three, four years out, that could be a concern. Another is analytics. I think that we have a huge opportunity because there's so much data that needs to be turned into information, and I think the tools that are associated with analytics can help present patterns and paths and directions that can allow for more informed decision making.

Yourdon: Hmm.

---

[1] International Traffic in Arms Regulations.

[2] (U.S.) Department of Defense.

Bohlen: The third one I see is the generational issue inside of the companies, including IT. Being a professionally educated IT person doesn't necessarily mean you're the best equipped, because they're graduating accounting majors who have computing tools they use on the side. So everybody is kind of an IT wizard—I won't say "professional," but they've got an opinion because they've used it.

Yourdon: Yeah.

Bohlen: I think that may create a tough leadership role in the future, even tougher than what we've got today. I watch my grandkids: 13, 14 years old. They're growing up with this thing that is significantly different. This is an interesting dialogue because historically, and as all the case studies suggest, you never take true advantage of the technology until you get rid of the traditional management over the top of it and usher in a new one. So how do we usher in the new leaders?

Yourdon: Well, in some cases they're starting at a much younger age than they were before. You and I are of the same generation, but when I talked to the CIO of Google—it's staggering to see. And Google as a company is … well, the average age must be 25, I think. So it's a whole different set of assumptions and expectations and experiences. Well, back to this issue of paradigm shifts. So I gather you think this move into cloud computing is one example where there are going to continue to be a lot more changes and things. Any other major things you'd add to that? Oh, and you said analytics. I'm sorry. That was the second one.

Bohlen: I think analytics is going to have a place in it. Another I'm beginning to sense is just the huge opportunity that exists for what I'd call "home computing."

Yourdon: Hmm. Yeah.

Bohlen: One of the things that we see at the utility is that that customers are going to consume more and more energy, but we've got coal that we don't necessarily want to promote and provide, for various reasons, and yet we know that renewables like solar and wind, probably only can make up 15 percent of our consumption by 2025. We are also seeing the true emergence of these home entertainment or smart home concepts. Honeywell's got some, GE's got one, Control4's got one, where you can begin to marry your thermostat to energy consumption models, so that during peak load times, you can cycle air conditioning and appliances differently. I think there's a revolution about to happen in that arena.

Yourdon: Ahh, interesting, 'cause we've been talking about it for 40 years, but maybe we're being driven by economic forces to really start getting serious about it.

Bohlen: I think we are. You know, you've got the boomers that dabble with technology, so they're kind of open. If you can put the thermostat readings on their TV so they can actually program and control it, I think they would actually do that. And the economics, to your point, you can now put … home systems in play for under a thousand bucks.

Yourdon: Yeah.

Bohlen: So all of a sudden, there's a market that I think the Googles or a different marketing franchise unit is going to come in and people are going to knock themselves on the head and say, "Why didn't I think of that?"

Yourdon: Interesting. Well, that will be interesting to watch if it develops. I haven't heard that one from anyone before. When you mentioned Google, by the way, you reminded me of one other suggestion that I heard from Google in this area of paradigm shifts, and that was the notion that for the first time in history, with the technology that we have and everything else, we have what one futurist, a guy by the name of Clay Shirky, calls a "cognitive surplus"—that is, an opportunity to take advantage of free brainpower and extra time to contribute to society things like Wikipedia or Linux. For that matter, the entire open software thing is one example. But this idea of contributing knowledge into some form that can be accessed by humanity is arguably what Google is all about, and several other organizations, too, and that just didn't exist a generation ago.

Bohlen: I agree with that. One of the things I've pondered recently here is: are there unintended consequences to free knowledge and growing knowledge? And my reference point is as I looked worldwide—I've managed engineering centers in India, too—and I began looking at what parents and grandparents were struggling with, with their children and grandchildren. And it led me to the thought that there is pervasive information before they're willing to have the maturity, the intellectual capability to interpret things. So as an example, you and I growing up, we didn't learn stuff because they were secret from you and me—because our parents said, "Well, they're not old enough. We're going to wait." In today's day and age, in this environment, I think that's a social environment that we haven't really thought through.

Yourdon: Ahh, I see what you're saying.

Bohlen: Because the information is so pervasive that the parents are no longer, or the grandparents or the nuclear family, may no longer be the source of information, and I think we're seeing that more and more as the new generation comes up. So I'm looking at humanity as an experiment and saying, "well, what's going to happen here?" because we've changed the very knowledge transfer of nuclear families.

Yourdon: There's a set of terms, vocabulary from an anthropologist, Margaret Mead, about a postfigurative, cofigureative, and prefigurative culture. Her point was that a couple of generations ago, it was just taken for granted that children would learn from their parents, much as you just said. And then there was a shift where the older and younger generations have to learn at the same time. It happens particularly with immigrant communities.

Bohlen: Yeah.

Yourdon: They both show up here in the United States, and they've all got to learn the language and customs and so on. And she argues that we're now in a new area—the prefigurative culture—where the parents have to learn from the children because the technology is changing so rapidly that the kids pick it up first. They learn how to operate the TV remote controls before their parents, which we've been joking about for 10 or 20 years. And the parents are struggling because they have to abandon old habits and assumptions, which is more difficult for them to do. So it's a huge transformation in that sense, and of course, IT is right in the middle of that also. Now, does any of that directly affect your industry?

Bohlen: I think it will and it does, but it gets back to that point we have all this data. We are all just learning how to interpret it.

Yourdon: Ahh. Okay.

Bohlen: For example, there's a feeling that the younger people are more energy-conscious. Well, some of the data doesn't show that. They may be even less energy-conscious as long as they get what they want in terms of data, information, so they don't care when they get it if it's cheaper. So there's some interesting debates that need to occur after we synthesize the data.

Yourdon: You know, there's a trivial example of that. I grew up in the '50s, and we were smacked on the hand if necessary to remind us that when you leave a room, you turn out the lights—because electricity was expensive. Today, of course, my kids wander from room to room and the entire house looks like a Christmas tree. Because it's always there and they have no idea what the bill is—so I think you're certainly right about that and you're probably right that we just don't know what data could be telling us because we haven't analyzed it properly. Very interesting.

Bohlen: You know, unfortunately, in the American culture particularly, we tend to operate best when we have a burning platform, and that platform's not quite there yet.

Yourdon: Yeah, I think you're right. Let me switch gears to the opposite side of this discussion we've been having, to the dark side of the force. What are the problems and things that keep you awake at night in terms of IT?

Bohlen: I think the Johari Window—are you familiar with that?

Yourdon: No, I'm not.

Bohlen: Basically, the things I know and you know are public. The things I know and you don't know, that's my private world. The things I don't know and you know are things that I try to discover. And then there are things you don't know and I don't know. That's what worries me.

Yourdon: Okay, that's what Donald Rumsfeld called the "unknown un-knowns."

Bohlen: Yes.

Yourdon: We used to have a lot of conversations about that sort of thing when we were planning for Y2K ten years ago. There are the known knowns and the known unknowns and so on. Okay, so you're concerned about the things we're not even aware that we should be worrying about.

Bohlen: It primarily comes from my work in the Department of Defense days, and you're familiar with the war games. But there are some people out there trying to destroy our way of life. And the more I know, the more I can make sure I protect myself or protect our society. So as an example, what's the potential of terrorists blowing up a microwave hub channel that would cut out power? I just don't know what I don't know. And that's bothersome to me because I think frequently the little things we should be doing—should I be worrying about it, you know? But those do from time to time cause me to sit up and shoot off a quick e-mail saying, "Guys, what are we doing on these channels or these distribution hubs or these remote locations?" When you think about the value or the criticality of them, they're huge.

Yourdon: You know, there's a related point that I heard from Google once again. The CIO there said it was humbling to realize just how much power could be brought to bear against you by an entire country. He said, "It's one thing to deal with hackers, or the kid in Moscow who's trying to break into your system. You deal with that, and you still have to worry about that at night. But when you've got a whole bloody country focusing its attention on you, that's terrifying." Especially if you're very visible.

Bohlen: You're right.

Yourdon: I interviewed the CIO of the New York Stock Exchange, and he said, "You know, clearly, we're a very visible target, as is Google, as is Microsoft, as are, you know, various other organizations." And I guess to some extent, energy companies in general are because of the attractive consequences that a terrorist might contemplate. You know, "If I can make all of Arizona go dark, wouldn't that be cool?"

Bohlen: Right.

Yourdon: Yeah, okay, so it's security on kind of a grand scale that still worries you.

Bohlen: The other one that I think I've always been vigilant on is not becoming complacent with where we are today. Keeping people on edge—because I think if you don't, it's too easy to make assumptions. And in some ways, I think if you ask by having somebody coming from outside the industry like myself, it allows you to ask the "dumb" questions. "Why do we do that? Why is that important? Why did we do it way back when? Do we still need to do it today?"

Yourdon: Right. That's a very good point. The other answer I heard in that area, which I'm pretty sure you would agree with, is listening more carefully to the younger people coming into the organization.

Bohlen: I've got several focus groups, they call them "skip levels," and my "Just Say Yes" program, as a matter of fact, came out of the young group. I've got them sponsored and I keep giving them the opportunity to keep telling me what I don't know so that we can provide leadership for the company, so I give them all the kudos.

Yourdon: Well, the other aspect of that that I would think would be very, very much of concern to CIOs in almost any industry is the risk of losing touch with existing parts of your marketplace, but also new parts of your marketplace.

Bohlen: And you've got to be quick. You know, I'm accustomed to planning for things nine months, ten months, a year out. We do it. But we've seen this massive switch. Blogs were a big thing for a long period of time. Now it's Twitter. They don't even go to blogs.

Yourdon: Right.

Bohlen: And you've got to be extremely sharp on the latest things that are coming out. Finding restaurants now, you go to Yelp—it's bizarre to me. But you're right. You've got to have the input of that generation because it is different.

We're going through discussions now inside the company. Should we be able to tweet high-power days out to our customer base so they can go and turn some of their lights or appliances off? So we've had those kinds of discussions and dialogs. Do we send out national alerts to our people on those high-energy days? So that's what we've been talking through. We're trying to gain some experience from the rest of the organization and other utilities. We're not a large utility so to speak. We've got 1.1 million customers. So we want to be mindful of how we do that, and I keep asking, "So if you send it, what do you want the recipient to do?"

Yourdon: Yeah.

Bohlen: We look at what specifically we can do beforehand, so that we don't annoy our audiences. Because that's another thing you learn. The young kids in particular don't like spam. They like stuff coming from people they know or it's actionable and meaningful to them. So you can't get on these wild goose chases where you've got to tweet everything. Well, why are we going to do that? Have we really looked at it? So there's a lot of old generational thinking and new value creation thinking that needs to occur, and I don't think we've got a good model yet.

Yourdon: Yeah, there certainly are examples of that kind of situation that I've seen. For example, the San Diego Fire Department used Twitter as a mechanism for allowing citizens to report in brush fires and these terrible fires that they have in the fall with everything getting very dry. And that's actionable and it conveys information back to the organization that they would otherwise not have known. Is there anything of that nature that might be relevant for you?

Bohlen: I think that is something that is available, because if you think about it today, we typically learn first about outages through telephone services. That's beginning to change with the smart meters. That's a whole new revolution beginning to occur, where you get instantaneous data. Our challenge is to figure out, "Do we want it every 15 minutes? Do we want it every 30 minutes?" Then the question is, "If we get that data every 15 minutes from 1.1 million customers, what do we do with it? What do we want them to do with it? How long do we keep it?" That's where analytics will really come into play.

Yourdon: Exactly. That is a good point. Let's see. I want to shift back to a topic we've talked about a little bit already and from a couple of different perspectives: this whole thing about the new generation, the younger generation coming in. Do you have any concerns about how they use technology or how they think about technology?

Bohlen: Not necessarily concerns. I think I have learned from that. I find it very intriguing. Some of my first meetings when I was at my previous company with the new-generation people is that they would ask questions that cause you to think: "Well, why do you send out meeting notices and expect all of us to attend the meeting? Don't you think that's a lot of wasted time, energy, and effort? Well, what are you guys talking about? Why do you have these meetings to discuss security issues?" is an example.

So I said, "Okay, then what should I do?"

"Well, why don't you send it out as an e-mail message to everybody, kind of an alert, let us all respond and dialogue,"—and at that time we were using a blog—"And we can respond from there. That way you'll get people feeding off of each other and you'll get ideas, and you don't have to waste all of our time in meetings. We can do it as a matter of course in our workday."

I'll tell you, that really shook me, because all of a sudden, I'm seeing their social media initiatives brought into the work environment that had the potential for changing the way we do work.

Yourdon: Ahh, interesting.

Bohlen: The other thing I found is that they're a whole lot more concerned and interested in teams. In one case, I had eight engineers, young ones, I wanted to keep two of them, so we told the two that we wanted to keep... "The other six, we're going to probably have to let go." They said, "Well, then, we're not staying. ... We hired on together. We've bonded. We're all in this together."

Yourdon: Well, I'm glad you mentioned that. It's the first confirmation I've gotten. I've asked several other people and I've gotten a blank stare. I heard first from the CIO of Marriott Hotels that teams are being hired together. It's very much—

Bohlen: Yeah, you talked to Carl?

Yourdon: Yeah, oh yeah, Carl Wilson.

Bohlen: He and I have shared similar examples that it just blows you away.

Yourdon: Yeah. I had not heard that before. I certainly have heard of teams demanding to stay together, which—when they finish one project and want to go on to another—which runs afoul of the HR policies in a lot of organizations.

Bohlen: Yeah, it does. The other one I ran into was when we started working through the teams of people and trying to figure out who should get what compensation. They wanted to have a say in that which, again, you would hold that close to your vest in the traditional management style.

Yourdon: Yes, I certainly agree with that. Interestingly, some of these kinds of issues in the IT field in particular have been discussed and debated for some 20 years now. I don't know if you've seen a book written by two friends of mine, Tom DeMarco and Tim Lister, called *Peopleware*[3].

Bohlen: Yes.

Yourdon: All of those topics are still relevant today because there are still a lot of organizations that insist on doing things in a very traditional way. But I think your point is that this new, younger generation is more and more resistant to just sort of buckling under and doing things the old way.

Bohlen: Exactly.

Yourdon: Do you have any concerns about how they work or what their loyalties or energies or anything else might be?

Bohlen: Well, I think that I've worked my way through it. They don't have any loyalty, but why should they? We've taught them not to.

Yourdon: [laughter] Yeah, that's been true for 20 years also, unfortunately.

Bohlen: I do think that they are a whole lot more mobile, but I've also found, particularly the educated group of people we're addressing—many of them are family-bound or root-bound. Or they saw what happened in their families. I had some experience with this in Wichita, Kansas, and Fort Worth, Texas—huge operations we had there. We were recruiting from the local colleges because the kids didn't want to leave those areas, the environment where they grew up. They wanted to stay close to their moms and dads.

Yourdon: Ahh, interesting.

Bohlen: I think the coasts were different. When I was in Rhode Island, I didn't find that as prevalent. However, in Providence, it did go on because,

---

[3] [Dorset House (Second Edition), 1999].

again, that community is very family-oriented. So they'd hire from Brown and Bryant.

So the shift is significantly different for me. I made offers to kids to go to Fort Worth or to go to Wichita. I know why they didn't want to go to Wichita, but that was another issue, but they wouldn't go. "No, I don't want to leave." And maybe that's a Midwest as opposed to coast issue. I don't know.

Yourdon: Would that still be true in today's economy?

Bohlen: I find it in Phoenix with ASU [Arizona State University] students. They want to stay in the valley.

Yourdon: Interesting. Even if it involves a lower-paying job than might be available in Silicon Valley?

Bohlen: Yes, and, you know, there are those highly motivated people I think will go wherever the jobs are and they'll grow through it. I was just back in the Midwest at John Deere in Iowa again, chatting with a bunch of young people, entrepreneurial startup people. I said, "What are you doing in Iowa?" These are geeky kinds of companies, and they're working through some analytics and open-source modules and what have you. And I said, "Do you want to go where the action is?"

"No, we're staying right here."

I said, "Well, you know, you're missing out on the huge opportunity of capital, because Iowa is a great place to be from, but you're not going to run into millionaires just willing to invest capital in startups." But they have no interest.

Yourdon: Well, in addition to that, one of the things we've begun to see with the Web 2.0 industry is that they don't need millions of dollars to get started.

Bohlen: Well, that's true, too.

Yourdon: A generation ago, you did. You had to go to Silicon Valley and find some rich person to give you a million dollars and then you did an IPO—but I could give you a long list of these Web 2.0 companies that have been started up on somebody's credit card with a spare computer that they had in the garage. And that means you can do it in Iowa, or for that matter, Bangalore or any other number of places around the world, so....

Bohlen: You're right and I agree with the context—they communicate on a worldwide basis. So maybe there's a little prejudice from my "what you are now is where you were when" perspective.

Yourdon: [laughter] The only negative thing that I have heard and the reason I kept asking about this actually comes from a man named Paul Strassmann [interviewed in Chapter 16], who was the CIO of the Defense Department and the CIO of Xerox and NASA and a few other places. He's very concerned about what he regards as kind of a superficial intellectual level of today's generation. They expect to get everything instantaneously from Google, their attention span is five minutes, and they may not be interested or perhaps even capable of deep intellectual concentration. Is that something you see at all?

Bohlen: I've seen a correlation to that. Math and science, depth in knowledge and skills, particularly in North American universities, is significantly less than other worldwide training programs. The reason I'd go to India is because I couldn't find enough skilled aerospace labor here in the United States.

Yourdon: Ahh, but …

Bohlen: But the depth of that knowledge was very light. So math and sciences, which is in support of that, are skills and avenues that require deep thought. So I do think that we're seeing Geraldo's "dumbing down of America." And I think the kinds of attention spans also are adding to that, so these are one of those social unknowns I was talking about before. And by the way, we're unconsciously doing it.

Yourdon: Well, consciously and unconsciously. It's something I began to hear about a while ago with something as innocent as *Sesame Street*, which are tiny little vignettes that are 30 seconds or a minute long because that's all a 5-year-old kid feels like concentrating on—and it stays with them all the way through their education these days.

So, we've got just a couple of minutes left, and I wanted to wrap things up with what I hope will be an appropriate final question and that is: where do you see yourself going from here?

Bohlen: Carl Wilson [the recently retired CIO of Marriott International] and I chatted about this about a month ago, and I think part of what we're doing is giving back to the profession.

Yourdon: Ahh, okay.

Bohlen: So, trying to do some public speaking. I speak frequently at Gartner events. I've been trying to get IT professionals to think about business in the terms of business. All the stuff we talked about, the desktop, yes, we've got to do that. But that's what we do in our private world. And I'm very concerned that today's IT people don't understand the value that they can bring to their organizations, nor do they understand the value and the worth that their organizations are to the companies. And many companies are being led and directed by traditionalists or boomers that don't really understand the technology movement and therefore aren't rewarding the IT people appropriately or rightly.

Yourdon: Hmm.

Bohlen: So I'm really on a campaign to push that message. That's one of the things I've been doing. Carl Wilson and I chatted about that. Can we work with groups like Concourse or Strive to get young leaders aware of the business language. So that's one of the things. Am I interested in another CIO? No, not at all.

Yourdon: [laughter]

Bohlen: While I miss the global environment, I'm into teaching the next generation. I get a ton of opportunities for this at APS and to speak nationally. I don't know if I want to travel anymore. I've done enough of that. So, being in Scottsdale, Arizona, is kind of nice because people come out here frequently.

Yourdon: That's true. It's a nice place to visit.

Bohlen: The dialogue my wife and I are having is like, "Okay, when will you be ready to go on to other stuff, like retirement and grandkids?" So, it's interesting.

Yourdon: Well, that'll be interesting to see how it plays out for you and for Carl—and there's another gentleman, the University of Miami CIO, who has just retired also and is going through similar kinds of questions for himself, so I'll be watching to see where all of you end up.

Bohlen: [laughter] You know, I took a step. I told Carl, I said, "You know, I'm a life learner. Being a chief innovation officer, you've got to re-create yourself." So I've decided to go back to school again. So I'm now taking seminary classes, Greek and Hebrew, because I thought I want to expand my mind.

Yourdon: That's interesting.

Bohlen: So that's been a very interesting dialogue, a complete change of agendas and learning, so that's one that I'm intrigued with right now.

Yourdon: Well, that certainly is unique. Nobody else has told me a story along those lines. And with that, I think I will wrap this up. I certainly appreciate your taking the time.

Bohlen: Thanks, Ed.

Yourdon: Thanks again. I really appreciate it.

Roger Gurnani

Executive Vice President and CIO, Verizon

Roger Gurnani is Executive Vice President and Chief Information Officer at Verizon Communication Inc., where he is responsible for information technology strategy, systems development, and operations. Before being named to his current position in October 2010, Gurnani was Senior Vice President of New Product Development for Verizon Wireless and was responsible for the innovation, development, and commercialization of consumer and business products.

Gurnani is one of the founding officers of Verizon Wireless. Until 2005 he served as Vice President and Chief Information Officer, helping to oversee and complete the integration of the domestic wireless operations of Bell Atlantic, Vodafone AirTouch, and GTE at the company's inception in 2000. He previously served as Vice President and Chief Information Officer at Bell Atlantic Mobile.

Ed Yourdon: So, why don't we start with the background? People do seem to be curious as to how a CIO gets into his or her position, because you obviously weren't born into it.

Roger Gurnani: Right, right.

Yourdon: Is this your first position as a CIO, at Verizon?

Gurnani: Uhh, no. So, you know, I was the CIO at Bell Atlantic Mobile. So, most of my career, I grew up in IT, and then…

Yourdon: Starting as a [systems] analyst, as you said earlier?

Gurnani: Yeah, yeah. I was telling you about CASE tools back in the '80s, and you worked on many different projects. I was with the Williams Companies. They had moved into telecommunications by laying out fiber optics. So that's how my telecom career from an IT perspective started, when we started laying fiber optic cables. So I got an early start with a startup business, if you will. But then I joined Bell Atlantic, and after a couple of years I became the CIO of Bell Atlantic Mobile, which was a very small wireless operation at that time in the mid-'90s. Today it's grown in the last 15 years, so I was fortunate to grow with that business as the CIO. And then the last six years I did other stuff. I ran Sales and Operations. I ran the Western Division of Verizon Wireless for a few years. Then I did new product development for Verizon Wireless, which gave me some other opportunities. My current role as the CIO for Verizon Communications, which is the corporate—I've been in this role for about five months now. So that's been my path to CIO.

Yourdon: One of the other things people seem to be quite interested in is the whole question about role models. Was there anybody that inspired you earlier in your career?

Gurnani: You know, I've had the opportunity to work with a lot of different people. Through my career, I have had many different bosses. It seems like I've learned some things from every boss I've had. But here in the last, I would say, 10 or 11 years, I would say I've certainly learned a lot from our CEO, Ivan Seidenberg, and our COO, Lowell McAdam. I've worked with them and watched them and learned from them, the last ten years or so. And I guess there's been just so much change in our industry.

Yourdon: That certainly is true.

Gurnani: And, there's been an opportunity to interact with a lot of different players—new players, you know, entering into our industry, so it's been an opportunity to learn from those guys as well.

Yourdon: I can imagine. Did you have any special training? Does one go to CIO School to learn how to become a CIO?

Gurnani: I don't think there's training per se, but it's really on the job, you know. I guess a couple of things helped me. One, my first job getting out of college was working for a German manufacturing company that had hired me and put me in a fast-start program.

Yourdon: Ahh, okay.

Gurnani: So the first six, eight months, I did like three weeks in the Sales department, a month in Manufacturing, maybe a few weeks in Accounting/

Finance department, a few weeks in IT working on very quick projects, working on a sales proposal or sales bid or a quick design program for IT or whatever. And that gave me a very good, broad perspective on how businesses work.

Yourdon: Hmm.

Gurnani: I think that was probably foundational, learning in my career. That's really helped me. The next thing that happened was when Williams Companies started WilTel, the telecommunications business. We probably did like 20 acquisitions in 5 or 6 years. And I got the opportunity to integrate these smaller organizations —and integrate the IT portfolios, the systems and streamline not only the IT side of things, but also the business side of things. So that came in very handy when Bell Atlantic Mobile merged with Nynex Mobile and then when we formed Verizon Wireless, which was bringing in lots of different companies together. So that experience in a small scale came in very handy about eight, ten years later.

Yourdon: Sure.

Gurnani: We were putting together the largest wireless operations in the country, right?

Yourdon: That's an interesting point that I've not heard from any of the other CIOs that I've interviewed, but I certainly have seen it, especially in the Wall Street area. When these enormous financial services companies merge, they've got enormous systems that have got to be consolidated or they have to just pick one and turn the other one off or lots of variations, so you get to see quite a variety of things. That is interesting. Certainly, the one theme that I've been hearing quite a lot is the value of a broad educational background, not only in university, but also in the first few assignments after. As you say, you get to see a wide spectrum of things going on.

Gurnani: Right.

Yourdon: Because I'm sure once you get into your current position, and obviously you have to interact with the business peers in all different parts of the company.

Gurnani: Right.

Yourdon: So that is handy. What about your current position as a CIO now? If you had to summarize your role in helping to make Verizon more successful, what would it be?

Gurnani: So my role right now—I have business unit CIOs, so we're organized in consumer telecom business, enterprise business, wireless business, shared services, wholesale, etc. So, each one of these business units has a CIO. And then we have a team that runs all our IT infrastructure.

Yourdon: Ahh, okay.

Gurnani: So that's how my function is organized. But what I spend a lot of my own time on is IT strategy: how do we drive IT forward? A lot of time on alignment, making sure IT is very well aligned with the business objectives, with the business goals.

Yourdon: Mm-hmm.

Gurnani: With the business leaders, looking at our business objectives and seeing what change needs to happen to achieve those objectives, both from a business standpoint as well as from a business process standpoint. Obviously, you try to look at things from the customers' viewpoint: what do our customers want? And I tell you, what's really helped me is the five, six years that I spent outside of IT.

Yourdon: Ahh, okay.

Gurnani: So the three years that I spent running all of our sales channels and operations, running the western part of Verizon Wireless, and then for two years doing new product development. So either thinking that, "Well, okay, 4G is coming. How do we take advantage of that? What would customers benefit from?" Working with others in the company as well, particularly marketing, but taking new products from concept to commercialization.

Yourdon: Mm-hmm.

Gurnani: So that experience really helped me a lot. Having grown up in IT and then spending six years and then doing other jobs, I think has given me new perspectives on how to better leverage IT.

Yourdon: I can imagine. I remember visiting a telephone company in Phoenix. This was about 1991 and they were showing me kind of the next generation of technology, and I'd never heard of call forwarding and call waiting and caller ID and all these things. That was pretty mind-boggling. And I have to imagine that kind of process continues on—there's going to be another generation of mobile technology next year or next week or the next decade.

Gurnani: Yeah. You know, mobile technology has obviously become mainstream. It is only about 20 years old. But this has become mainstream. Now people spend more time interacting with their mobile devices than they do with their computers and stuff.

Yourdon: Yeah.

Gurnani: If you think about personal computing, that's not that old either. It's only in the early '80s when personal computing came about. And it *is* shifting very rapidly. I think the traditional personal computer, the desktop computer, is now obsolete. New phone factors, tablets, and so on. So, that's happening. The devices, the people they track with, there's a lot of innovation that's going on there. There's a lot of innovation that's going on with networks. From a wireless perspective, we've gone from a 2G to 3G to 4G now. And you're talking about tenfold improvements in terms of throughput capabilities.

Yourdon: With each one of those?

Gurnani: With each one of those.

Yourdon: Wow.

Gurnani: And then obviously we rolled out fiber to customers' homes with our FiOS[1] product. The capabilities that we have with FiOS are unprecedented. So, that's happening. The other thing that's happening is digitization of content.

Yourdon: Hmm.

Gurnani: Whether it's pictures, multimedia, music. You know, you're talking about this [interview] is going to get recorded as an MP3 file. So everything is getting digitized with the amount of information and data that people want to consume. Now people want to watch movies and TV, download it through the Internet. So, we're seeing exponential growth with data consumption. And if you put all these things together, it creates huge new opportunities to create new innovative products and services, so ... we just announced the launch of our 4G smartphone, which is in the U.S. the first LTE, long-term evolution technology-based smartphone. And some of the capabilities it has are very high-end games, attractive games that you can play with people that are literally across the country. It's just amazing.

Yourdon: Now, it raises an interesting question, and I'll give you a couple of examples, because I'd be curious about your take on it, as to the CIO's role in helping shape or support information-based products. When I interviewed the CIO of Google, I asked him, "Are you in charge of Google apps?" And he said, "Oh, no, no, no."

---

[1] Verizon FiOS is a full fiber-optic-based service to a customers home with bundled voice, Internet, and digital TV.

Gurnani: That's a product role.

Yourdon: "That's a product. That's somebody else's job." He said, "I keep the lights on here inside the company and do a whole bunch of other things." And when I talked to the CIO of Microsoft, I asked him a similar question, and he said, "Well, we're the first in line in terms of dogfooding," as he put it. "You know, we interact a lot with the product people."

Gurnani: Tony Scott.

Yourdon: Tony Scott, exactly. Yes. "But we're the first people who actually try it out." So is there a similar kind of situation for you?

Gurnani: No. I would say for, for our company, IT is a bit more involved with product development, product realization. Let me give you a couple of examples. So IT does the normal things that you would expect. We enable all the back-office operations, you know, all our ERP systems. The financials.

Yourdon: I refer to that as "keeping the lights on," running the factory in the background. Back office.

Gurnani: Well, there's more to the back office in our business, because we're a service-oriented company, so keeping the lights on is making sure all the customer-touching channels are running as well, okay? So all our retail stores, all our centers, telesales, all our online touchpoints. You know, more than half our customer transactions, customer interactions happen with online mechanisms, or through cell phones, and so on. So that is keeping the lights on.

Yourdon: Okay.

Gurnani: So, definitely, IT has to be central to enabling that. But as it relates to new products, as we roll out new interactive capabilities on our televisions through FiOS—like recently we've rolled out, a product which is called "FlexView." It allows you to consume content from multiple screens and you can browse, purchase or rent, watch, archive, share, depending on the content, from your big-screen TV, from your computer in the house, from your smartphones and tablets, no matter where you are connected to the Internet.

Yourdon: Actually, I did see a commercial of a similar or an allegedly similar capability from Time Warner on TV last night, so I have a sense of it.

Gurnani: So, making sure the product itself works ... obviously it's a collaborative effort. There are technology groups within the company, people that build and operate our networks. Those teams are involved. Our marketing folks are involved: how we create demand for it, how do we price it, etc. And then IT has to not only be part of the product realization, from product enablement, but also operationalize the product. Make sure our sales channels can sell the product.

Yourdon: I see.

Gurnani: Make sure our customer support channels online and human-based customer support channels can support the product. Make sure we can bill and collect revenue for the products. Make sure we can collect a product, etc. So I would say 80 percent of products we roll out have to be supported by our central IT systems.

Yourdon: Interesting. That raises another related question that I've asked just about every CIO about, which has to do with the kind of role and influence that you have on your business peers. As you've been saying, you've got people in marketing and various product groups, and so forth, and they're all obviously very successful people because (a) they're smart, and (b) they have very strong personalities—and yet I'm sure you've seen situations where you're worried that they're going off in the wrong direction or they've not seen some opportunities that they could be taking advantage of. But, on the other hand, they don't work for you, so you can't order them. You can order people in your own organization, but certainly not your peers. How do you go about influencing people in terms of the technology that you think should either be used or not be used?

Gurnani: Yeah. So I think that it comes down to building those relationships. So now you've touched on—you know, a lot of people ask me, "So, what does it take to run IT?" And people obviously think IT is all about technology.

[both laughing]

Gurnani: And you know this very well: IT is more about people and relationships. So you can have the best engineers, technically speaking, but they are not totally aligned with the business objectives, no matter how good a technical system or product they create, it doesn't create business results, you know? It doesn't create the business benefits.

Yourdon: Right.

Gurnani: So making sure IT is totally lock-step aligned with the rest of the business, whether it's marketing or finance or customer support, operations, etc., is in my view just the most important factor that measures how successful the business is in leveraging IT.

Yourdon: Okay.

Gurnani: So it comes down to relationships and interaction and I spend a lot of time in that regard. I encourage my people to spend a lot of time in that regard. And I think this thing doesn't happen overnight. You have to build credibility, have that working rapport over an extended period of time. So once you get a couple of successful projects or a couple of successful laps, with your peers, whether it's marketing or business unit presidents or operations or finance people, then it becomes easy, right?

Yourdon: Yeah. And I've heard similar responses from other CIOs, who say, "You need to look for opportunities where you can achieve some demonstrable success, because when you get a track record of several of those, then they start to trust you more."

Gurnani: Yeah, and I think that over my 30 years—I'm rounding it to 30 years of my professional life—I have seen this become better, easier, simply because today's business environment, today's personal environment, in our personal life, everything is so technology-dependent and technology-interwoven. You know, we're so dependent on our PDAs and smartphones and so dependent on all the entertainment is now in some form of digital interaction. All our productivity tools and what we do around the house now are all very technology-driven. As a human being, you interact with probably 30, 40 different companies.

Yourdon: That's true.

Gurnani: There's so much technology that comes into play and we're so accustomed to it that it seems natural—so there's far greater recognition that technology is a key part of running the business today than it was twenty, thirty years ago. At least, that's been my experience.

Yourdon: Well, as you say, now it's a pervasive part of life in general. But certainly, if you're running a technology company, any kind of information company in the broader sense of the term, you're more likely to have business executives who have a higher level of understanding and appreciation and so forth than might be the case if you were a widget company. As you know, 30 years ago, there were a lot of business executives, vice president–level people who couldn't even do e-mail. Obviously, that has changed for everybody to some extent, but especially in an information company, I would think. There's, there's another aspect that just occurred to me that I'd be curious about because of the news headlines every day. A lot of the companies I've spoken to have some degree of global presence, and the CIOs have said to me, "Basically, we're on call 24 hours a day 'cause stuff happens around the world 24 hours a day."

Gurnani: Right, whatever happens.

Yourdon: How does that affect you, or Verizon?

Gurnani: It does. You know, we are a global business as well. We have a global IP backbone. We carry about 30 percent of the Internet traffic globally.

Yourdon: Wow. Is that right?

Gurnani: We provide not only network services, connectivity services globally; we also provide IT solutions and now we're getting into the cloud space as well. We provide those services globally.

Yourdon: Aha. Okay.

Gurnani: We have employees around the globe. Our IT organization is also global. That gives us a little bit of flexibility in terms of running a global around-the-clock operation. So we've got systems work, for example, going on around the clock. We've got people watching the stuff and doing stuff from different parts of the world. And then there's a handoff, which is like the "follow the sun" model.

Yourdon: Ahh, okay.

Gurnani: Now, we haven't perfected it, but we are maturing. We're getting better and working out the kinks, but today's business does require that type of a model for our customers.

Yourdon: Does that mean that you might get a phone call or an e-mail at three in the morning saying, "There's been another earthquake someplace?"

Gurnani: Yeah. Having been in IT most of my career, I've been pretty used to that.

Yourdon: You mentioned a familiar buzzword a few moments ago, and it's one of the next sections that I wanted to get into, which is new trends that might influence the industry in the future—cloud computing being one example. There's a lot of debate about whether it really is new, but putting that aside, what kind of new technologies do you see really having a big impact on the Verizon kind of industry?

Gurnani: So, cloud is definitely a trend. What's happening is more and more customers want a one-stop shop and they want not only the network services; they want the infrastructure, the software, the applications, all together and packaged, flexible, on-demand, right? So, more and more customers are adopting that model. This concept is not new, but the adoption is picking up speed, and this is a natural for small and medium-sized businesses, because they don't have a large IT organization and it's difficult for them to make an investment, support it themselves, and going to a cloud model lets you not have to worry about upgrades. As the technology evolves, they can be assured that they will be able to play … it's more of a utility model if you will.

Yourdon: Right.

Gurnani: So it's definitely penetrated the small to medium segment. The large enterprise customers are also interested in this model because the economics make a whole lot of sense. It's a different economic model. We offer a full stack of cloud services and we've been pretty aggressive in expanding our capabilities in this area.

We acquired a couple or three years ago, Cybertrust Security practice, which is very well known, has done very well. Recently we acquired a Terramark, which runs a lot of data centers. We own lots of data centers around the globe. We obviously provide the network-based services, but we have been also providing the infrastructure services and now it's the full cloud utility. So that's a trend.

Mobility, there's lots happening. Now enterprise customers are beginning to say, "Well, we provide our employees a computer and a smartphone or a tablet. Why can't the employee do everything they need to do on one device?" Or, "How can we virtualize the device?"

Yourdon: Hmm.

Gurnani: "When they come to work, it's a business device. When they go home, it becomes a personal device. How can you make it more secure?" All that stuff. So, the enterprises have their unique needs. The individual consumers have different needs, you know. The other trend that's happening very fast is, in the '80s, '90s, information technology used to be created for, primarily for businesses and enterprises. But today what's happening is, you know, a lot of technology is for consumers and then it's being applied or practically pulled into the enterprise environment.

Yourdon: Well, to some extent that's a form of what you were just talking about a moment ago with cloud computing, that it's initially very attractive to the startup companies and then maybe somewhat later on that the Fortune 500 companies begin to say, "Hey, this is interesting."

Gurnani: The Fortune 500 are also, you know, getting into it because from an economics standpoint, you don't have to spend a lot of capital. So it makes a lot of economic sense.

Yourdon: Sure. But the general trend that you mentioned a second ago is one that Ben Fried of Google mentioned to me: "Instead of starting with enterprise-oriented apps and then seeing how we can push them down to the consumer, now it's flipped around."

Gurnani: It's flipped around.

Yourdon: "And we're starting off," with Google being the classic example, with Google Mail and Google Apps. They start at the consumer level, and then they go up and make it more bulletproof and secure and so forth so that it has a market in the enterprise."

Gurnani: You know, a lot of the devices, the consumer electronics devices—the phone you're holding there, the tablets and so on—created for the consumer and then very quick, rapid adoption by businesses, right?

Yourdon: Right.

Gurnani: Whereas in the old days, it used to be we created a computer, what it was for the business, and then pushed it down.

Yourdon: Yeah. Now, part of what makes this interesting, is that some of these trends have been underway for 5, 10, 20, 30 years, and we imagine that they will continue on. Do you see any brand-new things that we basically didn't have five or ten years ago that will become significant trends over the next decade?

Gurnani: We're still in the early stages of those trends. So digitization of information—that trend, we're still in the early days. Now you're talking about digitizing healthcare records and other records. So the future is all about digitizing. It's a digitized world, and I think we're still in the early stages of life, and it's only accelerating.

We talked about how, as the demand for information and data consumption continues to grow and people now are consuming and demanding lots more data, with lots of choice, flexibility, freedom. So they don't want to buy the package, they want to buy a la carte: "I want to watch this show at this time at my convenience," rather than when the show comes on.

Yourdon: Right.

Gurnani: So, I think that thread is only going to accelerate. I think it's only going to accelerate—all the advances with networks, broadband networks, 4G networks, etc., advances in devices are going to enable virtual corporations, virtual enterprises. So, sometime in the future, you won't need buildings like these to run a large business. People could be anywhere. That is happening. For example, we run our IT help desk with a lot of people that are in different places. Three days, four days, they can work from home. We have the ability to route the calls to their house. And the customers, the end users, don't even know the difference. In fact, we've seen our user satisfaction scores go up, our productivity levels go up.

Yourdon: Ahh, interesting.

Gurnani: And so that's just a small example of what perhaps the future might hold.

Yourdon: One other thing you said earlier may shed some light on it. You were talking about the evolution of these networks, from 1G to 2G to 3G and so on, and saying that each one of them represented a ten-fold improvement. There's an old saying that if you improve technology by 10 percent, it's incremental and will kind of be ignored—but if you make it ten-fold, a factor of 10, that changes the very quality of the technology, the experience and so on.

People do things fundamentally differently if they have to drive 30 miles per hour versus getting in an airplane and flying 300 miles per hour. So if that continues—well, Moore's Law, I think, is safe for another decade or so. So whatever we've got today is going to be 100 times faster, cheaper, smaller within a decade, which is pretty amazing. So that will probably create, as you were saying, new demands, new uses, things that we can't even imagine right now.

Gurnani: So, people working from home—that's happening. The other thing, how it's manifesting itself in the business environment, its value is starting to shift at very fast speeds now. You have major businesses, like Netflix, for example, that didn't exist a few years ago. Now it's so big. So new business models shift in value. You know, innovation can come from anywhere, 'cause it's a digital super-interconnected world.

Yourdon: Right. That's an area that I've been trying to explore and I've had great trouble doing, but I'll give you an example: I was hoping to be able to talk to the CIO of, let's say, Avis or Hertz on one side and Zipcar on the other side—'cause there's an example where technology has facilitated an entirely different business model. Do you see that kind of disruption taking place in the telecommunications industry?

Gurnani: Well, it has and I think we've already gone through a couple of waves of disruption. Mobile is huge, and you look at how the ecosystem continues to evolve and change. Like Apple was not in the mobile business until four years ago. Today they're big. And they've created a nice spot for themselves.

So, yes, there are a lot of disruptive forces in our ecosystem. However, our bedrock, our foundation is making sure that we build very reliable, state-of-the-art networks.

Yourdon: Okay.

Gurnani: Which takes a lot of expertise, a lot of capital, and people who need that at the end of the day. So, that's the core part of our value chain if you will.

Yourdon: Interesting. How do you take into account the changing marketplace, attitudes, especially from one generation to the next? Notwithstanding the technology, I would not be willing to watch a movie on a tiny screen like my iPhone, but my kids will. I'm willing to read the newspaper on a Kindle, but my wife won't. Do you build that into your planning as well?

Gurnani: I would say, in the last few years, yes, we have to build that into our planning because we, just like everybody else, we are realizing what's happened, how fast things are changing. So there's no doubt, the younger generation, they don't want a wired phone, a telephone line to the house, apartment, or whatever. Wireless is good enough for them. We started seeing that trend several years ago.

Yourdon: Yes.

Gurnani: We are also seeing trends—as I mentioned to you before, people are spending more time in front of their mobile devices than they are in front of their stationery devices. We rolled out our service, which allows you to browse, purchase or rent and consume and share content on multiple screens, because we know customers want choice. They want flexibility. So that's what it's all about. It's called "customer is king." It means flexibility, and the younger generation demonstrate those traits. [laughter]

Yourdon: And how do you go about finding out what it is the younger generation wants or is thinking or dreaming about?

Gurnani: We hire the younger generation as well. [laughter]

Yourdon: And just watch them?

Gurnani: No, we talk to our younger-generation customers as well. We get feedback from our customers. That's the other change that's happened—getting feedback from customers, I think, over the years has become a lot easier.

Yourdon: That's true. If they can just do something right on their mobile device and just send it in.

Gurnani: Or go online, blogs or customer forums, get feedback that way. You get feedback from a lot of different sources. So the online properties of Verizon.com, it's become a very central customer-engagement channel for us.

Yourdon: Interesting. Now you mentioned the younger generation coming to work here, either in the IT department or anywhere else. Aside from their greater sense of comfort with technology or familiarity, do you notice any other changes with the younger generation of employees that are either good or bad?

Gurnani: I think it's mostly good, but there are a few things. I think the social interaction and the face-to-face communications, interactions I think are still important. Maybe I'm from the older generation. I'm biased with my view. But in my opinion that face-to-face interaction and that teaming collaboration is still important. And I think the younger generation does not pay as much attention to that.

Yourdon: They'd rather just text you than just look you in the eye and tell you something.

Gurnani: Yes. But I think this is mostly positive, right? I wouldn't say there's anything that stands out that's something that's a big issue.

Yourdon: One of the answers I expected to get in this area, from CIOs in particular, since part of their job is protecting the information asset, one of the things I expected was that the younger generation has less regard for the traditional kind of…

Gurnani: See, in my notes, I wrote down "intellectual property rights."

Yourdon: Ahh, okay.

Gurnani: But I didn't know if you wanted to go down that trail or not—but you're right. You're right. We see some of our younger employees, they're very comfortable going on Twitter, going on Facebook and talking, and sometimes they need to be guided a bit in terms of what's appropriate and what's inappropriate, in terms of what gets put where.

Yourdon: Guidance certainly is quite understandable, but one of the things that I started seeing maybe three years ago, when the whole Web 2.0 world took off, was companies just completely outlawing blogs, saying that, "Basically, we just don't trust our employees. We're not going to let them blog because they might allow some of these intellectual property things to get out in the open."

Gurnani: I think we've been through that phase.

Yourdon: That may be another example of things changing far more rapidly than they did when I was a young man.

Gurnani: And in my opinion, that doesn't work, just completely blocking. So there are some controls that you have to put in place. But I think what's more effective is training awareness, coaching, guiding employees, and making them understand the responsibility they have in protecting information assets and what's the right business judgment versus not.

Yourdon: Sure. I agree. And I've always said to people, "You've had that same problem 20 years ago, that your employees could go out into the public and attend a technical conference or write an article for a magazine and the same issues applied." Now it's more instant. And sometimes people do act in kind of an impetuous fashion without thinking about what they're doing.

Gurnani: So we have a code of business conduct. We do a lot of training and communicating what's the right thing to do. Once in a while we have a violation, and we take appropriate actions. I think that's something that you have to do all of the time. Sometimes you see even our older employees.

Yourdon: That's a good point. It's not just the young ones necessarily.

Gurnani: So I think it's part of maturing and becoming a responsible employee. And I think the employers or the companies have to facilitate that.

Yourdon: There's another aspect of younger employees that I'm curious about… a phenomenon of kids coming out of college and applying for jobs as a team. Have you seen that at all?

Gurnani: As a team?

Yourdon: As a team. "Hire all of us or none of us."

Gurnani: No, we haven't seen that.

Yourdon: Okay. Well, maybe that was an exception then. Because he was telling me about four kids who came out of MIT, and they studied together, worked together, learned software together, and they wanted to work together. And three of them got a job offer from some very good company, and the other one didn't, so.

Gurnani: So they declined.

Yourdon: So they all turned it down.

Gurnani: Oh, wow. No, I haven't heard that, but I have seen people from MIT seem to be connected and want to do things.

Yourdon: [laughter] I'm an MIT graduate, and we were loners when I went to school there. What about the degree of control you impose on new hires with regard to the personal devices that they either bring into the office with them or take home with them?

Gurnani: We have certain standards, and we have certain guidelines, okay? And, given that we sell a variety of devices to the consumers, our policies are quite open. And I often have this dialogue with the peer community, other CIOs—who want to restrict the devices. We can manage multiple devices as the security solutions work fairly well. So we practice and eat our own dog food there as well.

Yourdon: That's a good opportunity that a lot of companies don't have, I suppose.

Gurnani: Yeah, exactly right. Now, we also work with our partners, people who make these gadgets and make these operating systems and make the apps and services that run on these—we work with them as we see certain opportunities to improve and solidify, strengthen security aspects. But enterprises have to pay attention to security. You have to protect. You have an obligation to the customers, plus in many cases it's the law. We have to abide by the law as well.

Yourdon: Yeah. So there may be security regulations. Yeah. Well, I'm getting a consistent theme from just about everybody on that score as well. Again, it was not too long ago that you would hear CIOs saying, "Our employees are only allowed to have a BlackBerry or only allowed to have a Windows PC or whatever. That's it. Period." And now they can't impose that degree of control. They can certainly deal with guidelines and security policies and things of that sort, but not everybody has the variety of devices that you're providing to the consumer marketplace. But almost all of the CIOs I've spoken to have backed off and have said, "Within some reasonable limits, you can bring any gadget you want into the office. As long as you behave with it properly."

Gurnani: Right.

Yourdon: Okay. That is interesting. Now you mentioned a second ago comparing notes or chatting with other CIOs—and I'd like to pursue that for just a second. How important is that in your role as a CIO?

Gurnani: I think it's very important. We obviously pick up different tips or ideas, suggestions. If one's got a particular need, you can always bounce off different ideas to see if it helps there. Many times, our companies are trying to do business together and there is partnership, collaboration, between the business development executives, between the marketing, the sales executives. And if you strike up a conversation between the CIOs, that can further along the partnership or the collaboration.

Yourdon: It makes a lot of sense. I hadn't thought of that, but you're right.

Gurnani: So, I find that becoming a key part of that dialogue with the CIO community. It comes in very handy.

Yourdon: I would think that a CIO in any company is going to be dealing with vendors, whether it's hardware vendors or software vendors or whatever—so connecting to the CIO of those vendor companies is a given. And I certainly have gotten the impression that there's a fair amount of—it's almost like a club, particularly because some CIOs do move around from one place to another, and there are annual conferences and so on, and after a while you get to know who you can call up and or e-mail to ask a question.

Gurnani: Yep, yep, yep.

Yourdon: What about the people who work with you as part of your own team? In your case, you said it was CIOs of the various business units and so forth. Are there particular skills or criteria that you look for to have somebody on your team? What things really matter to you in that area?

Gurnani: You know, I have a fairly seasoned team—which helps out a lot. To answer your question, it's really focused on business results—but I wanted to get to one of your questions here. [sounds of looking through papers] Umm, here it is. You know, I think you were asking what would prevent my subordinates to do my job?

Yourdon: What weaknesses might prevent them from doing a good job as the CIO?

Gurnani: So, what I wanted to mention to you was two of my good subordinates are ready to do my job. And they've been with the business for a long time. And a couple of them I hired many years ago. I feel like I've been groomed for my job for the last many years. You got rotated into the business, worldwide sales, operations, global product development. But I think two things are important. It's really focusing on business results.

Yourdon: Okay.

Gurnani: So getting an IT project done is not sufficient. Yeah, you have to get that done. That's table stake. But then are you extracting or leveraging that IT capability to drive business results—so that's what I, encourage my team to do. So I always tell them, "Big project. Long project. A lot of hard work. You got to get it done. It's in production. Good job," but that's day one of that project.

[both laughing]

Yourdon: Right.

Gurnani: "Now we gotta make sure it's really delivered, what we said we'd deliver." So is it driving sales? Is it driving revenue growth? Or is it driving efficiencies or product acceptance? So that's one. The other is really making sure you have very strong business relationship management, business alignment. So making sure IT is working on the right stuff that's really going to matter for the business.

Yourdon: Okay.

Gurnani: As I said, I've been through like 60 mergers and acquisitions in my career, so I've worked with many different companies and had to integrate IT pieces and so on. A lot of times you see IT is working on stuff that's really great stuff. But does it really matter for the business? You know, if you think about it from a business standpoint. So those are the two things that I think are the key points, where CIOs can make a huge, huge difference to a business.

Yourdon: Now how can we turn that into advice for the young IT professional who's aspiring to become a CIO 20 years from now? What would you tell him or her?

Gurnani: So a couple of things there. One, learn the business.

Yourdon: Learn the business. Okay.

Gurnani: And the second thing is, you not only want to be an IT leader; you want to be a business leader. So I'll tell you a story. This again goes back to the '80s, you know, my early days. Within IT, you had midlevel managers, leaders, and the business people actually had to fund the projects, okay? And what that resulted in was, within IT, a lot of internal competition and politics and it was intended to create good alignment with the business, but what I saw was, it was actually hurting the IT to business objectives alignment. And I saw what was going on, and even though the business said, "Okay, this is what we want, and this is what we are funding," within IT there were competitive forces where—someone would try to undermine the project for the other, because that's the way the environment was.

I think that's where I learned a few lessons about how important it is for IT and all the business functions to be totally aligned and all moving together.

And if you can create an environment that does that, you just get the maximum leverage, maximum benefit in terms of IT.

Yourdon: Okay. Very interesting. I've got some questions about problems and concerns and issues. What is it that keeps you up at night—if there is anything that keeps you awake? [laughter] And I think I know the answer to this, but it's one that I've asked all the CIOs.

Gurnani: I think your question was, "What political problems and issues do you face?" And, I would say—I've been with our company for a long time. I know all the business leaders, all the way from the top down and across very well. So if, if there's a minor issue, I'm very easily able to work through that—and having said that, our business culture is such that there's a lot of emphasis on teamwork and customer focus and results, so politics is not an issue per se. Your other question on problems, threats, issues, concerns over the next year or two: security—obviously, we talked quite a bit about that—is top of mine. And that's because it's such a large business. You know, hundreds of thousands of employees, millions of customers, global, and, you always have to keep that top of mind, not only in my mind, but everybody else's.

You know, some other things I would say in that area is, our industry, our ecosystem, is going through some phenomenal changes. We talked about how value is shifting between players and if you look at what's happened in the music industry and all that. So digitization is creating some great new trends. And as I also mentioned earlier, our bedrock foundation is making sure that we build very powerful and very reliable networks, because everybody at the end of the day is going to need networks and the ability to communicate, whether it's wireless or through fiber or a global IP backbone.

Yourdon: Something you said earlier is relevant here. I would think that one of your possible concerns might be that the technology is changing so rapidly that you may not have enough time to amortize or to depreciate the capital investment you've been forced to make in these very expensive networks. When I was just getting out of college, the old story was that AT&T/Bell Labs built stuff that lasted for 40 years, and that gave them plenty of time to write it off. But if a whole new generation of technology comes along three years later and you've already sunk *x* billion dollars into the previous technology—maybe it doesn't keep you, but the CFO awake at night.

Gurnani: No, that's almost become a core competency of ours, okay? That's what we do for a living. [laughter]

Yourdon: Okay.

Gurnani: Okay, so going from 2G to 3G to 4G—our 4G program is a three-year program, a four-year program to build up, and our 2G is still going to be around for the next 10 years, 12 years, because we have still millions of customers that are still using it.

Yourdon: Okay.

Gurnani: Okay. So, an example I would give you is, in the early '90s we built analog cellular networks. We just shut down analog about three, four years ago. So even though new technology had been overlaid on top of the old technology, it's the same thing that happens with IT or a computer in your house. You don't shut down your old computer the day you bring in your new computer. Either you give it to your kid or you keep it as a side computer, maybe for a special task or something. So all that gets factored into how we do our planning, technology planning each year.

Yourdon: Well, that's a very good point. And the other software example, of course, is that we're still running COBOL, in legacy apps, 50 years after they were written and probably will for another 50 years. Umm, I scribbled down another note that just occurred to me—I don't know if it relates to your industry at all, but you had mentioned music before. You know, the whole music industry rested on the idea that people respected intellectual property. And now society obviously has begun looking at that entirely differently. IBM and Microsoft depended on the notion that proprietary software would always be a profitable venture, and now open-source software changes that quite a lot. Is there anything equivalent for the telecommunications world?

Gurnani: Not really because we are a distribution channel for the people who create the bits and bytes and stuff, right? So, we don't necessarily get into the bits and bytes per se.

Yourdon: Okay.

Gurnani: But we connect the end points that the bits and bytes move between, whether it's a movie or a video or a song or e-mail or a voice call or a voicemail. We don't get involved with those. We're the distribution channel. And the other thing that we do is facilitate the commerce that takes place—so billing customers, collecting customers, doing revenue sharing, or whatever the case may be. We will produce the bits to the people who consume the bits. So I don't believe there's something equivalent directly as it relates to telecom, but there's no doubt as those things happen, they are massive value shifts that happen within the ecosystem.

Yourdon: Okay.

Gurnani: We are players, right? So we have to be agile enough to make sure that we recognize those value shifts and we don't do anything stupid to get caught in the undercurrents.

Yourdon: Okay, one last question for you, and it's kind of the obvious ending point: Where do you see yourself going next? What is life after CIO?

Gurnani: I don't know. As I mentioned to you, I just got to this job five months ago, so I'm having fun. Intellectually, I find my job challenging. Professionally, it's rewarding. There's lots to be done here. We've got some challenges and some things to do, for the next two, three, four, five years, I'm busy.

But, a couple of things I will add. Throughout my career, I've done a lot of things, moved into different roles. As I said, I spent six years or so outside of IT, ran Sales, Operations when I was the West Area president for Verizon Wireless, in new product development. None of my moves throughout my career—and I know this sounds unbelievable—have been planned moves. They just seem to have happened.

Yourdon: I've heard that from at least one other person.

Gurnani: So my current job, I didn't plan to be in this job. But I got the call. My previous job I wasn't planning to be in, but I got the call. The previous job I wasn't planning to be in. So I've not had to plan my moves throughout my career. It's things have happened.

Yourdon: Opportunities have presented themselves.

Gurnani: Yes. So, so I don't tend to worry about or think about, "Okay, what's next?"

Yourdon: I, I had kind of expected when I started putting this together that an awful lot of CIOs would say, "I enjoy this, but the next step would be something up to the CEO level." Almost nobody has said that.

Gurnani: So, three, three and a half years I was the West Area president for Verizon Wireless. I was running the business, I had all the sales channels, I had all the customer support operations, I had P&L responsibility, marketing, PR, etc. So it was not a CEO job, but it was close to that.

Yourdon: Pretty close.

Gurnani: Yeah. Pretty close. You know, I used to get involved with some state-level regulatory issues and stuff like that, so a lot of different dimensions. And I learned a lot, but I also realized that, "Okay, where I can create more value for a company and business is in the job I'm in."

Yourdon: In the CIO job.

Gurnani: CIO. And I can definitely do that job, but all my experiences, 30 years or so, I would say have prepared me for this job better than they have prepared me for anything else.

Yourdon: I would think also part of the answer that anyone would give to a question like that would be based on your own belief about the future relevance or importance of the CIO position. And I gather that's a common area of debate among CIOs when they get together or at the CIO.com conferences. Will there be a CIO ten years from now?

Gurnani: As we were talking earlier, IT, information technology, is now so central to running any business. It's like making sure you're managing your finances. You've got to manage your IT, you've got to manage it. It's that central. And I think most businesses right now realize that.

Yourdon: The CIO of Detroit Energy, whom I spoke to, had the same answer. She said, "I've never planned my next position, but, you know, out of the blue the phone would ring, and lo and behold."

Gurnani: Yeah.

Yourdon: She said she got really good at deciding what opportunities to turn down, but she never worried about whether something eventually would come along. Very, very interesting. Okay, well, I could go on all day, but I'm sure you've got tons of other things to do, so I think I will turn this off.

Ashish Gupta

Managing Director of Service Design, British Telecom (BT)

Ashish Gupta is Managing Director/President of Portfolio & Service Design (P&SD), BT Global Services. BT Global Services provides networked IT services to its multi-national customers across the United Kingdom, other European countries, the Middle East, Africa, Asia-Pacific, and the Americas. Mr. Gupta has dual accountability reporting to the CEOs of both BT Global Services and BT Innovate & Design (BTI&D), which designs and implements BT's network, systems, and business processes for BT units globally. In his capacity as Managing Director/President, P&SD, Gupta has the responsibility for implementing global services network and IT strategy.

Before joining BT in 2004, Mr. Gupta spent about nine years with Tech Mahindra, an IT outsourcing company, in various roles, including as an IT delivery director responsible for the company's CRM practice. Gupta holds an MBA in General Management from the London Business School.

Ed Yourdon: I like to ask a starting question, which is basically how you got to where you are now, because people were obviously not born into the position of CIO. So, how did you get here?

Ashish Gupta: Okay, so, how did I get here? If I just clarify the role that I do, because I am the CIO for BT Global Services. But I also have many other functions as part of my role.

Yourdon: Okay.

Gupta: Actually, the way we're organized in BT is we have a federated CIO structure, so Clive Selley is the CIO for BT Group. We have four legal entities that are listed, and not separately but as part of BT Group, and each business unit has in effect a CIO that represents the interests of that group but also perform a wider function, so we call them not CIOs, but MDs or presidents of service design.

Yourdon: Ahh, okay.

Gupta: And we call them the presidents or MDs of service design because in effect, the responsibility of the role that we carry is more than the management of the IT infrastructure for the company. It's also all about taking the ideas and product innovations functions and getting them converted into a set of designs and a delivered combination of people, process, systems and tooling capabilities for the business to use.

Yourdon: Okay.

Gupta: In effect, that's what I do for GS. I have other roles: BT Global Services is into IT outsourcing, so network IT services is what we do. And I also have the responsibility for the function which is responsible for transforming the estate that we manage for our customers. So I have the team around the world—of 3,200—that works with the accountants to transform customer accounts, when we win bids, to move them onto the BT infrastructure.

Yourdon: Okay.

Gupta: So it's a little bit wider than a typical CIO function. I do the systems for Global Services, and I make sure that we create the right tooling and capability for the operations teams. But I also run the portfolio for Global Services, so the product portfolio team works for me, and I also run this service delivery organization, on transition and transformation.

Yourdon: Okay. Well, it's similar to what I've heard from virtually everybody else in terms of their responsibility for just keeping the lights on, just running the operation—but you're much more involved in the product area than some of the other people that I've spoken to. But back to my original question.

Gupta: How did we get here?

Yourdon: Were you a CIO somewhere else before you took this position?

Gupta: No. It's basically been an upward career progression. I started off as an IT engineer out of the university. I got through several different functional roles, whether they were development, design through project and program management. I used to work for an Indian IT outsourcing company.

Yourdon: Which one?

Gupta: Called Tech Mahindra, which I joined out of university in India. Tech Mahindra was a joint venture between The Mahindra Group and BT. Which is how it was instituted. And I worked there for a good nine years, at which point I basically moved to BT to join Clive Selley's team when he was the CIO of BT Wholesale, which is one of our divisions.

Yourdon: Okay.

Gupta: And then from that it's just been essentially career progression roles. I took on a role running the entire estate in BT, which was about 4,000 systems across the world. And then when Clive moved on to be the group CIO, I took on his erstwhile role—which was the CIO of Global Services, all the product president of portfolio and service delivery.

Yourdon: Okay. Well, that was the kind of story I expected to hear from everybody, and I've been staggered by the variety. And that's given me the opportunity to ask you a question as to the importance or non-importance that you might feel about your foundation, your starting core as an IT engineer. How important is that to what you do today?

Gupta: For me, it is pretty important. You know, I feel the need to understand what it is the teams are doing, so it's not management by management but by understanding how the nuts and bolts work. I do think though that it is a balance, because the CIO role is a lot wider as it's defined today. It's a very integral part of the business than it maybe has been in the past, when it was just about doing IT, so I think it's not very surprising that we have economists or erstwhile chemists or whatever that are doing CIO functions because I think the way it's evolved, a lot of the technology aspects.

A lot of CIOs are now actually increasingly people who are very good at outsourcing stuff because lots of corporations are deciding that maybe there are certain aspects of what the CIO did that aren't core competencies. It isn't something that they want an IT department for in-house and it actually might be better done through an outsourced partner.

Yourdon: Mm-hmm.

Gupta: And then what you need is somebody who's very good at managing the partner as opposed to somebody who's good at doing the IT itself. So I think there's a good sort of mix and balance depending on what the core strengths and what the aspiration of the organization is, in terms of the individual that runs the booth as opposed to whether or not you graduated from engineering school and then made your way up through the ranks. So while it might be surprising, I think it's actually quite healthy. It keeps it current.

Yourdon: One reinforcement that I heard from somebody is that having a strong engineering or IT background gives you, as he put it rather bluntly, have a good crap detector. If somebody is trying to sell you a story, you have a more fundamental sense of whether it's exaggerated or complete rubbish or…

Gupta: I'd agree with that. I think that's pretty fair.

Yourdon: One last question in this kind of starting area. As you've kind of moved up through the ranks, did you take any special training or go back to school to get any special degree?

Gupta: I did. I attended a set of business courses, just through the career, and then I actually invested two years doing an executive MBA. So I was doing that at the same time I was doing my previous role. I was doing it at London Business School. I did it while still on the job. That was pretty tough, because those programs are very extensive. But I found that to be extremely useful. A good grounding in the wider context.

Yourdon: Sure.

Gupta: I brought a whole bunch of "home truths" back to bear in terms of how engineers think about the world and how the broader context thinks about work, and I found that to be a very useful experience.

Yourdon: Well, I had expected to hear that from almost everyone, and it's not been true very often. And the reason I ask these questions is that I run into a lot of junior IT people who say, "Someday, when I grow up, I want to be a CIO, just like the man sitting up there in that office." So they're very curious about how people get started and what kind of additional training might be appropriate or useful along the way, which is the reason for all those questions. But in terms of the main assignment or the main job that you do, you'd already mentioned that there were three main parts of it. How extensive a job is it just to provide the IT services to the internal organization? Is that a minor job or a major one?

Gupta: Well, no, it's not. It's not minor. Global Services is a very broadly distributed organization. We have employees in 170-odd locations around the world, and so making sure that they're all connected to the corporate network and they have the right tools to do their job, whether it's pricing tools, whether it's all the management functions, whether it's just functions that allow them to feel part of BT as an organization is quite a difficult thing, because we have rules and regulations about data protection acts. Each country has…

Yourdon: Each country has a different issue.

Gupta: Yeah. There's all sorts of technology issues in terms of how people connect. There's differences in the quality of different networks in each of the countries. But luckily for us, like I said, we have a federated structure, and a lot of the nuts and bolts, laptop services and what goes on the desktop, etc.—I don't worry about that. It's done by a group function that's done centrally for every employee in BT.

Yourdon: Okay.

Gupta: I think my focus area is more about making sure that the people in Global Services have the right systems and tools that allow them to do the Global Services job, which is mostly to do with the billing or the management sales functions and the services operations function for managing the network and capabilities of that nature. So I think that is a pretty substantial element of my role. Especially given that we've built up through acquisition, and like every other big telco, we have challenges in terms of consolidating our systems instead.

Yourdon: Right.

Gupta: Keeping it current and making sure that we are on top of it as the technology evolves. You know, if you look at iPads and stuff, how do we make sure that we're bringing them to bear at an affordable pace?

Yourdon: You know, you've mentioned the global nature of your work, and it's very understandable from what you've said. But I must say, I've been surprised by the comment I heard from CIOs whom I had thought were just running a U.S. operation or a somewhat more local operation, who still said that basically they live in a global world now and if something happens, if there's a revolution in Egypt or a tsunami in Japan, they expect to get a phone call at three in the morning because even if they don't have their own employees in that affected part of the world, their company is expected to jump in. And, of course, you've got your own employees and operations that are affected by whatever may happen in the world.

Gupta: Absolutely. Japan's a valid example because we had a team of people there and we were communicating with them every day to figure out how they were working and it's very interesting to understand the dynamics of the fact that the tsunami affected the standard phone lines a lot more than they affected the voice-over-IP connections that were in their offices.

Yourdon: Oh, really?

Gupta: So actually, in some cases they were able to connect in their offices as opposed to from some of their homes. So, you know, it's interesting how all the technology actually eventually finds a way to help in hard and terrible situations like Japan.

Yourdon: You know, there was a concept that got a lot of popularity a couple of years ago, called "hastily formed networks" about the need for local groups on the scene to somehow put together a network to support relief services and so on. Of course, in many cases the cell phone communications infrastructure is the most affected by an earthquake or something of that sort. Was that true in Japan?

Gupta: I don't have data points, to be honest. I do know that there was disruption to the communications infrastructure. You could see it on the broadcasts on BBC, there were a lot of people communicating over Skype and all sorts of other things when they were doing interviews with broadcasters. But the extent to which they—well, clearly, in the towns and cities that had pretty much disappeared, the masts went with them, without a doubt.

Yourdon: Ahh, okay.

Gupta: I don't know if there was a big amount of disruption to the mobile communications network in Tokyo and other parts because of the earthquake. I would have suggested that Japan, being a country that knows so much about earthquakes, they would have made sure that there was enough backup. I was amazed at the, the level of movement that some of these skyscrapers we were seeing without them coming down. I mean, those buildings must be engineered amazingly well. So I don't really know the level of disruption that happened on the mobile network, but there was definitely disruption to the communications capabilities in that country.

Yourdon: Fascinating. Now, a second area that you mentioned a moment ago in terms of what your job involves has to do with the whole product area, and I wanted to explore just one aspect of that for a moment. When I spoke to the CIO of Microsoft, he said that while his department is not responsible for the products—they don't create Microsoft Office—they are evolved enormously in the activity that he referred to as "dogfooding," that is, being the first users of what will eventually become a product. Is there a lot of that here at BT?

Gupta: Yeah, it's very interesting because, actually, our biggest customers for Global Services are CIOs. If you think about what we do in Global Services, because we provide outsourced network IT services, which is WAN, LAN, voice capability and infrastructure for CIOs around the world. So, yes, in a lot of ways, clearly, we dogfood our own stuff, because we provide our own network. We have our own voice communications capabilities, and we productize that stuff, and we sell that as a managed service to other CIOs. So in a lot of ways, yes, we eat what we produce because in a lot of ways that's what we actually go to market with.

Yourdon: All right, one last question in that general area. To what extent are you expected to help invent possible products that just don't exist at all right now, as opposed to taking a product idea that might have originated from a business unit and productizing that? That's more understandable, but the idea of helping to invent the future...

Gupta: Yes, so, like I said, we run the portfolio team. I have a product management team that is keeping tabs with what's going on in the market from an innovation perspective and bringing those ideas to bear in terms of innovating the next sets of products and how we take them to market.

Yourdon: Okay.

Gupta: So we do define the propositions. We do look at how we take those propositions and make sure that they fit the customer needs to the market segments we're going into. We obviously do it very closely with the market units, because they have the customer relationships. But we're also working very closely with the technology companies, be it the Microsofts, the Avias, the Ciscos of the world that produce the telecommunications capability, and then we look at how we can bring some of that technology to bear with a wider portfolio, including the network, to make life easier for the CIOs and to improve the productivity of their employees. That's the value-add that we look to bring to the market.

Yourdon: Now does your group get involved in putting the services on, say, a mobile phone, or are you more just on the network side of things?

Gupta: No—our core proposition—we don't have a mobile network division, but we do a lot of mobility services. So we will look at mobile-enabling voice, for instance, we will look at creating mobility applications for telecoms to do equipment management services for CIOs so that they can manage the mobile estate within their organization, they can manage spend levels and look at how they can control that.

Yourdon: Okay.

Gupta: So tools that allow CIOs to manage their own organization better. And, yes, we do have products and services that we can put onto mobile devices like iPads and iPhones and other things of that nature, but what we're not doing is selling mobile networks, because we don't have a mobile phone network, for instance, right? We have a different target marketplace.

Yourdon: Okay. The reason I asked that question is that the CIO of Verizon reminded me that among the many business partners they have to interact with, of course, there are all of the smartphone vendors. You know, the Apples and Samsungs and Nokias and so forth. And, of course, they're busy, hopefully, innovating.

Indeed, one of the amazing things I heard in Japan—I can't remember which mobile phone company I visited—was that they have to come out with at least two new models each year, because Japanese workers get two bonuses every year—which they often spend on telephones, so there's a spring season and a fall season, whereas in the U.S., Apple comes up with a new iPhone once a year, not twice a year.

Gupta: Well, I just think that the productive cycles and the life cycles are getting much shorter and shorter all the time. And I think that's a bit of a challenge for us as CIOs because we need to keep pace with it so we don't start losing the advantage that some of those tools and technologies create for our employees. And, of course, in big enterprises like us, there's a lot of other things to worry about, like how secure is the data on those devices? Are we making sure that we're not opening ourselves to a threat of important company confidential information getting leaked out just through accident or through theft of these devices? And how do we secure all of those things, which to a large extent, makes our ability to now consume an iPad every year a lot harder? Because some of those things are not fixed in a day.

Yourdon: Yes.

Gupta: And I think a lot of policy thinking and shift needs to go on before we can fully exploit the ability to use these devices more widely through the organization because a lot of companies still have very locked-down estates, very stringent firewall rules, and they're there for good reason. All we need to do is figure out the flexibility for an employee to use a mobile phone personally and for business use, yet not open the organization up to a threat—and I'm not sure we've all cracked how we do that just as yet.

Yourdon: [laughter] I would agree. Well, that moves me into the next area that I wanted to talk to you about, which is just the general question of new innovations and new developments that you see coming along. The one that has been universally mentioned by everybody, of course.

Gupta: Cloud? Well, yeah, I think the buzzword is "cloud computing." How do we get rich on what is now well agreed as being the way we do computing going forward? And how do we make sure that we can leverage that asset and go back if you will to the—it's very interesting to me because we all started off with big mainframes, that were all multi-tenanted and multi-processed and multi-tasked to our client-server model, to our mini-microcomputer model, back towards a mainframe model, which is really what cloud computing gives us.

Yourdon: Right.

Gupta: Except, of course, it's way more powerful and way more flexible, and a lot more distributed, and so for us, it's very important that we exploit that, not just for ourselves, but also for the propositions we take to market for our customers. And the architecture's evolving rather well, isn't it? So you've got more and more of the computing becoming virtualized and available on demand, on a sort of utility basis. You're getting a lot of the application platforms getting more standardized. So you can exploit the broader developer community to create apps, and through the explosion of the app stores, be it on the iPad or on Android, or maybe even increasingly on the BlackBerry and the Windows platform, which are the four big ones as I see them at the moment.

Yourdon: Mm-hmm.

Gupta: See, you've got the IOS, you've got Android, you've got Windows Mobile, and then you've got the platform that BlackBerry uses.

And, clearly, others will make plays in that space, but at the moment, from an enterprise market segment perspective, most people have one of those platforms. And then the combination of the ability to put applications on those devices is running on a more distributed, cloud-based computing infrastructure, with more platformized capabilities that allow application development and innovation to happen at greater speed is all good for us as enterprises.

We have the same challenges in terms of data protection, if you're multi-tenanted, are we secure? And all of those policies have to be resolved and clarified. But, without doubt, people are moving toward virtualizing their estates, to getting to more applications that can be written on standardized platforms. The challenge we have, obviously, is a lot of enterprise businesses are heavily today dependent on big software manufacturers like Oracle, like Microsoft.

Yourdon: Right.

Gupta: Like all the others, and we have thousands and thousands of users deployed using these applications with licensing that's based on old models. And how does that evolve to exploit the new compute-utility-based, per-use-based model? That's the key challenge, and I think it's very exciting for us, in terms of where the industry goes next.

Yourdon: One other aspect, of course, of the cloud computing concept is the scalability, the instant scalability that it provides. I heard a lot about that yesterday when I was visiting Ladbrokes because they like to say that their whole business is "peaky." I think is the word he used. In the moments before a big race, a big football game, the demand spikes. Do you see that becoming more and more common among all of the major computer users, this idea of extremely rapid and fluctuating demands for scalability?

Gupta: Well, to be fair, what happens today is *everyone* has a set of peaky processes in their business. You know, whether they're bill runs that happen at the end of the month, or whether there are events that happen at a certain time on a certain week on a certain day that needs a certain volume to be able to deal with it.

Yourdon: Right.

Gupta: And I think at the moment, most enterprises end up creating more capacity than they need, on an average running basis, purely because they have to deal with those peaks because they're so important to their businesses. And so the benefits of being able to take different peaky businesses that peak at different times and run around a common shared infrastructure, economically just makes total sense.

Yourdon: Yeah.

Gupta: The challenge is getting the right mix of businesses on that platform and being able to deal with all the challenges around data protection and security and all of that stuff. But it's inevitable. It makes so much economic sense to be able to do it on that basis where you're not building hundreds of extra servers in your data centers. only because you're going to get that peaky event on a Saturday night if you're a broadcaster or end of the month because you run billing cycles or whatever the model might be. It makes total sense.

Yourdon: Well, that's a good point. So you're saying that it really affects everybody, because everybody has got their own peaks.

Gupta: And whether you are willing to live with the peak because it is so critical that if it failed, you'd be out of business.

Yourdon: Good point. Now, there's another phenomenon that you've touched on with a couple of your comments already that I'd like to explore. Maybe one way to explain it is to say that the traditional world that most of us grew up with involved new products, tools, apps, etc., coming into the enterprise and being controlled and locked down and managed very carefully, if appropriate, pushed down to the employees, to say, "Here's something that you can do at your desk." And now you see a world—it's certainly illustrated by Google and some of the individual phone apps—things come in at the consumer level. You know, "We're going to sell something to the consumer out on the street."

Gupta: Yeah.

Yourdon: And then it may come up into the enterprise, with some problems and opportunities, but the obvious example is that all around the world now, employees are bringing into the office some handheld thing and also the memory of what they were doing last night at home on a computing device that's much more powerful than what's sitting on their desk. How does that impact your day-to-day world? This kind of upward movement, from the consumer up into the enterprise?

Gupta: So, if I was honest, that in itself isn't our biggest issue. From my perspective, right? I think we might be missing a trick in terms of exploiting it better, but we have other challenges to sort out at the moment. I think the bottom line is there is increasingly becoming a need for convergence of devices between individuals and their personal use and what they do in the enterprise, because everything is getting so seamlessly integrated. People work all sorts of hours.

Yourdon: True.

Gupta: You know, they'll be working at eight o'clock in the evening over dinner sometimes and sometimes they're at work and they might want to do something that's personal, and that level of flexibility though creates a stickiness of the employees with the organization 'cause it gives them the flexibility to maybe work, achieve their objective in life and at work. And not feel like the two have to be separated out, which is, "Nine-to-five I use a PC. It's locked down. I can never do anything else. And when I go home, I can look after my bills and whatever else on a different and more powerful device and with a set of apps."

Yourdon: Right.

Gupta: So I think increasingly we have to leverage the convergence of an individual as an individual at work and at home and find a way to exploit the upward-based apps, but we have to find a way to make sure that we do that in the context of securing the enterprise data, make sure that we are within the bounds of the regulation we operate within, and those are the problems that we have to tackle and be able to deal with.

Now, I haven't got all the answers, and we do have lots and lots of people that have abilities today to connect their working with their iPads or their iPhones. We have sort of agreements as to how that's managed and what the expectations are, like it has to be password-protected, it has to go through our VPN, it will get scanned, etc., so that we're keeping all of those checks and balances in place. But has that got us to the point where it's a single-device model and your home PC and your work, or your home laptop and your work laptop looks exactly the same? I wouldn't say that it is.

Yourdon: Okay. But, if I understood you correctly, at the moment your primary marketing thrust and your product development thrust is still aimed at the enterprise first and foremost. With the expectation that it's eventually going to involve all of these employees who are doing things at home and bringing into work, and somehow those worlds have got to be married up.

Gupta: Well, if you look at what's happening—we do a lot of work in the unified communications space, which is all about unifying the messaging capability with the voice capability with your contacts and your e-mail and all of that good stuff. Increasingly, all the tools that we would take in the enterprise would provide capability, would federate your contacts between your personal contacts and your work contacts, so that you can bring them all together and make it easier for employees to use a more unified capability for how they work.

And so we have tools and we have products that are targeted and aimed specifically in that area for employees within enterprise organizations. So, by definition, with the nature of the architectures that are being built up, there is a convergence happening in terms of innovation and application development anyway, I think.

Yourdon: Okay. There's another aspect of all of this that I'd be curious to hear your opinions about. Partly because of all these developments we've talked about, the price of technology and devices is dropping to the point where almost anybody can afford it, including large parts of the world that previously could not afford anything at all. And so we're now seeing enormous new markets in Africa and parts of Asia, with hundreds of millions of people having handheld devices that allow them to do productive, useful things. And I'm curious to what extent a company like BT is trying to capitalize on that or seeing that as a tidal wave?

Gupta: Well, I think, in a lot of ways, we enable a lot of other enterprises that are growing in those areas. If you look at FMCG[1] businesses, you look at what companies like several of the ones that we work with today are doing; they're all expanding, they're all seeing growth in Africa, and in a lot of ways we are building the network infrastructures that allow them to get there.

Yourdon: Okay, okay.

Gupta: To be able to then connect their employees in those countries back with the rest of the world. So, the mobile traffic explosion that's going on and the connectivity and the ability to be able to get stuff into those countries and enable the factories, enable the employees is happening. We can see it going on.

And we're absolutely at the heart of empowering companies going into these growth markets but also making sure that we're not just helping them with their employees there, but also bringing back and connecting those employees to make them part of the bigger, broader enterprise that they work in. So in a lot of ways, us and a lot of other telcos, our core business is to make sure we keep people connected, wherever they might be. And I think we're playing a very important role in terms of keeping the world more and more connected. It keeps getting smaller, every month, every year.

---

[1] Fast Moving Consumer Goods.

Yourdon: Yes.

Gupta: There are technologies that bring people closer together, and we're certainly at the heart of making sure that the networks we build, the resilience we put into them, the capital we're investing allows companies to do that easier and easier all the time.

Yourdon: Well, that's an interesting point, because it does all require a network. Vast networks. That sometimes gets overlooked, but you guys are kind of in the background, so to speak, making all that possible. It really is an amazing kind of shift that you see. Google Apps, for example, is free. It may be supported by ads, but it's free, so the social transformation is just phenomenal. But I think that your point is well taken. If you didn't have a network there in the background, it would be irrelevant.

Gupta: We were having this conversation as part of one of the subforums of the IMF[2], which has to do with cloud and enablement of communities, through the ability to leverage the cloud and what the cloud brings to them. And I think one of the big discussions we were having there is, "The cloud's all well and good if you can get at it." And, really, that's why there needs to be continued focus on the infrastructure that allows communities to access the cloud. Because if you can't get at it, it's not really there to help you with.

Yourdon: Hmm.

Gupta: So, yes, you can get Google Apps for free, but if you didn't have a mobile network operator building a mobile network or a telecommunications operator connecting that country up with the World Wide Web, providing the bandwidth that's required to be able to truck all that traffic through, yes, you can deploy smart phones, make them cheap as chips, but they couldn't get anywhere near what customers actually need to be able to use.

Yourdon: Yes. Very good point. Now, you mentioned bandwidth, and I can't help but ask a question here. Being an iPad user or an iPhone observer, I'm sure you can anticipate this, which is that the bandwidth requirements of a lot of those devices are an order of magnitude greater than they were when we were just doing simple voice communications. I almost never use my iPhone for ordinary phone calls. It's all web browsing and that kind of thing. How much of a problem is that going to

---

[2] International Monetary Fund

be in the future, and as the people who have smart devices are doing far richer things with astronomically greater bandwidth requirements than would have been the case ten years ago?

Gupta: It's a very significant problem already. You only have to roam around in India to figure out how difficult it is—you can have a full signal but still not be able to do anything with it 'cause the networks are getting heavily congested by the devices. You know, the operators are investing huge amounts of capital to increase the size of the pipes, to bring new technology to bear. We're helping a number of the operators here in the UK, for instance, with being able to trunk more and more data off the cells. Providers are providing fourth-generation LTE networks.

Yourdon: Right.

Gupta: All of it is being accelerated because of the speed at which the smart devices are gaining traction, the success of the platforms and the applications on them mean more and more people are using it, much, much faster. How many iPads were sold in the first six months? Was it over a million devices were sold in two months or so? Some ridiculous number like that.

Yourdon: Well, they had sold 15 million when Steve Jobs got up to announce the iPad 2.

Gupta: There we go. So I think it sold a million in the first four weeks or so. And the more that happens, the more pressure it will put on bandwidth and network infrastructure. I think people also expect them to be more reliable, 'cause they get so used to using some of these applications. They become so integral to their day-to-day life. There is now more than ever the expectation that these networks are not only quick and fast but also very reliable. So I think the core network infrastructure is still a very integral part of the speed at which all of this is happening.

Yourdon: Now in terms of growing all that, is that primarily a capital problem or a technology problem?

Gupta: Well, it's a bit of both, because the technology needs to evolve at a pace which allows us to build those networks at price points that are commensurate with the price points at which customers are expecting to be able to pay for some of this stuff.

Yourdon: Right, right.

Gupta: So the cost per unit of bandwidth or the price per unit of bandwidth drops significantly year on year, every year. The costs of building those networks needs to trend the same way and a lot of that is enabled by just more innovation, better technology, and greater scale clearly helps. But a lot of that plays in the mix. It's a very interesting dynamic on cost and price and how do we as providers of networks enable this ever-growing desire and requirement for bandwidth but, equally, make sure that we're making good positive returns in helping the businesses, other businesses and customers flourish?

Yourdon: Interesting. Let me turn the conversation around about 180 degrees now and talk about the dark side of the force, the problems, the things that keep you awake at night. You've already mentioned security. That's kind of an obvious one, and the related issues of privacy and so forth. Are there other problems associated with the technology that you work with that keep you awake at night?

Gupta: Yeah, I guess the big challenge for us is speed. How do we make sure that we can innovate and deliver products and services, both to our internal users but, importantly, to our customers at the speed at which they're expecting us to?

Yourdon: And also maintaining enough control and integrity.

Gupta: Absolutely. So how do we get through the innovation part and how do we build the tools, how do we build the capabilities, how do we take them to market at a price and at a speed that is commensurate with the rate at which customer demands are changing? So one of our big challenges is how do we do that? And then underpinning that on a whole bunch of other challenges in terms of skills: how do we capture the right skills that we need to be able to move the business forward from a technology perspective? How do we retain them? How do we keep them excited? How do we stay relevant?

Yourdon: Ahh, okay.

Gupta: There's a big, there's a big war out there in terms of skills. There's a lot of people working in very different ways. I saw one of your questions about, you know, what differences are we seeing in terms of the graduates that are coming through?

Yourdon: Yes, I'm going to get to that in just a moment, because it is a big area, yeah.

Gupta: But I think the big challenge for us is really as an IT function, we need to continue to reduce the cost of IT for the organization, but do it at the same time as improving the quality and speed at which we get capabilities delivered. And then from an innovation and product perspective, we have to do much the same in terms of delivering new products and services, innovating but doing it quicker, doing it cheaper, and getting it out there faster. And I think those would be some of the biggest challenges that I face on a day-to-day basis.

Yourdon: There's a slight variation on this that I've asked all the other CIOs about. When you're dealing with these issues and problems, you're also working with other business units and product managers and marketing people, and so forth.

Now, in the old days, when I got started in the field, we were the experts and they didn't know anything about computing, so they would come to us and say, "Please tell us what we need to do." And even then, these peers of ours were very smart and very successful and had very strong opinions and certainly felt that they knew how to run their business better than we did.

Now they sometimes feel that they know how to run the IT business better than we do, so that you can't order them about what to do and what not to do, even though you may seem some opportunities that they've missed or some dangers that they're unaware of. How do you influence them to deal with these problems and developments that, that you've talked about?

Gupta: Yeah, it's a very, very good point because there are lots of people out there that do understand the technology better because it's become so integral to how people work, not just at work but at homes. I think it comes back to engagement and governance and being clear about what it is the objectives are the organization is trying to achieve and then aligning around them. I don't think there's any IT organization that does everything everyone wants at any given point in time.

Yourdon: [laughter]

Gupta: The issue is agreeing and being able to communicate effectively what challenges we're trying to resolve, make sure that we have the broad governance and buy-in from that organization, be it through capital investment forums or decision-making bodies that can agree and then communicate not just what we're doing, but why it makes sense.

And then good quality execution of those elements, because I think people get frustrated at two levels. One is, "I can't have what I want," but, more importantly, "I can't have what was promised I could have." And I think you need to sort of solve problem number two before you can start tackling problem number one.

Because if you're not resolving what you promised to deliver or what you offered you would do for the organization in time and cost, then there's a level of issues in terms of confidence and the willingness to go on the journey.

Yourdon: Yeah, a lot of the other CIOs have said the first thing you need to do is establish trust. Because if they don't trust you, particularly because you've not delivered what you promised, then it doesn't really matter what you say.

Gupta: Yeah.

Yourdon: So that's got to be the first point. I had an interesting comment from one of the electric utility companies in the U.S., who said, "Just because you can use Excel doesn't mean that you're a programmer." Everybody thinks they understand a lot about IT, but she said, "We have to sometimes bring our outspoken business leaders into some of our more complex areas and show them that, in fact, it's a hell of a lot more complex than they ever imagined." And I have to assume that's true for some of what you do as well.

Gupta: Yeah, I think there is absolutely a broad expectation out there that fundamentally there must be a way that they could do it faster than us if they just had control of all the functions, so we centralize all this stuff. Without doubt, we have to have those conversations and say, "Look. Here's the reasons why that aspect of the problem that we're trying to solve cannot be fixed through a quick fix, which takes two weeks and is done."

Yourdon: Right.

Gupta: Because, actually, in doing that, we create a whole suite of other problems that will come back and bite us later, and this is the reason why it has to be done this way, this is why it costs what it does, and we'd all like to do it faster, but this is the reason why the plan looks like the plan and that's why we will execute this plan. So those conversations, just like every other department, or IT department, in the world—in fact, many other functional service departments in organizations, not just CIOs, have to go on that journey.

Yourdon: Yeah.

Gupta: Because you have the same conversation with an HR manager or the head of HR: "Why can't I just get XYZ skill and hire them at will?" Well, there are reasons why you want to balance your resources a certain way, you want to do things, you want to train your light body of a strategy for what you're enforcing in an organization to look like, the same way you need to have a strategy and an execution plan for what the technology looks like. And you have to go through those hard conversations and have those discussions.

Yourdon: You've used one other word in that answer that also resonated with me. When I asked that question of the CIO at Educational Testing Services, the people that do all the college placement exams in the U.S., he said, "We constantly have users coming to us saying they want to outsource. They don't want to have to everything through central IT. And our response is, 'Fine, if you want to, but let us show you the detailed cost breakdowns, the detailed measurements, and then make sure that the vendors you're talking to give you equally detailed measurements, and if you can get it cheaper, God bless you. Do it.'"

Gupta: Absolutely.

Yourdon: But if you don't have the measurements, you don't have the data, he said it's very hard to carry on a rational conversation. And, of course, one of the dilemmas we've always had in the IT profession is that we've, we've not been all that good at measuring things.

Gupta: My personal opinion—this is a personal thing—is it's very dangerous to outsource something that you either ill understand or couldn't resolve yourself.

Yourdon: [laughter] Yes.

Gupta: Because how do you know that the outsource is actually being effective? And how do you know that in the outsourcing, we aren't mortgaging away a capability that is actually required to drive the business further forward? So, you know, at a minimum, you should be able to fix it yourself.

Yourdon: Right.

Gupta: You might be able to do it faster 'cause the skills might exist somewhere else or the organization that's taking on the outsourcing has economies of scale and can leverage a certain type of people that can do it better, but if you don't understand what you're trying to achieve, and you're outsourcing it because outsourcing is what the mantra is, then in a lot of such cases I would suggest that the outsource doesn't work.

Yourdon: Yeah, I would agree with that.

Gupta: You end up with contract breakages, unhappy customers, big fights with your suppliers about what you thought you were getting and what you're then going to get, and all of that to me is about not having been crisp and clear about exactly what we're trying to achieve through the outsource.

Yourdon: I agree. The last major area I wanted to talk about before I ask you my final question had to do with this generational issue you saw in my list of questions. You know, every company these days is now facing a new generation of employees, not just in the IT department but throughout the organization, that grew up as digital natives, and I'm curious what your opinion is of them. Is it good, is it bad?

Gupta: Well, I don't think it's good or bad. I think it's different. I think the population coming to work at the moment does expect to be more mobile. They expect to be more flexible, and I think they are more easily frustrated by the constraints that you might put around lots of procedural processes that they feel, because of the way they've grown up—you know, when I grew up in Mumbai, I used to have two TV channels that were only ever available from six o'clock in the evening till ten o'clock at night. These days, you know, the TV is on 24/7.

Yourdon: With 500 channels.

Gupta: They're watching 500 channels. They're watching something on TV and communicating with their friends and SMSing away on their mobile all at once. And they're just used to being able to be better connected to be able to do things in a certain way. And then when they come into an organizational construct, they kind of don't expect to be able to radically change their mind and work in a context that's very different, not just from an IT perspective, but just generally in terms of the processes and the procedural rules that exist within an organization and how they work.

So I think that as the mix changes and as the population gets more Generation Y or X, I think we will need to and will see a shift in the dynamics of how organizations work. Just by the pure nature that a lot of these people that will come through the ranks know a certain different way of living, not just working, and they will hope to mold the way they get work done in that way.

And I think it will bring innovation, so it's a challenge, because they have to be integrated, they need to feel like they can take the business forward, and they need to feel like they can be successful. But at the same time, they'll want to start seeing a collection of them trying to change the way certain things get done. Through better collaboration, through tooling, through whatever. And I think we all have to just at least be conscious of that and deal with it as best as we can.

Yourdon: Do you see any, any disadvantages or risks or problems with the younger generation? Do they create problems for you?

Gupta: I personally see that the generation at the moment is a little disadvantaged. The state that the younger generation is in, because the state of the economies at the moment and the fact that pension ages are being increased, basically means that people will have to stay at work for longer. Which means, by definition, that the average age of an organization will move to the right, just because everyone needs to work longer to create the nest egg that they can use in retirement.

Yourdon: That's true.

Gupta: Which then means, by definition, we're not creating as many opportunities for the younger population. So I think they're going to struggle a bit, which is not fair for them, but it's the reality of where we are, and I think that's going to create a level of tension in terms of figuring out how they get frustrated about not being able to get into the workforce, into the right sort of jobs and roles as quickly as they might want to.

So I think that while there was the opportunity generation, I think at the moment the guys coming out of the university face some reasonably challenging times in terms of the number of jobs that are available and how they get hired, which is why companies like Google and others are doing so well, because they've started up fresh, they don't have a legacy of lots of people and a very strict employment contracts that have worked in large organizations for many, many years, and they are being able to hire all of these newer generation people with new ideas, and that, I think, is an advantage for them.

Yourdon: I'll give you an amazing statistic. When I spoke to the CIO of Google, I had just seen an article in the paper, and I confirmed it with him. They get 75,000 job applications a week.

Gupta: That is amazing.

Yourdon: It is. He said, "We have millions of résumés on file here." Just staggering. Well, let me ask one final question—and it's kind of an obvious ending question. Where do you see yourself going from here? Are you going to be a CIO for the rest of your life, or do you have aspirations for anything other?

Gupta: To be honest, I'm 36. I've done a lot of stuff in a reasonably short period of time, so when I get asked that question, I guess for me it's about constantly being able to achieve outcomes for the business and for customers. I haven't sat down and mapped out the route to being a president or to being a king or anything like that.

Yourdon: [laughter]

Gupta: It's worth it for me at the moment to be able to be reasonably opportunistic in finding things that are of interest to me, and then moving on. I move on when I feel like the job and the role I'm doing is done. I can move on and let somebody with new ideas come in and I can go do something else. Do I want to be a CIO all my life? You know, it wouldn't be the end of the world. I quite enjoy working with technology. I have a good background in it, and actually, it's quite a fulfilling job. It will kill me, though, because the CIO function is not a 9-to-5 job.

Yourdon: No, it's a 24-hour job.

Gupta: It's very, very intensive, obviously. And obviously, that needs to play in to how long and how far you wish to go in the work-life balance sort of sense, but equally, I'd be more than happy—'cause I already do some of this in terms of portfolio and business alignment—to look at opportunities to move laterally, to doing more P&L escrows or deciding to do something different. But, we'll see what comes.

Yourdon: The reason I ask that question is that the traditional picture of the CIO is that it's the end of the line, and a lot of the people I've interviewed are in their fifties or sixties. In fact, I interviewed one CIO who had just resigned—in fact, I take it back, there were three. One man was in his eighties—it's understandable that he said, "I don't want to be a CIO anymore." But, particularly in the technology companies, you, the CIO of Google—I guess he's in his thirties, but a lot are young people who have risen relatively quickly and they're in an industry that's moving quickly, and so they've got still 20 or 30 years ahead of them. And as several CIOs have told me, they never planned for this job, and they're not going to plan for the next job. Opportunities present themselves, and when the right opportunity comes along, they'll—

Gupta: Jump and decide what to do then. Yeah, it's a way of doing it. There are certain people who have a career mapped out and know where they want to get to. There are others like me who are happy that I've achieved what I wanted to achieve so far. I'm happy with what I'm doing, and I'm not out looking for the next step or the next thing just yet.

Yourdon: It'll come, right?

Gupta: It'll come.

Joan Miller

Director of ICT, the UK Parliament

Joan Miller is Director of Parliamentary ICT (Information, Communication, and Technology) for the United Kingdom Parliament and sits on the management boards of both the House of Commons and the House of Lords. She was recruited to set up a new department in 2005, centralizing nine separate ICT offices to create a new and more strategic ICT function for the UK Parliament.

In previous roles Ms. Miller managed community development programs and European partnerships, becoming involved in managing ICT in 1993. She managed award-winning ICT programs and services in local government in Essex, Suffolk, and London from 1993–2003, in the course of which she centralized ICT services three times and established substantial organization-wide change and savings programs to create new contact centers, new face-to-face services, and new transactional web services for citizens. She also led two UK national projects in this period, one to connect electronic information and records across several organizations and the other to set standard methodologies for public sector programs and project management.

Ed Yourdon: One of the things that I've been quite curious about with everyone I've spoken to is basically how you get to a position like this. Obviously, you weren't born a CIO—but had you been a CIO at previous organizations or was this your first appointment?

Joan Miller: I should probably tell you a little bit about my earlier career, because it is relevant. I did an economics degree. Which I think is quite unusual for CIOs.

Yourdon: You'd be amazed at the variety. The CIO of the New York Stock Exchange has a PhD in chemistry, so I'm no longer surprised by anything. But economics in your case.

Miller: Economics lives between science and art. And I think the CIO job lives between science and art with what people do with technology. And that's why it's not so unusual. There are a number of CIOs who also come from the social sciences. I began working in an insurance company.

Yourdon: Ahh.

Miller: But I took a 14-year gap to have children. So I was not working other than caring for the children for 14 years, and I did lots of voluntary work in that period. When I came back to work I was working with community development, which is a long way from IT.

Yourdon: That's true.

Miller: But when I was organizing voluntary organizations that work with social care services, in Essex—a part of that was project planning. It was business planning, project planning for a voluntary center, creating contracts with the social care services to provide services, and that's very much a people-based, but organizational planning–based role. And then I moved and worked for the director of social services, doing a staff officer-type job, and that meant that I did anything that wasn't social work that the director needed done. When I was working in that area, I was working on things like voluntary sector development, European policy, and projects. And then this new topic of information management came along.

Yourdon: Ahh, I see.

Miller: I'm talking the early 1990s here, we were looking at information management as the big development for social care, in order to be able to keep records. In 1993 we did a very big project, a community care project, which was about creating in an eight-week period a paper–based records system that crossed all of the council's social care services. It was primarily for older people, people with disabilities, and people with mental health problems. Looking at the workflow process and how you could record the record of the individual being helped by social services when that individual would see a lot of different social workers and care workers. We did it all on paper in 1993.

Yourdon: Hmm.

Miller: When I'd finished that project, the director said to me, "So, what's your next project?" And I said, "Well, I think you should computerize this. I think databases do this work much better than paper," because we had 30 different forms in the process.

Yourdon: Mmm.

Miller: And for each one you had to do basic repetitious stuff, like write names and addresses and relationships on each form, and the obvious opportunity is to create an electronic record that would do that for you. I wasn't thinking very much more than just being able to transfer information from one form to the next and build up a record. So we went into a period of looking at what computer systems might work. And we were lucky, I think, to find a computer system specifically for social care but which was a very well-structured computer system. I learned my IT data management, project management from that project.

Yourdon: Ahh, I see.

Miller: Buying a computer system that works and that social workers could use. Social workers are not the easiest people to persuade to use computers — their focus is much more on the person they're working with than it is on the computer they need to give them the information, and they were very much at that time used to writing paper records, long files, so my introduction to big-time computing as opposed to home and personal computing was managing and leading a project to implement an electronic social care record.

Yourdon: Interesting. Well, there's a related question then for which you might give a very different answer than from what I've heard, and that is the question of role models or mentors along the way, because I would imagine they might have been somewhat different than what I've been hearing from other interviews.

Miller: I'll take a little roundabout way to give you the answer to this question. Having implemented a social care record in Essex, which is quite hard work, one of the things I really discovered is that in a social care organization, you need good leadership. Unless the leadership understands what you're going to do and what you're trying to do, implementing technology doesn't work.

The next job I was headhunted to Suffolk and implemented a social care computer electronic record system there. And probably the most important lesson from Essex was the need to engage with the senior management.

And the person who influenced me probably the most in Suffolk was the Director of Social Services there, who although he did not know about computers or technology, his point was that this technology would be good. And so he invited me, not as director, but as the head of information management, to sit with him and his directors on their management board.

Yourdon: Okay.

Miller: So he allowed me to give strategic input to the business and decisions being made from an electronic record and support role. That meant that when we developed the electronic record at Suffolk, it had primary support from somebody who thought it was a good thing, with the freedom to work with Directors to find out why it was a good thing, and the authority to work with the users to help them to invent the use of the system, so that I wasn't implementing technology. I was implementing a new way of working.

Yourdon: Hmm. Okay.

Miller: And so my prejudices around CIOs is not that they're technology-based, but that they are work-based. It's how people work that's important. Technology just supports it.

Yourdon: Okay, fair enough.

Miller: Now there are two things that came out of that. One is that you have to mediate, I think, as the head of information anyway, between what packages do, what systems do, and what users want to do. You don't just go with the choice of the user because you may not be able to support the technology. But neither do you implement a perfect technology and expect users to adapt their working practices without understanding what they're trying to achieve in their work.

And I think the principle of all IT management that I've had experience with is around that mediation CIO role, which is about discovering what is it the business wants to do and finding the technology that supports what they want to do, and the negotiation with the business that says, "Don't go window-shopping for IT systems; come and let's work out the principles. We're the experts in technology, or at least I know some friends who are who work for me. Let's make technology that supports your workflow that we can then support and that works together across the piece."

Yourdon: Okay.

Miller: So I think the Director of Social Services at Suffolk was probably a key influence then because he was an enabler of technology. He didn't understand it, but he enabled it.

Yourdon: A champion, so to speak. Very interesting.

Miller: A champion, yeah. I think another person was also very influential, and that was the owner of the company, the software house, that we bought the system from. He was influential because he had a huge understanding of how to simplify IT. And I learned from him around the principles of data management, data flows, simplification, and the ability to give the same result to many different people by showing them a screen that looked the way they wanted it to look, but built into a common database. So I learned about simplifying IT, but providing it in a very intuitive way to users and how important that was.

Yourdon: Interesting. There's one last introductory question that I'm curious about. When people start to become groomed or moving in a career path toward a CIO, some of them have had additional education or training, and some have not. And I'm just curious, did they send you off to school, to CIO school of any sort?

Miller: No.

Yourdon: So all on-the-job training?

Miller: I don't think I've had any specific CIO training. I've had business management training, more generic training. I've been to many conferences. I've been to good practice-sharing groups with other people who are aspirational CIOs. But I've never had any specific training. I'm perhaps of a generation before the people who did the specific training. I don't think there were many courses around for CIOs, in the early 1990s.

Yourdon: [laughter] Probably not.

Miller: But I think also this role of CIO is not a Technology Officer. It's about a business manager who is that translator between business requirements, and therefore the training in the business skills is as important as the training in the technology or the understanding of the technology. So my training has been much more about organizational change. And I've had some good training on organizational change. It's been about principles of business management, not about technology. I rely on other people to be experts in technology.

Yourdon: Okay, interesting. All right, probably the central question I've been asking everybody, for which the answers are all over the place, is how you see information technology playing a role to make your constituents, or the people you serve, more effective. What are your dreams in terms of using it to make the world a better place?

Miller: That's a really good question because I work in the public sector. And I work in the public sector because that's my driving motive, to make the world a better place.

Yourdon: Ahh.

Miller: So why am I in technology? I would say by accident. And I would say the accident is that experience working in Essex when the Director said, "Go do the computer system." So my experience, and just what happens in IT, is about using IT to make organizations work more efficiently. It's about being able to control the information flows to help people be more efficient; to be able to automate the stuff to make the organization cheaper and more efficient. About the end of the 1990s, I think it was about '98, the big word "e-government" came out.

Yourdon: Mm-hmm.

Miller: And I was in that bandwagon of people who were saying, "E-government is an incredibly important force to change the way (local government is where I was working then) government works," so rather than being an organization that thinks itself as silo departments, it becomes an organization that's customer-focused, that says to the customer, "You are members of the public, residents of the local authority. You have a collection of things that you need from this authority. How would you like to interact with the authority?"

And the principle then was to create customer service–focused, front-end services to the county council, to make them easier to approach and work with. To make it easier. If you had a problem that crossed social care and education and some of the other services of the county council, you didn't have to go in five different doors to find the services you needed as an individual, but you could go into one door, and from that one door the person in the front-office service would connect you to the services you needed.

Yourdon: Okay.

Miller: In fact, this is the New Brunswick model in Canada. I was very influenced by reading about those services, where they had done things about more efficient front-line services that allowed the resident, the citizen, to access those services in a more intuitive way. When I was in social services, if you looked at the kinds of services provided, the management team was focused on 10 percent of the customers who had high-level needs and had high-level costs. Ninety percent of the customers with low-level needs and low-level costs were in queues waiting to see the social workers.

Yourdon: Aha. Interesting.

Miller: And the way we were able to restructure the organization was to create front-office services to give them the information they needed or even to be able to say, "We can't help you with this problem because it doesn't meet our criteria, but you can try this service." We were able to put in a service that gave a faster, quicker, more responsive service to that citizen than the 90 percent of people who just got stuck in long queues. Also, note that the 10 percent who needed intensive social worker input were able to get to the social worker because there wasn't such a long queue.

Yourdon: Ahh, interesting.

Miller: And that's about—it was not about saving money, although we did, but it was actually about making the organization more responsive to the person who wanted that service. That is how I see IT working, because IT was able to support the front-office service and connect the information back to knowledge and workflow and processes that allowed the 90 percent, the people who were dealing with the 90 percent, who had fewer qualifications to effectively deal consistently with the members of the public and enable them to pass back to the social workers those who did need higher levels of care in a quicker, faster, and therefore cheaper way.

Yourdon: Now you say this movement began in the late '90s, so it's now more than ten years old. Do you still think it has a long way to go, or is it fairly well established at this point?

Miller: I think in many local government areas it's well established. I think there are many services government provides, both from central government and local government and other quango-type organizations, which are still not connected. There are some very good developments in thinking, but it's such a big problem in the public sector to connect everything up. So it's a long time scale.

Yourdon: Does it become progressively more difficult as you go from a local government focus to a national focus?

Miller: Yeah.

Yourdon: Is it a linear scale or an exponential scale?

Miller: It's an exponential scale. It's easier to deal and partner with the people you can see. It is much more difficult to deal with people who are remote to you and to trust and partner, because working together—for instance, in the late '90s, early 2000s to today, Health and Social Care, which is a national and a local organization, have been working much more closely together. That's supported by electronic records.

Yourdon: Ahh, okay.

Miller: That's a national organization dealing with a local organization, so two different trust environments needing to work together.

Yourdon: And exchange information. Appropriate information.

Miller: Confidential information.

Yourdon: I was going to say, "With all the privacy issues associated with that."

Miller: And that's been quite fascinating to see. The developments probably took five years to get off the ground, because nobody knew how to do it. I'm not at all sure that there's comprehensive coverage yet, but there are some very good areas of good practice.

Yourdon: Okay.

Miller: There is the ability now to share information because people mostly work on electronic records. I suppose the working population have become more familiar with working on electronic records. When I was talking back in the mid-'90s, when I was implementing social care systems, this was anathema to social workers.

Yourdon: Hmm.

Miller: I think most are now used to it and indeed demand mobile electronic information, which was a big thing. But the ability to share information with Health has become an expectation rather than a threat. So the mind changes affect the use.

Yourdon: Mm-hmm.

Miller: And I think the role of the CIO is to keep track with and push, when necessary, the agenda. And I think constructive input from the CIO can change the world, or at least a little bit of the world. You have an influence by helping organizations to share and therefore partner and work together, and therefore the citizen gets a better deal.

Yourdon: Now you had mentioned that the buzzword that kind of launched all of this 10, 12 years ago was "e-government." Another one that I wrote down here that we're hearing a lot now about is "Government 2.0" as the counterpart of Web 2.0 or Enterprise 2.0. Is that something that has become significant here in the UK?

Miller: I think that that was always significant. I think that right from the end of the 1990s we were saying, "So how—if we're taking people through the door or on a telephone service, can we even prevent that by giving them Internet information and transactional services?" I think that Health is probably one of the organizations that has gone the farthest to help diagnostic information appear to the citizen on the Web.

Yourdon: Hmm, interesting.

Miller: And they've done that from early 2000 onwards. I think that's developed in a very intensive way. I think the complexity of how we provide services makes it really difficult for citizens to interact on the Web in a comprehensive way, but there are some very good examples. Having said that, there are some very good examples of how government is now trading, doing transactions with citizens through web-based services.

Yourdon: Mm-hmm.

Miller: So income tax forms you can do entirely on the Web. Things like driver vehicle licensing, you can do entirely on the Web, and it's so much easier for citizens to sit at home and do this work rather than try and do everything on paper or go and visit an office. So, yes, I think it's probably at the 25 percent success level at the minute. Rough figure, for government, but the direction of travel is to help people to get what they need quickly and therefore more cheaply for the government and for the individual.

Yourdon: I was actually referring to something—I think of it differently philosophically—which is instead of having the information essentially go top-down, turning it around and having it go bottom-up.

Miller: Ahh, yeah, so the social networking-type of environment.

Yourdon: Yes. For example, in New York City we never did, as citizens, trust the official government information about whether the public transportation was running on time. If you went to the train station, could you catch a train on time? And now we rely on citizens, who contribute the information themselves into a social network. And there are more and more attempts to provide mechanisms for citizens to either input information or actually contribute services that would otherwise be provided in a top-down fashion.

Miller: Well, I think there are two ways citizens can influence their services. One is through using them. The information they provide is then collected based on the way they use them and will modify the way governments react with them, but the bigger one, I think, is the citizen voice.

Yourdon: Yes.

Miller: I think in the UK we are still very unsure as to how to use this citizens' voice. We have had some experiments in the UK. We have a representational democracy, which means that in the UK, if you elect somebody, you elect them to make the decisions for you. So they sit in Parliament to use their judgment to engage in the debate about what are the right laws, what is the right government and for the people.

Yourdon: Mm-hmm.

Miller: There is this wave of opinion, people's opinions, what in the UK we might call the "X-factor" type of opinion from people that comes through the electronic media. This is now providing information to those elected representatives in a fairly prolific way. And the problem that those elected representatives have is to first understand if that electronic voice is representative? How can it be made to be representative? And, secondly, how to hear all those individual comments? How do you possibly pay attention to the volume of electronic comments that are coming from the population, to help them to understand what the public view is.

In Parliament, we have some experiments in some of our committees, which are about inviting comments on bills, on committees' scrutiny of bills. And as the process goes through Parliament, those are difficult to manage because it's difficult to understand if what you get is the true public voice or the lobby public voice or just the electronic-enabled public voice.

Yourdon: Yes.

Miller: So there is an experiment, but not yet a great deal of understanding of how that should and can influence the members when they make decisions. It's the same in government where Number 10—that's the prime minister's office—has been very engaged in trying to connect to the public. They've had a petitions website to try to gauge what issues the public are focused on, what are their priorities? But, again, it's very difficult to know from the petitions they've had, the experiences they've had, what is of value, what is representative, what is lobbying, what is irrelevant to government because they can't do anything about it? It's quite difficult to be able to receive the information and do something with it.

And I think this "Government 2" thing is less about how you enable the comments, although there's something about making that representational, it's what do you do with what you get? How do you process it? How do you manage it? I don't think there's an answer to that yet.

Yourdon: But does your office get involved in these ongoing experiments?

Miller: In as much as members require there to be experiments, and therefore to be able to facilitate public comments into some of the scrutiny going on in Parliament, or some of the legislative activity going on in Parliament, yes. But this has to be a member-led activity because they are the elected representatives. They have to understand what the options are, but then they have to know what to do with the options. And we can't tell them.

Yourdon: Well, I think that's the classic example you were talking about before, the relationship between the business community, in this case, members of Parliament, and the technology people. Now, that is interesting.

Miller: We're very much in a facilitative role in that.

Yourdon: Yes.

Miller: Parliament is 700 years old and it's lived on petitions, paper petitions, and the public being able to access Parliament for 700 years, or perhaps it was probably for the higher class originally, but nowadays, Parliament's main function is to be open to the public. "Electronically open" means something different.

Yourdon: Yes.

Miller: And we haven't got our heads around yet what that means and how to deal with that.

Yourdon: That's a very good point. And I suspect we're going to be seeing a lot more about that in every dimension in the years ahead, especially with all the current news that we're seeing about activity. One of the questions I had was whether IT in your case is expected to enable entirely new things which the business, whether it's Parliament or other parts of government, simply cannot do today. Are you expected to bring completely new possibilities up for their consideration?

Miller: Yes.

Yourdon: Or just improve on what they're now doing?

Miller: Well, I think it's an interesting place to use technology, because we have an interesting customer group, very diverse. It ranges from people who don't really like using computers or electronic mechanisms, to people who are probably world leaders in using electronic information.

Yourdon: Okay.

Miller: So one of the roles for IT in this organization, and our function in this organization is to be able to describe the possible, but also to be able to follow the impossible demands of those people right out at the front. So, for instance, we have had in the last few months debates in either chamber as to whether people can use iPads in the chamber.

Yourdon: [laughter] Ahh, okay.

Miller: Now in both chambers they have voted and said, "Yes, they can." That doesn't sound like a great big thing, does it? Because initially what that means is that Members in either house will have their papers electronically, which is good because it saves printing, it's environmentally efficient, it's timely—there are lots of very good things about it. The impact behind that, the opportunity behind that is to be able to provide the Member in his chamber with more information, instantly, than they've ever had in the past.

Yourdon: Mm-hmm.

Miller: That changes the way the debate happens. It allows Members in the chamber, if they wish, to be able to see what the public is saying about the debate as it's happening.

Yourdon: That's right.

Miller: If they wish. In fact, there was an experiment in the House of Lords where they did a parallel debate. So they did a debate in the chamber, and there was a parallel debate that was open to the public to engage.

Yourdon: Ahh.

Miller: The public didn't engage very much, but, you know, it was a one-off first try. But how does that change democracy and the democratic process? Obviously, if you take it to the extreme, it will change the way democracy works. It will change the way the democratically elected Member is fed information. It changes a tradition. If you just have it as a source of your paper, it won't change very much at all.

Yourdon: Right.

Miller: And our job is to display the opportunities for Members to decide at what pace they want to move.

Yourdon: Okay. That's very interesting. Of course, iPads are a good example of another whole area that I wanted to ask about, which is the new trends that you see helping to shape the future. Almost everyone I've spoken to has focused on mobile technology in one form or another. Is that near the top of your list in terms of new technologies?

Miller: Absolutely, totally. It's mobile individual.

Yourdon: Yes.

Miller: It's not just "mobile," but it's "individual." "I want to use the technology I want to use; please IT organization, don't lock me down."

Yourdon: Aha, okay.

Miller: That's specifically true because our customer group is not a homogeneous group of people. They are people of independence, who can and do make their own choices about what technology they use, what software they use, and how and when they use it.

Yourdon: Okay.

Miller: So our preoccupation at the minute is with a new ICT strategy. Being as old as I am, I can see some trends appearing in IT, and I can go back to the days of the mainframe in the 1980s, when IT told everybody, "This is what you get, and you get it for five hours a day or one hour a day, and we'll crunch numbers for you."

Yourdon: Yes.

Miller: And then about the mid-, early '90s, it was about e-mail and messages. Electronic communication replaced letters. I'm quite surprised when I get a letter these days.

Yourdon: [laughter]

Miller: That was sort of the 1990 to 1995 invention of IT. At the same time, we took IT out of the mainframe environment. It became the business owners' product, and they had their own systems, and they set up IT departments, one of which I managed. And they created small, discrete, beautifully formed IT for very specific purpose.

You get into the late 1990s, and people want to join up this small, discrete information, so you centralize IT again, and you become enterprise IT, and that brings back control. It brings back format; it brings back locked-down information that says, "You work this way because you have to because we can't keep it all safe and we can't predictably manage the information flows unless you do." I think what we're seeing in the late 2000s is a move away from that integrated, hard integration of IT into individual IT.

Yourdon: Ahh.

Miller: People at work want what they get at home. And what they get at home is massive. They can use any product they like to do e-mail by signing up for free. No controls that they are aware of stops them from accessing that from any device anywhere. There is software that they can download anywhere to do what they want to do. And if they can do that at home, why not at work? I think that our ICT strategy here is to try to preserve security around data and to open up the opportunity for people to individually use that data, in whatever software, whatever hardware they want to use.

Yourdon: Okay.

Miller: And that's our challenge: how do we make that happen and keep the data secure? Because the data is about confidence, trust, security, interoperability. So that's our challenge and our strategy over the next five years. For instance, we currently provide a big e-mail service. It's secure. It has network perimeters, security. We barbwire on it. And it means that if you travel out of the Estate, you have a heck of a problem dialing into the network because of all of the security we have.

Yourdon: Right.

Miller: So our question is, where can we put that e-mail service to allow people to get it easily on the move where individually it's secured to them? Can we use Microsoft's cloud service or Google's cloud service? Would it be secure enough for our Members' requirements? Can we do that for the administration? Those are our big questions. Those are the questions we have to ask, and when we look at "can we put it into the cloud?" we're asking, "Is it secure? Can other people crack it? Is it safe? Has it got sovereignty if you put it into a U.S. company's servers?"

Yourdon: [laughter]

Miller: Would the U.S. government be able to demand they could see it? You can imagine, for a UK Parliament, that's an absolute veto.

Yourdon: Oh yes, yes.

Miller: Can we transfer it? If we buy a Microsoft service, can we ever go out of it again?

Yourdon: Actually, a more fundamental question is, do you know where it is? You know, before you ask whether the U.S. can get it, you have to know where it is, that the data is in the U.S. or on some island in the Pacific Ocean.

Miller: Yes, that's exactly the sovereignty issue. So we have big questions about this very attractive offering because it looks like a good cost break if we can move into these big-scale services, these utility services. Can we afford the risk of these other issues, which are security, sovereignty, and transferability?

Yourdon: Is there a fundamental feeling in your world that these problems will eventually be solved?

Miller: Yes.

Yourdon: That it's just a matter of time?

Miller: We think they can be solved. We think they can be solved in the next 12 months. We are actively investigating how to solve them. Our role in IT is to look at our customer group and say, "Actually, what you want is that kind of flexibility. Do we provide it ourselves, or do we provide it cheaper from somewhere that already does it?"

Yourdon: Mm-hmm.

Miller: If we did that, how do we solve these other problems? So our active work is to solve these problems. If, after six months, we say, "We can't solve these problems," then we have to hold until they will be solved. But they will be solved.

Yourdon: Yeah. I certainly find general agreement that this whole cloud model of having an infinitely scalable resource is one that is inevitable—it's a tidal wave.

Miller: Mm-hmm.

Yourdon: It's just a question of whether it's this year or next year or the year after. You know, there's another kind of new trend that a few people have mentioned, and I'm curious to see if it's relevant for you. There's an author in the United States by the name of Clay Shirky who refers to this as the "cognitive surplus." He argues that ours is the first generation now, maybe the generation that's coming out of college, that has the time and interest and computer resources to contribute some part of their surplus brainpower, so to speak, to free things like Wikipedia and thousands of things like that—and that things like this have never happened before in society. Is that sort of concept one that is relevant in your work?

Miller: I think knowledge is a key issue. And I think people like to be engaged in knowledge. I think there are two problems for us and the work that we do. One is about authoritative knowledge. How can we be sure that the collective knowledge has authority? The Wikipedia issue.

Yourdon: You're aware of the comparisons with *Encyclopedia Britannica*?

Miller: I was just going to mention it. There's a one percent maybe variation in the authority and accuracy.

Yourdon: Yeah, and the most amazing is the mean time to repair.

Miller: And look at the administration behind Wikipedia that makes it work that way. Look at the increased controls on Wikipedia.

Yourdon: That's true, that's true.

Miller: Now why did that happen? And that's my second point, information goes out-of-date very quickly. It also needs managing.

Yourdon: Yes.

Miller: And I think that the key for us is to understand whether unmanaged sources of data can sustain themselves over the long period. Or will it need increased management? Now Wikipedia has chosen to put in that increased management in order to keep up its authority level.

Yourdon: Yes, that's true. That's true.

Miller: So my question back is, is that a necessary step?

Yourdon: Ahh. I certainly don't know. [laughter]

Miller: I don't know either. And it's the same question if you like which our Members face when they try to listen to the electorate voice.

Yourdon: That's a good point.

Miller: How can you judge the validity of what you're hearing? How can you deal with the volume of what you're hearing? These are two important questions I think the world has to concentrate on, but there will be an answer. I just don't know what it is yet.

Yourdon: Meanwhile, there's also the economic aspect to this. This whole concept of essentially free software, databases, open source, you know, all of that stuff, has completely transformed the economics of large parts of Africa and other countries. I certainly think that that may be significant—and the CIO of Google thinks that this is going to be transformative in our time.

Miller: It absolutely is transformative, and it's about making software a utility that people engage with and engage on.

Yourdon: Yes. That's true.

Miller: I think it is, I can see the point. I just don't know what the sustainable model is. If I seriously look at investing in a Google model for our users, what do I then do about sustainability and growth and future-proofing? What happens in the now if it's free?

Yourdon: Good question, yeah.

Miller: I don't know, you see? And I think the job of CIOs is to be able to read the market a little bit further forward, and be able to explain it to our customers, so they don't fall off a cliff by trying something too brave.

Yourdon: And too early.

Miller: Or too early. Well, I'm not sure about too early. To me, the Google model is just so attractive. I don't think that it will fail. But what if it did, and we'd invested all our knowledge in that?

Yourdon: Good point.

Miller: On the other hand—there is another hand. We could invest in the very well-known Microsoft and find that we're locked in and have no options. And can't take a future anywhere else. So our job is to make both possible for the future, because there is no answer yet. That's why transferability is the key.

Yourdon: Interesting.

Miller: That we don't get locked in. We own our own data, and we can move it to whatever service is best at the time.

Yourdon: There's another broad area that I want to make sure we have a few minutes to talk about, and that is the opposite side of what we've been discussing so far, the dark side of the force. What are the risks and problems and so forth that keep you awake at night?

Miller: [laughing] Interesting place to work here. You see, I don't get kept awake by the future of technology. I think if we proceed with ambitious caution, we'll find a solution. I don't think it's a difficult impossibility to proceed at a pace that allows you to change track if necessary, as long as you understand that's what you may need to do.

I think the things that keep me awake at night are the more immediate, what's happening now. And that's about the instant services required here.

So when we are working on the electronic services that support the work of the House, there is no time adjustment allowed for failure. They have to work the moment that it's done.

Yourdon: Ahh.

Miller: So immediacy is the thing that is critical because IT is never fully, 100 percent going to work 100 percent of the time. But it has to. So that's a critical business imperative. You know, if you create an agenda for the House business, it has to be available at the time, to the minute, when it has to be available. It has to be available so many hours before it's used in the chamber. Information has to be updated immediately and online within two hours of what they said each day.

Yourdon: Hmm.

Miller: So, you know, you have these time-critical issues. Big-scale text issues are a little bit worrying, I guess, because the technology's so irritating. The thing that worked yesterday fails to work today. Why is that?

[both laughing]

Miller: So that's the irritation factor. And the other things that probably keep me awake are very much more to do with the user. How to keep the communication, how to keep the information flows at the right level, in that right language, that people get it. They get the opportunity, they're not afraid of it, because they trust the solution without it all being proved to them, and not being proved to them in technical language but in language that they understand. How to get that trust, that relationship between IT and the users and how to maintain it?

Yourdon: Interesting.

Miller: That's the key issue. And that is really about hearing, living, breathing the experiences of the user, and showing that you're doing it all the time.

Yourdon: And that leads very naturally to my next question then, which is about the generational changes, because how you live it and breathe it and so forth with an older user may or may not be the same as how you would go about doing it with somebody fresh out of the university. Have you seen fundamental changes in the generation of people not even out of the university these days, they could be teenagers?

Miller: No, it's fascinating. When I joined Parliament in 2005, one Member would not have any computers in his constituency office.

Yourdon: Is that right? My goodness.

Miller: Would not have it. He unfortunately died soon after I joined here. Now every Member, whether enthusiastically or reluctantly, has IT and is dependent on IT. And when I look at the user surveys, Member surveys that we've just done, one of their top needs, across all the services they're given, is IT.

Yourdon: Hmm.

Miller: That's the top key issue for them, so something has significantly changed. In 2010 we had an election, and a third of the House changed. So what I have noticed is, amongst the new Members, a much higher proportion of people who are self-sufficient in IT and ambitious to use IT. The other thing I've noticed, interestingly, is a move away from using the IT that they're just given. A small number, but still a growing percentage, and they're using their own products, mostly Apple. A big change for us.

Yourdon: Interesting.

Miller: From our products to Apple products. So whereas in the last Parliament we had maybe 20 members who were devoted Mac users, we now maybe have 80, maybe more. And with the growth of the iPad, first on the market as that device, without a real competitor yet, it may be twice that number.

Yourdon: I just got my iPad 2 the day before I took the plane over here.

Miller: Ahh, well done! And not very widely available in the UK yet. But we have a queue of people who are waiting for it. We're in fact running a trial with two committees, one in the Commons, one in the Lords, where the members of those committees who have very wide-ranging experience with IT will use these iPads for their committee papers.

Yourdon: Ahh, interesting.

Miller: And they'll take them away and use them however they use them privately, probably e-mail, Word documents, and so forth, but use them in their committee. And of the two committees, which are about 16 members each, one Member on each committee has said no, for different reasons. But only one has said no. The rest are all engaged and saying, "Yes, we see the point. We'll give it a go. We're not all confident, but we'll give it a go."

Yourdon: Interesting.

Miller: To find out what it's like to use that kind of electronic device, to use their imaginations to tell us what's next. And I think that would not have happened in the last Parliament. The change is very fast.

Yourdon: That fast?

Miller: Very significant, led by consumer products that people like. I mean, a little quote for you—this will delight Apple—I gave somebody their iPad, got a little message back a couple of days later: "I think I'm in love!" It's what I call "forgiving technology." It's like the iPhone, you know, it's forgiving technology.

Yourdon: Yes.

Miller: It may even be like the BlackBerry, which is awkward technology. But forgiving technology because people can get their signal.

Yourdon: Yes.

Miller: There are other products that we have provided that are technically superior, but unforgiving, because if they go wrong, they're too complex. They go wrong because they're too complex, a lot of user error. And then people do not forgive them. So I think forgiving technology and the adoption of it is a big change I've seen.

Yourdon: Interesting.

Miller: It makes people more interested in it, more able to experiment. The iPad is representing everything. We've had tablets. They didn't do it.

Yourdon: No?

Miller: They didn't do it because they're too complex. They would take too much time. We've had Berry Lites and laptops.

Yourdon: Mm-hmm, netbooks.

Miller: But it creates a barrier between me and the person I'm talking to, and in our debating chamber, it doesn't work. So the flat divide that is forgiven when it goes wrong has made a huge user turnaround.

Miller: So we have been issuing iPads for probably six months, which is quite advanced for organizations, but I watch users and how they use their IT. That's what the CIO has to do.

Yourdon: I agree.

Miller: Watch, listen, learn, reflect.

Yourdon: I think you've summed it up. Now, I have one minute left, so the final question, and I think it's an appropriate final question, is, so where do you see your own future? Where do you go from here?

Miller: [laughter] That's such a difficult question for me, because I've never planned a career.

Yourdon: I'm astounded at how often I've gotten that answer. Maybe there's some deep truth to that.

Miller: Well, I think, well, the deep truth as far as I'm concerned is I'm fascinated about what I can change. What can I do that has an impact that changes stuff and makes it better? So if I'm interested about what I can change; it's what I can see that I can do that I do next, and mostly that's just been accidental for me. So I haven't ever planned it. So I'm not planning the next phase.

Yourdon: Fair enough. All right, well, thank you.

Vivek Kundra

First CIO of the United States of America

Vivek Kundra is the first Chief Information Officer of the United States, and was appointed to the position by President Obama in February 2009. The Federal CIO is responsible for directing the policy and strategic planning of federal information technology investments, as well as oversight of federal spending on information technology. Three months after his appointment, Mr. Kundra unveiled an IT Dashboard that tracks over $80 billion in federal IT spending, and which is designed to provide CIOs of individual government agencies, the public, and agency leaders unprecedented visibility into the operations and performance of Federal IT investments.

Prior to his current position, Mr. Kundra was Chief Technology Officer for the District of Columbia, after serving as Assistant Secretary of Commerce and Technology for the state of Virginia.

Mr. Kundra was born in New Delhi, India and moved to Tanzania with his family at the age of one, before moving to Washington, DC at the age of eleven.

Ed Yourdon: Given that we do have such a short time, I thought I would focus on just three things. First, what exciting things do you see coming along, somewhat like the cloud that I see you've really latched onto?

And then the dark side of the force, you know, what are the things that keep you awake at night? And the one thing I'm very curious about is your opinion of the impact of the next generation, the kids coming out of school right now and their assumptions and attitudes about social media and technology and the whole works. Do you see that as a significant thing? So in terms of futures, the cloud is a good example of something that's already here but do you see other things coming down the pipeline in the next couple of years that could dramatically change?

Kundra: There are three megatrends that are going to disrupt our current technology landscape. So, if you look at how we deploy technology, the word that I've coined is "digital oil."

Yourdon: Ahh, okay.

Kundra: And the reason I think that technology is like digital oil today is because if you look at just the federal government, we went from 432 data centers to more than 2,000 in about a decade.

Yourdon: I saw those figures.

Kundra: Average utilization of servers in these datacenters is under 26 percent. So you could just imagine the compute power we're throwing out that's not really being utilized. And storage utilization is under 40 percent. Yet, when you look at manufacturing, asset utilization in most industrialized countries, whether it's the United States or Canada, Brazil, the entire European Union, it's about 79 percent.

Yourdon: Wow.

Kundra: So the question before us is why do we accept a 50 percentile differential between how we deploy IT versus our manufacturing base? And the reason I'm calling it "digital oil" is because it is so vital to the prosperity of the country and the prosperity of our economy.

Yourdon: Okay.

Kundra: We are as dependent on IT as we are oil to drive the economy. And what we need to start doing is figuring out what is the equivalent of alternative fuels for technology—and that's why I've been very passionate about the move to the cloud.

Yourdon: Mm-hmm.

Kundra: The ability to massively scale and provide resources on demand and a consumption-based model, rather than just overbuilding, underutilizing, harmful for the environment assets is extremely inefficient and unsustainable.

Yourdon: Okay.

Kundra: There is a tectonic shift in technology driven by three megatrends: one is mobile, two is social, three is cloud.

Yourdon: Okay.

Kundra: All driven by consumerization of IT and the fact that every person, every endpoint is becoming a sensor that's not only consuming information, but it's also generating digital-borne content.

In the public sector scenario, consider this: The National Archives archives one billion pieces of paper a year, and that's all historical content. Think about all the new content this is being generated: blogs, videos, information from sensors across the board—the demand for computing and for storage is beyond anyone's comprehension today.

Yourdon: Okay.

Kundra: Sensors are generating data from intelligent transportation systems to the electrical grid, which requires us to fundamentally rethink our computing models as a result of these megatrends. And underlying all of that is obviously going to be issues around security and privacy.

Yourdon: Right, which is probably the first thing on your list on the dark side of the force. Security and privacy.

Kundra: On some of the issues there, it's not just that it's simply looked at as security and privacy, but it's also when you start making available geospatial data, when social becomes an integral part of human behavior, when it comes to leveraging a lot of the mobile devices, the privacy issues are very serious and they're very real. And from a security perspective, when you look at nation-states building massive capabilities, and in the context of cyber-warfare, when you look at organized crime and you look at the number of phishing attacks and how they're exponentially increasing, we put in charge a four-star general to build that cyber-command because we realize that this new landscape, when you look at it from a military perspective, our command and control systems, and we've gone through many revolutions since the days of the Pony Express.

Yourdon: Right.

Kundra: Our adversaries were constantly trying to disrupt the military command and control systems; the same was true during the telegraph era, and today it's cyber. The other part is to think about how larger parts of our economy are moving to the digital world. Wireless transportation, banking, health care, and energy require that we hardwire security up front.

And we must make sure that we are not focused on the silly notion of "perimeter security," because that's dead.

Yourdon: When you had mentioned the whole consumerization thing, one of the interesting things that I wasn't anticipating—which I've heard from several people in my interviews—is a shift that has taken place from when I got into the field, where everything was top-down. If you go back 50 years, it was the government that first bought computers, to build bombs and things like that, 'cause they were expensive, and now, probably typified most by Google, but really, across the board, it's bottom-up.

Kundra: Mm-hmm.

Yourdon: A lot of the vendors are building products for the consumer marketplace first, 'cause there are lots more of them, and everybody brings their gadget into the office, and then eventually everybody says, "I want an iPad," and so now it's going bottom-up, which is a pretty significant change, I think.

Kundra: I actually think that's a great change. That's how it should have been.

Yourdon: [laughter]

Kundra: One of the first things I did when I came into office was to launch the IT dashboard. To drive transparency on how all of our IT assets were performing across the board. And what you realize very quickly is there's a huge gap between the public and private sector when it comes to information technology. And a big part of that gap is because the villain is mostly the CIOs. They act like villains, they are still tied to the old IT model of command and control while all their customers hate the enterprise IT solutions they are forced to use.

Yourdon: Right.

Kundra: And they pretend, under the guise of security, that they are more secure. To give you a data point, I went up to the Silicon Valley and I spent a lot of time in the Bay Area.

Yourdon: Mm-hmm.

Kundra: And I was talking to all these startups, and I was telling them, "Well, why don't you compete for government business?" because part of what I'm trying to introduce is Darwinian pressure in the public sector because we spend $80 billion a year on IT.

Yourdon: Mm-hmm.

Kundra: How great would it be if we could get some of the most innovative companies in this country to compete for some of these really large contracts? And a lot of the startups told me, "Well, some federal government employees are already using our solution."

Yourdon: [laughter]

Kundra: It's a new world order, and I ask the CIOs a very simple question, which is, "Why is it that everybody hates enterprise software? Nobody's ever said 'I love my user experience.'" And people love some of these consumer solutions.

Yourdon: Right.

Kundra: And part of the reason is also because these guys have monopolies; it's like an IT cartel. Once you win the contract, there aren't really incentives to innovate. So if you have a five-year contract, your incentive is to increase margins. Compare that with the consumer space where every day you're one click away from extinction.

Yourdon: That's right.

Kundra: You're constantly innovating and that isn't happening in the enterprise space. And those companies are actually obsessed with the customer experience, and that's part of what we've done in the federal government. That is why we have focused on going after some of these wasteful projects by killing them or turning them around. We've been able to save $3 billion. These are huge changes in federal IT.

Yourdon: Another thing that I heard which I know you've been involved with for quite some time—I think the best phrase is from a futurist named Clay Shirky with his term the "cognitive surplus"—this idea that probably for the first time in history, society has an excess of brainpower that can be contributed using computers for the greater good, the classic example of which is, of course, Wikipedia.

Kundra: Mm-hmm.

Yourdon: But your *Apps for Democracy*[1] I think is a wonderful example. Now you did that for the city of Washington, didn't you?

Kundra: When I was the chief technology officer in the District of Columbia, one of the problems I was trying to solve was in introducing disruption in government IT, and I realized the only way I could do it was to

---

[1] www.appsfordemocracy.org

change the paradigm, because the way the government buys IT, it's usually through these contracts or grants. And the model was broken, and I realized, "Well, wait a second. What if I put up a challenge and tapped into the ingenuity of our citizens?"

Yourdon: Right.

Kundra: And if by democratizing data and challenging developers to build useful applications? What was amazing about this initiative is we only spent $50,000.

Yourdon: And $3.2 million in savings?

Kundra: Right. I gave people 30 days, and I got 47 applications, which ended up saving about $3.2 million. What would normally have cost millions, I got for 50 grand. And that is why when I came into the Administration, one of the first things I did is launch data.gov.

Yourdon: Okay.

Kundra: We started with 47 data sets, and now we've got over 400,000 data sets. And we also worked with Congress on the America COMPETES Act that now gives every agency the same authorities that DARPA and NASA have to launch challenges and prizes up to $50 million.

Yourdon: Really?

Kundra: Agencies can say, "Here's our problem. We want it solved and are willing to pay $50 million." And crowd-source solutions.

Yourdon: You know, it's fascinating because I present seminars in Rome on Enterprise 2.0, and up until now, the pharmaceutical industry has been one of the best examples of, of this concept.

Kundra: Eli Lilly?

Yourdon: And Pfizer. There's one other one. And the people that I meet in Rome are just astounded and can't believe that anybody would be doing this.

Kundra: Well, have you heard my other example that I use about Rome and the Agora? In the Agora people would convene in a public square to petition their government, to conduct commerce, to socialize.

Yourdon: Right.

Kundra: Now through technology, what you have is a digital public square that's global. So the ability to convene and to harness, especially for this president, who really cares about tapping into the ingenuity of the American people, the power of technology can be used actually to tap into millions of people across the country to solve some of the toughest problems this country faces, rather than a few people behind closed doors, which has been the old, traditional model.

Yourdon: Well, I'm delighted to hear it—it's got this kind of central thrust behind it because the examples I've seen so far have been very few and far between. There's one in New York called *Clever Commute*[2]. But, again, those have been isolated examples. I've had trouble tracking down some. I'd mentioned there was a third area I wanted to chat with you about since I'm watching the clock: your thoughts about the impact that the next generation, the digital natives, or whatever you want to call them, and their impact on how they're going to use technology to impact government or society. Are you optimistic or pessimistic?

Kundra: Well, I'm actually very, very optimistic. And I'll tell you what one of the things that the President did when he came into office. He said he wanted to make sure that government service was cool.

Yourdon: [laughter]

Kundra: We've looked at what the next-generation workforce will look like. Not a year or 2 from now, 10, 15, 20 years from now.

Yourdon: Ahh, okay.

Kundra: The leading trends, whether you're in the Bay Area, you're in Austin, Boston, New York, Silicon Valley. It's nothing like a government office today.

Yourdon: Right.

Kundra: But there are two shining examples. The Patent and Trademark Office is one of the leaders in teleworking, and what they've done is rejected the old model of managing through sight. "If I can see you, I know you're working. But if I don't see you, you're not working."

Yourdon: Right.

Kundra: They've got 50 percent of their workforce teleworking, all over the country. And they're able to attract some of the smartest people across the country, and they've been able to quantify work. It's been an amazing success. The other one is the Government Accountability Office [(GAO)].

Yourdon: Hmm.

---

[2] www.clevercommute.com

Kundra: Now that happened because after the anthrax attack the Senate had to evacuate. They took over the GAO building. And GAO employees had to look at innovative technologies to continue their work. But beyond that, I think, for us to be able to attract the best people in the country, we've got to be able to fundamentally rethink the nature of work and this notion that people are only productive 9-to-5 in a single location.

Yourdon: Mm-hmm.

Kundra: But the most important thing for us is to make sure that what we're doing is that we're recognizing this trend of the rise of employee-owned.

Yourdon: I see. Aha, okay. Do you see any impact coming from the next generation outside of the so-called First World countries? You know, when you get devices that are cheap enough that anyone in the world can afford them, I think that also changes the balance of power in a lot of ways, pretty much illustrated by what's going on in the Middle East right now.

Kundra: Well, absolutely. For example, with what's going on in Egypt and the use of social media, or frugal engineering in India, which is an area that we pay a lot of attention to. When you think of the scale of a country like India and the problems it has to solve with 1.1 billion people, or China, with 1.3 billion people, the approach and the underlying technical architecture is fundamentally different than when you're designing solutions for 310 million people.

Yourdon: Right.

Kundra: We're very interested in looking at some other leapfrog technologies, whether it's in South Africa or in India or in China, in terms of how are they are leapfrogging; what does mobile commerce look like; and as I mentioned, the three megatrends in social, mobile, and cloud, and how they will fundamentally alter development and commerce.

Yourdon: Some guy just found one of his spare PCs in the garage and used that and $500 from his credit card to get it started. And if you extend that, then I assume that the next obvious step is that entrepreneurial startup model is going to operate in China and India and Africa and all over the world. Umm, fascinating.

Kundra: It's exciting.

Yourdon: Yeah, it is exciting. And I'm delighted to hear that there are initiatives underway that, you know, I was unaware of.

Kundra: President Obama has said that we're going to win the future by out-innovating, outcompeting on a global scale. And we're in a very good position because the U.S. economy, and the innovation that's happening, especially in all of these three megatrends is actually leading-edge, whether you look at cloud, you look at what we're doing in the context of digital oil.

Yourdon: Yeah.

Kundra: How do we disrupt that? The key is going to be to make sure that as Clay Christensen says, that the "innovator's dilemma" doesn't kick in.

Yourdon: [laughter]

Kundra: Unfortunately, I've got to run.

Yourdon: I very much appreciate your time.

Paul Strassmann

Former CIO for Kraft Foods Inc., Xerox Corp., U.S. Department of Defense, and NASA

Paul Strassmann *is currently a Distinguished Professor of Information Sciences at the George Mason School of Information Technology. Previously he was the acting Chief Information Officer of NASA, with direct responsibility and accountability for the NASA computing and telecommunication information infrastructure. Before that, he was the Director of Defense Information, where he was responsible for organizing and managing the corporate information management (CIM) program across the U.S. Department of Defense, and where he had policy oversight for the Defense Department's information technology expenditures.*

Mr. Strassmann's earlier career includes the Xerox Corporation, where he began as director of administration and information systems, with worldwide responsibility for all internal Xerox computer activities, and from which he retired as Vice President of Strategic Planning for the Information Products Group. He also held the job of Corporate Information Officer for General Foods, and Chief Information Officer for Kraft Foods Inc. He is also the author of more than 250 articles and nine books on various aspects of information technology.

Ed Yourdon: One of the things I want to ask you about, because of your position, is your opinions about some of the trends you have seen over the years as [a] CIO.

Paul Strassmann: Yeah, there are clearly trends. You must understand that I've been a CIO since '61. And it's all I've done. In other words, there are very few people that I know of who have been in the CIO position as long as I have. Because even today I am basically a professor teaching CIOs.

Yourdon: Fascinating.

Strassmann: And there are very few people who made it over two generations. In other words, they used to fall out and fall off at the end of a generation. And maybe they fell off after the second generation, but the life expectancy of a CIO has always been very short.

Yourdon: Yes. That definitely is true.

Strassmann: And I've been pulling this stunt now for a long time.

Yourdon: [laughter] Ahh… that obviously will give you a better perspective.

Strassmann: If you're looking for a catchphrase for the book, for whatever it's worth, you could say you talked to the oldest holder of the CIO title in, perhaps in the world. Perhaps. You have to validate that.

Yourdon: Well, why don't I start on something that I gather is part of what you're lecturing on, about new trends that might influence the industry in general, whether it's the military or any other industry. Are you spending a lot of time worrying and thinking about things like virtualization and cloud computing and so forth?

Strassmann: Oh absolutely.

Yourdon: Or are there, if you're looking further into the future, are there other things?

Strassmann: Yes. By the way, my course, that I'm starting … has 13 lectures. And they are three-hour lectures, and two of those lectures are on virtualization and cloud computing.

Yourdon: Okay, well, that obviously gives it some great significance.

Strassmann: And the significance is really driven by the economics, the shifting economics of how do you equip an enterprise with information technology that's long-lasting? And so you have to go towards cloud computing.

Yourdon: The less exotic sort of form or sister of that is the virtualization approach, which also seems like a clear-cut economic issue for any large organization. They would have thousands of servers on all over the place.

Strassmann: You know, so-called cloud computing, which means lots of things, is really an extension, a progression from virtualization. The foundations of cloud computing were really laid by a Stanford professor by the name of Mendel—who created the idea of a universal virtualization with capability. That firm became VMware.

Yourdon: Ah, okay.

Strassmann: VMware has now about an 80 percent market share of virtualization. And the virtualization then became the [springboard] for going to the next generation—namely, if you can virtualize all these things, that means you can suddenly draw in huge complexes.

You know, we're talking about billion-dollar data centers. The economics will drive you. Economy of scale will drive you to a huge scale, namely, a cloud. But then you have to do something with software.

Yourdon: Right.

Strassmann: So, I've been following VMware, I'm a shareholder and my son is one of the ringleaders. It's looking at the whole issue of virtualization and cloud computing as a transformation, a whole shifting of the cost structure. And what is really happening with all of this environment is the shifting from a dominant part of the IT budget, which is hardware, to less than 10 percent.

Yourdon: Okay.

Strassmann: And you achieve that through cloud computing and virtualization. And then all of the other stuff is then devoted to other objectives. But when I got started in computing, 90 percent of my budget was hardware. You know, IBM manpower didn't matter.

Yourdon: Right. [laughter]

Strassmann: Manpower was cheap. Today manpower is extremely expensive.

Yourdon: That's right.

Strassmann: I don't know where you are leading with this, but I just want to comment that the whole underlying issue is one of economics.

Yourdon: Well, certainly, I can appreciate that that's the driver, although it's interesting that I participated in a cloud computing conference in Rome a couple of months ago, where you could see there's still enormous resistance—showing that the barrier, the obstacle, is not economics but rather the more familiar things like security and privacy.

Strassmann: Oh, yeah, sure. Sure, that's the usual stuff. That's what's called "friction."

Yourdon: Meaning what, you expect it to fade away?

Strassmann: Oh yeah, it will all be swept away because the economics, the power of the economics will totally, totally dominate, see?

Yourdon: Aha. Interesting. You know, the kind of separation that's more readily apparent right now in the industry is the big, regulated companies versus the smaller companies that have no regulation—where there's less concern about security and privacy and more of a willingness to really take advantage of the economics, versus the more established firms.

Strassmann: Let me give it to you: those are not inconsistent. Security and economics are not inconsistent. Security, depending on how you do the architecture, can be very cheap. The question is, where are you going to put this security?

Yourdon: Ah, okay.

Strassmann: See, you've got lots of places where you can put your first line of defenses.

Yourdon: Right.

Strassmann: Right now everybody's loading their power with firewalls and antiviruses and so forth. You are really like the guy in the cottage 200 years ago—going to Kansas and building a house out of local wood, making his own latrine, and buying a can of kerosene. Now the thing has shifted. Now we are in an urban area now, you are a New Yorker, and the economics of you as contrasted with the farmer in Kansas is totally different. And in the old days, the farmer in Kansas had his own Winchester. That was the security.

Yourdon: Okay.

Strassmann: Well, now we have a different security, but the economics of the police department in New York is totally different to the economics of the guy with the gun in Kansas.

Yourdon: Okay.

Strassmann: So security is a thing that is thrown out without any really thought given to the whole question of what the security issues are and where do you spend your money on security. The Department of Defense now spends over 50 percent of its budget on security. Most of it is wasted.

Yourdon: Because they put it in the wrong place?

Strassmann: Too many places.

Yourdon: Too many places. Oh, okay.

Strassmann: Many places.

Yourdon: Ahh, interesting. And is your argument that because the economics are shifting so rapidly … the security friction will be taken care of because there's so much more money available?

Strassmann: Yeah, well, one of the ways of dealing with the problem of security is to look at the cost of protection, and what do you protect against? Are you protecting yourself against infiltration? And you know, there's all kinds of infiltration. Or are you protecting yourself against exfiltration?

Yourdon: Stuff leaking out?

Strassmann: Yeah. You know, I've been involved with Citicorp, where money went out because of insiders. So every bank today and every financial institution has a problem with exfiltration. And certainly the Department of Defense has a big problem with exfiltration.

Yourdon: Sure.

Strassmann: So then the question is, if you are confronted with infiltration, exfiltration, what are you going to do about it? And how are you going to protect against it?

Yourdon: Okay, interesting. So those technologies are big ones in terms of your vision of the future. What I see of virtualization is that it's no longer a leading-edge or early adopter stuff. It's becoming mainstream.

Strassmann: Yes, it is.

Yourdon: Cloud computing is a little further out.

Strassmann: Well, it depends. You know, I have a list of cloud computing companies. I don't know if you've looked at the list. They're global now. I looked at companies that provide servers that have over 100,000 servers in one building.

Yourdon: Wow.

Strassmann: So a huge amount of business is now being channeled to cloud computing. One of the intriguing things is that many of the startups are experiments—in other words, if you are in a given corporation, and you want to experiment with something, and they don't want to let it into the protected area, you just go out to Amazon and you buy yourself a server, for 25 cents a minute. And you buy the server, a big Dell server, for 25 cents a minute.

Yourdon: Yeah.

Strassmann: So you can feed in an application, a complicated application, and for less than $14, get it done. Pay with a credit card, and you're done. It's thoroughly accepted today.

Yourdon: Yeah, I agree. And then you can try out your idea, and if it fails, you've got no capital.

Strassmann: Well, sure, no problem. And some of the stuff that is available as a service like Google Apps. There are hundreds of thousands of people using Google Apps now.

Yourdon: You're right. A lot of the articles that I've been seeing lately about government agencies switching to Google Apps and Google Mail[1] is driven by the economics, so that if there are concerns about privacy or security, those are dwarfed by the savings.

Strassmann: No, no, no, no. No, they are not dwarfed. They are being taken care of.

Yourdon: Ah, okay.

Strassmann: In other words, you cannot just go and do this without taking care of security. My point is that the security on Amazon EC2 is cheap. They give you very good security. They may actually give you, for the same bucks, 25 cents an hour, a security that's better than anything that you have right now in your data center.

Yourdon: That's a very good point. I hadn't really thought about that: that for a lot of companies, if they do make a comparison, they would have to acknowledge that their existing security is not very good to begin with.

Strassmann: Yeah, the existing security, particularly because of legacy instances, implementation. There are too many damn servers. I'm looking at a population of approximately a quarter of a million servers.

---

[1] Gmail.

Yourdon: Wow. [laughter]

Strassmann: Doing 7,000 major applications and untold number of local homegrown fixes. You know, I'm looking at 750 data centers just in the Department of Defense. You try to tell me that they have security? I mean, you must be kidding.

Yourdon: I remember you giving me similar numbers back in the early '90s about the number of payroll systems you had seen in data centers all over the Defense Department.

Strassmann: Oh, yeah. Oh, yeah.

Yourdon: Well, aside from virtualization and cloud computing, what other key technology trends do you see on the horizon that we should be thinking about or planning for? Particularly if you have a longer horizon than the rest of the CIOs that I'm talking to.

Strassmann: Well, the heart of an enterprise is data. The heart of the enterprise is software.

Yourdon: True.

Strassmann: When you look at the budget of a typical installation, you'll find that the bulk of the people are not in the computer room, but are running around fixing things, downloading things, improving things, and most importantly, doing bridges between system A and system B.

Yourdon: Okay.

Strassmann: Interoperability. So when you look at your budget, you will discover that you may tie up almost all of your available resources on maintenance. It's a killer, absolute killer. And, and in addition to this, what you find is that there's always somebody who needs something—an operator, a financial analyst, a venture capitalist. You know, "I want to do something different. You know, I want to have millisecond response." So they just go and buy something, and they buy it, put it in, and use it. But then somebody either merges it, or combines it, or needs feeds, and that's when they start hiring somebody to do feeds. Protecting the feeds and so forth.

Yourdon: Aha.

Strassmann: So you are really looking at an environment where the technology is largely misused because the integration isn't there. So the big question of integration is, what kinds of applications and through what protocols are you going to be writing those applications? Are web pages to be interoperable?

Yourdon: Okay.

Strassmann: So to answer your question of what is the technology that I view in the next 20, 30 years, it really deals with the subject of integration and service-oriented architecture, where you have a billion-dollar network called the Internet and inside the network survive thousands, sometimes millions of applications that depend on each other. And you don't have the human intervention labor to do all of that. You have to automate the interoperability between data and applications and then have a layer which then will allow a new application to come in, a new app—or 99 cents.

Yourdon: Right.

Strassmann: A button. And that button will have the protocols, so it will go to discover where the pieces are. And from multiple databases it will do what's called a mash-up and bring back an answer to you in the protocol that deals with a certain human interface. So the future is not virtualization, the future is not cloud. The future is really in how a CIO will create an environment which will provide his customers with the ability to operate in an extremely information-rich environment that is extremely complex and that must be secure.

Yourdon: Are you essentially talking about the buzzword that for years and years has been known as enterprise architecture integration?

Strassmann: Sure. Well, this idea has been around for a long time.

Yourdon: And I guess that's my concern. It's been around and it hasn't happened yet.

Strassmann: Well, it hasn't happened for a number of reasons. First, the technology has not been mature. The emphasis on people building their own shanties in Kansas, digging their own latrine, and having a can of kerosene has been very strong.

Yourdon: Right.

Strassmann: There is a whole cohort of contractors who live like that. I mean, the place is full of people who do maintenance programming. That's their business. They would be all blown away.

Yourdon: You've mentioned another aspect of this that I wanted to touch on, and that is the transition from a CIO environment where the enterprise owns and controls the technology versus the world that we're beginning to see more and more of now, of employee-owned technology.

Strassmann: No, no, no, no, no, no. No, the employee owns the buttons, the apps. The infrastructure —which may be either local for a number of reasons or part of a cloud environment—it's somebody else's.

Yourdon: Oh, okay.

Strassmann: So the employee still owns … you know, when you sit down at a Mac, you don't own its code. You don't even know what the code is. So if you think you control technology, don't kid yourself.

Yourdon: Well, you control it in terms of whether you buy a Mac or a Windows machine.

Strassmann: Well, fine, but technology is not the issue anymore. See, for people to go in the way I did it 20, 30 years ago. When I wanted an application, I went in, got a bunch of programmers, we designed it, got a computer and debugged it and did all of the other stuff. But that was home-cooked, that was home-improvised; it was all put together by a bunch of amateurs.

Yourdon: Sure.

Strassmann: Now you have a bunch of people like my son who are really deeply embedded in real fancy software. I mean, *really* fancy software. And they're doing all of that. And it's all available for you by pushing a button.

Yourdon: Okay. One of the battles that I see going on in companies all over the place is the CIO who says, "You can't have one of these. You've got to have a BlackBerry. And I don't like the fact that there are 300,000 apps and you can choose. I want to choose for you."

Strassmann: Well, yes and no. It's an issue because behind all of that thing is the interoperability. Because if I give you an iPod, I have cut a link with my interoperability and my security. I cannot allow that.

Yourdon: Okay. So that's where the real control comes in; it's the interoperability.

Strassmann: It's a question of whether the CIO of the future will really be a sort of master orchestrator, like a conductor—although it's a poor analogy. But it's more in that direction than the CIO of the past.

Yourdon: Okay, interesting. Well, the related question I had is: What was the most significant change or development that you've seen now that your career is, as you say, much longer than anyone else's? Two generations of a career, looking back over 40 or 50 years, what would you say have been the most significant changes?

Strassmann: Maybe a few things. Now you buy everything. And the entire progression since '53 or '54. In other words, in '54 I actually plug-wired the plugboards. Nobody does that anymore. So now you are in a much higher level. The technology is in the wall, and now the issues are much bigger. They have to do with the issue of how the computing environment is going to be harnessed to support your business. And so you've gone away from technology. You still have to understand how to orchestrate the technology.

Yourdon: Mm-hmm.

Strassmann: But then you are moving to a much higher level. And one of the most interesting things that happened in the U.S. Navy, which I consider one of the leading organizations. Last March they decided to abolish the function of information technology as a separate function.

Yourdon: Really?

Strassmann: They created information technology and intelligence into one unit. Because they basically decided information technology is really an arm of intelligence. Totally brought in, totally new character of people, including some technologists. But when you look at the staffing in the organization, it's an intelligence organization.

Yourdon: Interesting.

Strassmann: Because with all these Predators running around doing color video data and stuff like that. The issue is what do you do with this massive, gigabytes-per-second downloads in Afghanistan? That is not an IT problem anymore.

Yourdon: [laughter] Of course not. I could go off on that tangent, but let me go back to this question of what has been significant over the last 40 or 50 years. You had mentioned earlier an obvious transition from the era where hardware was expensive and people were cheap, compared to where we are now. What about kind of an even broader version of that? Certainly I remember when I started, because hardware was so expensive, it was a controlled commodity. We were not allowed into the computer room or even the Xerox room.

Strassmann: Look, I built the Xerox video center that ran the United States. I built it in 1971. It was a block building with a deep cellar for tapes and what-have-you with a nuclear resistor.

Yourdon: [laughter] So that the tapes would survive.

Strassmann: And it had a wire fence, and it was called "Strassmann's concentration camp." And it had guards at the beginning. In other words, the whole thing, I built a data center. And its own uninterrupted power supply, and nobody could come in without permission and clearance and God knows what.

Yourdon: So now 40 years later, we're in a world where the hardware is cheap and is a commodity and available to everybody in some form.

Strassmann: No, not cheap. It's in block houses. You must understand. You can go to Secaucus and see buildings that look like block houses. Those are data centers, and you can't get in. No way.

Yourdon: That's true.

Strassmann: And those block houses, you go in, and there's a row of cages, and in those cages are either dedicated servers or utility servers. And you may have forty, fifty thousand servers in that room. And, by the way, the cost of electricity and air conditioning costs more than the servers. It's just totally different.

Yourdon: Yeah. Certainly, that's an interesting transition when you see the effort that Amazon or Google are making in terms of supporting conservation and, finding sources of energy.

Strassmann: What choice do they have?

Yourdon: Yeah. That's amazing. Well, on some level, though, wouldn't you agree that there are many forms of technology that are almost free for the individual in terms of being able to go down to the local store and buy it and use it?

Strassmann: Oh yeah.

Yourdon: Versus a generation ago.

Strassmann: You know, anybody can go to Radio Shack and buy some fantastic technology.

Yourdon: Right.

Strassmann: The question is, if you have an organization, how do you bring the technology? I have no problem with people going to Radio Shack and buying some widget. My problem arises when they come with technology and want to draw on data that I own. Under what conditions will they be allowed to do that?

Yourdon: What if they create their own data and communicate it with their friends, sort of outside your borders entirely?

Strassmann: Oh, if they want to do social computing—and by the way, we have that problem. In the Navy, 60 percent of transmission today, particularly on ships, you know, the ships go out for 8 months. The guys get bored silly. They do social computing.

Yourdon: [laughter] So it would seem!

Strassmann: And so the real issue is, how do you make sure—because they are using the same transmission circuits, which [are] satellites—how do you make sure that they are not used for infiltration and exfiltration?

Yourdon: Right.

Strassmann: That becomes a very dicey issue. And it's a very detailed issue. It has to do with the design of the software. It's the design of the client or how much do you permit an edition of a browser to be in that machine?

Yourdon: It's obviously a very serious issue within the military. Do you see that elsewhere?

Strassmann: No, it's also in every financial organization.

Yourdon: Well, that's where I was going. Do you see it gravitating, that financial organizations will be the next one?

Strassmann: All commercial. You know, right now, you have this big thing in France because in Peugeot, much of the drawings of their electrical car leaked out to the Chinese.

Yourdon: Ahh, I didn't know that.

Strassmann: Oh yeah. Everybody's got the same problem. Some people talk about it; some don't, but there's a disgruntled employee sitting in a cubicle, with access and password access. And then, then you have things like intelligence like [Aldrich] Ames. Ames who was in counterintelligence. And he rode through CIA and accessed files, which he had no business accessing, but nobody knew.

Yourdon: Is he the one that provided it to the WikiLeaks guy, to [Julian] Assange? Or is that someone else?

Strassmann: No, Ames provided to the Russians.

Yourdon: Yeah. I thought he was the more traditional one. Who is the guy who gave all of the Wiki stuff?

Strassmann: Oh, you know, a low-level sergeant.

Yourdon: But the same problem?

Strassmann: Same problem, exfiltration. And by the way, the stuff that is being reported is defective. The stuff that is reported that he downloaded, he cut a CD, and sent out by mail for WikiLeaks.

Yourdon: Really?

Strassmann: So now you are dealing with a problem. I have several trays in there [pointing to his desktop computer] with CDs. Now, are you going to permit people to burn their own CDs? And, you know, today on a DVD, you can put a big database. Right now, WikiLeaks has a list of all the people who had accounts in the Cayman Islands. You know, that's a three-million download.

Yourdon: Right. [laughter] Amazing. Any other significant changes and developments that you think have really been worth mentioning over your career?

Strassmann: Yeah, the awareness of money. You see, it used to be that everybody was budgeting the cost of money. Much of the cost used to be capital purchase. So everybody, the controllers, were watching capital purchases and head count, and that was it. And it was head count in the data shop. Well, I beat this thing very quickly by deciding to move my output out to the user.

Yourdon: Ahh.

Strassmann: And the clerks loved to be computer operators, so I put the printer out with the users. I reduced head count in my bursting decollection room, which was enormous. Where I showed that it was someone else's payroll. I'm just giving you little tricks you can play, you see? It's a CIO against a moving . . . it's a shell game. So, the real issue is that when you start looking at these big trading rules and you say, "What are these people doing?" Much of what they are doing is actually data processing.

Yourdon: Okay. So that has been a shift.

Strassmann: So you are suddenly seeing a shift which is externalization of IT from an enclave, which was identified as a capital cost enclave to something which is now part of overhead. It's part of the overhead cost. It's a totally different way of looking at it. In other words, the people who are sitting in the room are actually information processors. They do very little trading.

Yourdon: Right.

Strassmann: So, you know, I've been tracking the costs of overhead in the United States, and one of the most interesting cases comes from General Motors. General Motors bought EDS.

Yourdon: I remember that.

Strassmann: I was very much involved in that. What really basically happened is that it showed up as an acquisition capital cost, but the operating cost moved into the overhead of General Motors. So as General Motors started outsourcing ... by the way, General Motors, at the worst time, 87 percent of their cost were purchases of parts.

Yourdon: Wow. Really?

Strassmann: The rest of it was overhead. Information processing. So the ratio of the truth-to-tell ratio went the wrong way. So, coming back to your question, what I do see is recognition that today the bulk of the population of America [are] information processors. Hardly anybody makes anything.

Yourdon: That certainly is true.

Strassmann: So one of perhaps the major insights for your book is that when I look at America and where we are going, I'm seeing the dominant occupation is information processing jobs. Which is not just people in jobs labeled as IT, but people who do information processing.

Yourdon: Across the board.

Strassmann: And, basically we don't have secretaries anymore. So everybody got upgraded. The women became administrators. The women *love* computers because it allows them to upgrade themselves from a secretary position to an administrator.

Yourdon: Aha. Interesting. If there was a list of really significant developments over the last 40 or 50 years, would you include the Internet or the Web or Google or those things?

Strassmann: Oh yeah, yeah. Sure, the Internet is very important.

Yourdon: Okay.

Strassmann: Sure. Very important and growing in importance. There are going to be billions of nodes on the Internet, and it's growing in complexity and there are issues of cost. There are some deep issues of cost—who is actually paying for Internet?

Yourdon: Right.

Strassmann: Who is making a profit out of the Internet? There is increased demand for high bandwidth, so you're talking about 10- to 30-gigabyte circuits. There's also the question of computing at the edge rather than computing in the center in order to reduce latency because if you are in a certain situation, particularly in Wall Street. Some of the trading is now, people are fighting nanosecond delay in differences.

All I'm saying is there's some deep, deep issues here of latency, availability, up time. In other words, is 99.999 percent an acceptable level of reliability? Very difficult to do.

Yourdon: Yeah.

Strassmann: And also that with technical issues, where do you put your redundancies? Because there is no way of improving reliability on a single server. No way, can't be done. I mean, it goes only so far and then you're dealing against the inexorable problem of electrical or mechanical failure. So then you have to start working on the redundancies. So the issues are enormous.

Yourdon: I certainly agree. Let me jump on to an area we've not talked about and I'm certain you have some strong opinions. The whole generational issue. Do you see significant differences in the behavior or attitude of the generation of workers, IT workers, in particular, coming out of college today as opposed to a generation or two generations ago?

Strassmann: Well, it varies. The funny thing is, at the elite end—I have a grandson at Carnegie-Mellon. He's taking a degree in software engineering. You know, this guy is going to be a hotshot.

Yourdon: Right.

Strassmann: And I have another one at Virginia Tech, also doing electrical engineering. So, you know, I'm keeping everybody on the narrow. Those guys are going to be hotshots and they're going to do very well, unless they do something crazy. My son has a PhD from MIT. He's doing extremely well. He's a programmer. Nothing wrong about that, my friend.

Yourdon: Right.

Strassmann: He doesn't want to be a big boss, because that is not where the fun is and where the money is. They pay him extremely well.

Yourdon: But as you say, those are all examples of the elite.

Strassmann: It's the elite. And by the way, that's what the Chinese are going into. You see, the big problem we have is when you look at the Silicon Valley software factories, half of them are not Americans. The class I'm going to be teaching, half of my class will not be Americans.

Yourdon: I think that's only a problem if we make them so miserable that they want to go back or we make it so difficult to get in that they can't get in. I think it's wonderful if we attract them in and they stay here.

Strassmann: Well, it varies, and we cannot get into this. The big problem I have is with the young generation. They're no good, they're really no good. They are superficial. You know, I'm also an educator, so I have them at my class. They don't bore down; they are not engineers.

Yourdon: Ahh, okay.

Strassmann: Their mental state is behavioral, PowerPoint slides, the gloss. And I'm talking about fairly high-level people. I'm talking about rear admirals and up. They're an outgrowth of an education that is not rigorous, that is not science-oriented. I really despair of the current generation. The bulk of it is not good, not suitable.

Yourdon: And you think this has been going on for a generation?

Strassmann: Oh, this has been creeping up since the '60s.

Yourdon: Certainly you hear a lot of people complaining about the level of superficiality of the younger generation, that they don't bore down.

Strassmann: They don't bore down. In other words, you cannot have an in-depth conversation; they will just glide away. They don't have the mental mechanics of an engineer, a scientist to start going into the details and starting to examine how the thing works.

Yourdon: Do you know why that is true? Or how that has happened?

Strassmann: I absolutely blame grade schools, and from grade schools up. It's all this grade school, high school stuff. You know, I have seven grandchildren who have gone through the public school system, so I watch these kids. And some of them are doing very well, and I have one grandchild who is a marvelous kid. He's in California, he's in Davis, the University of California in Davis. He's a nice kid, a very nice personal kid, but he's a fluff. By the way, he's a better personality than my geeks.

Yourdon: [laughter] Well, all of these kids, obviously, are coming out of high school or college with an exposure to technology and information.

Strassmann: Oh they think they know technology. They think they know computers.

Yourdon: Okay.

Strassmann: I mean, please, give me a break. They have learned how to operate toys.

Yourdon: True. And I'm not just talking about the ones that are going to go into a formal career of IT but, generally speaking, the white-collar workers who come into the workforce with their toys. And, as you say, they don't have the ability to bore down into any problem. Do you see them making bad use of their toys or superficial use of their toys?

Strassmann: Well, it varies. They just can't cope with it, so you hire more people to do less and less. And then you always find a contractor. And then you hire a contractor to do the contract. And then the contractor provides the brains, the analysis, but the contractor will make sure that whatever the contractor does for you is not fungible, which means that the contractor will stay there for a long time.

Yourdon: Or come back periodically to tweak it?

Strassmann: Yeah, yeah. And, so, I'm very unhappy with the modern generation. They are just not . . . this is not an information society.

Yourdon: Could it also possibly be, at least partly, that they have a whole different focus instead of the priorities their parents' generation did? Let me give you an example. I went out to California in the fairly early days of the whole Web 2.0 movement and talked to one guy in a start-up company who said, "Today's colleges have never seen Microsoft Outlook. And if they did, they would be horrified, not just by the ugly user interface, but by its task orientation." Which appeals to me, because I get up in the morning and my first question is, "What tasks do I have today?" which is often a function of the e-mail messages I've gotten overnight, with people demanding this or that and everything.

Strassmann: Yeah.

Yourdon: Well, this fellow in California said the average college kid gets up and his first question is, "Where are my friends and what are they doing? And how can I find them?"

Strassmann: It's social. It's social.

Yourdon: So they need tools, calendars, and things of that sort that cater to that orientation. And they find the older generation of tools completely alien from that perspective.

Strassmann: Let me just say, everything was fine until three years ago, when things went to hell.

Yourdon: What happened then?

Strassmann: We have now $15 trillion's worth of debt and going up.

Yourdon: [laughter] Okay.

Strassmann: So everybody was fiddling and singing while it looked like everything was just great. Suddenly, the young people have 20 percent or more unemployment. Can't get jobs. There are no jobs there, because the manufacturing jobs are gone. The information jobs are not available because I need now less and less information people, and I will only hire the Carnegie-Mellon guys who can really do the job for me.

Yourdon: Yeah.

Strassmann: So we've got a problem. We've got a social problem. Now in Tunisia, you know, there was 30 percent unemployment for people under 25. Well, they're going to have a revolution. You are going to have a social problem in the United States with a large mass of unemployed, young, college-educated people who think they're entitled to a job of consequence.

Yourdon: Aha.

Strassmann: So the growth in America among the intellectuals has been in government-supported activities. Enormous growth.

Yourdon: Interesting. Well, does all of this provide any guidance or recommendations for the CIO? What should you do with this wave of graduates coming in now?

Strassmann: Do exactly what I've always done.

Yourdon: Which is what?

Strassmann: I've done this consistently. What I've done starting at General Foods, I made sure that I gave summer jobs to people that I could handpick.

Yourdon: Okay.

Strassmann: So you handpick them. Now, half of them will be gone. But you watch them, you give them a summer job, which is better than any other summer job they can get.

Yourdon: Absolutely. I'm one of those people. [laughter]

Strassmann: Yeah, and, and some of these guys actually went to grad school and were still working and then they got full jobs. And then when I moved to Xerox, they moved with me.

Yourdon: Oh, that's right. You started that way, too, when you were at the Sloan School.

Strassmann: So, my advice to the CIOs today is what the baseball people do. Have a training farm somewhere. You just train them and then you get the good guys.

Yourdon: So that's how he or she can groom their own IT staff. What do they do with the hundreds or thousands of people they see being hired into the marketing department or finance department, all of these other people?

Strassmann: You can't do that. You're a CIO. You have a given power position. You have a budget.

Yourdon: Okay.

Strassmann: Everybody has a budget, okay? So the question is what are you going to do? You're asking me what practical recommendation do I have for CIOs, and my answer is, grow the young guys and nurture them. And bring them along.

Yourdon: But, as for all those other people? Because part of the problem is that they're bringing their own toys with them and their own expectations about the technology they'll use.

Strassmann: Yeah, but up to a point. They can bring their own toys, but you cannot allow those toys to come into the database. You must understand, when all is said and done, the CIO is a guy with a big stick. He has a budget, he has a big stick, and he has power.

Yourdon: Right.

Strassmann: Now, if you don't have power and you don't have budget, you are nothing. So, let's talk about practical politics, the Machiavellian view of the situation. As a CIO, you must maintain a position of power. Otherwise, you're gonna find yourself out of a job.

Yourdon: And how do you do that? How do you maintain this position of power?

Strassmann: Well, it varies. At General Foods I created an alliance with the CFO, who really then was willing . . . that was the first time ever. You must understand, the battle between the CFO and the CIO is as old as … this is classic.

Yourdon: Sure.

Strassmann: The CFO always used to own this thing. And also sucked off most of the output out of the IT. And this lasted for a long time, for some organizations.

Yourdon: Probably a generation or more.

Strassmann: Oh, almost a generation. It varies from place to place. What happened was that at General Foods, the controller—a guy by the name of McDade—used to be MacArthur's intelligence officer.

Yourdon: Really?

Strassmann: Yes. And so McDade and I go out for lunch, and McDade is just trying to size me up. I'm the new guy on the block. And I said, "You know, the problem is that you control it all now, and you think you have control, but these marketing guys are really on their way out, doing their own thing." And the big issue in those days was advertising. And the money that Finance would spend and control and the stuff they were controlling at the factory was this much [gesturing with thumb and index finger close together]. The big money at General Foods was for advertising. And I said, "Well, Tom, you now, these guys go out to BBDO[2] . . ."

Yourdon: Right.

Strassmann: "And renting 7090s and really playing the big game, and this is getting away from you." So McDade looks at me. He said, "I understand now." Now, I was just a low guy when a week later I become the director of information for General Foods.

Yourdon: [laughter] Aha.

Strassmann: And so that's when the game played, and I had an alliance with McDade; then McDade decided to retire and I was his retirement play. I mean, he was an elderly gentleman, a very fine, educated, Harvard kind of person that used to gravitate toward CIA. Yale and Harvard people used to go to the CIA.

Yourdon: That's right.

Strassmann: See, that's the way it used to be done. The moment McDade retired, of course, all the knives were out. The positions of all the controllers was, "We're going to cut his throat." Well, as they were ready to cut my throat, I get a phone call from the controller of Kraft: "You know, we hear good things about you. Would you like to come over as director of information for all Kraft worldwide?" And I said, "Kraft? You know, I'm not sure, you know, as compared with General Foods." He said, "Well, you know what? Why don't you have a look at our financial statement?" It turns out Kraft was much bigger than General Foods.

Yourdon: [laughter]

Strassmann: And there was a raise. So I just inherited one controller and went to work for another controller. So you create alliances. When I got

---

[2] A global advertising agency.

into the Department of Defense, the issue was one of alliances. I came to the Department of Defense when the Soviet Union gave up.

Yourdon: That's right.

Strassmann: Congress decided to declare a peace dividend: $74 billion. And Congress can just take the money, yank the money out, and it's gone. So as they yank it out, they say, "Oh, by the way, we're going to leave you three billion to do efficiency. You're going to make it up with efficiency." Cheney turns around and brings in the vice chairman of General Motors as his deputy secretary. Now if you understand politics, the secretary is Mr. Outside, the deputy secretary is Mr. Inside.

Yourdon: Right.

Strassmann: Okay. The deputy secretary, an outstanding MIT engineer, a spectacular engineer, had enough of General Motors and Mr. Perot, so he was ready to roll over. He comes into the Pentagon, looks around, and well, months later, he says, "I'm going to start a corporate information management initiative. And I know just the bastard who knows how to do it."

Yourdon: [laughter]

Strassmann: Because I did a hatchet man's job at General Motors. I took about $300 million out of Mr. Perot. So he brought me in. So I was Atwood's man, and everyone knew in the building that I saw Atwood once a week. You know, the rest of it is just details.

Yourdon: Yeah.

Strassmann: So from a political standpoint, if you want to be a CIO, you must have an alliance with a source of power. Otherwise you can't play.

Yourdon: Interesting. Well, that plays into my next question, and, in fact, you may have given the answer. Obviously if you're a CIO and you've got lots of people below you, you can usually spot one or two aspiring CIOs— the person who says, "Some day I want his job."

Strassmann: Oh sure.

Yourdon: What's the key advice that you would give that person?

Strassmann: Give them hell. Just give them as much work as they can carry, just overload them, just break them.

Yourdon: Break who? This aspiring CIO?

Strassmann: Break them with work.

Yourdon: Oh, I see.

Strassmann: Just see how much they can do. A good man can do an infinite amount of work.

Yourdon: So your advice to aspiring CIOs would be: show your ability to take on an enormous amount of work and succeed with it?

Strassmann: Oh yeah. And they may stay with you, they may go somewhere else, who knows? But you're going to get a couple of years of good work out of them.

Yourdon: Oh, okay.

Strassmann: But some of these are loyalties, which then persist. So when you move from Kraft to Xerox, there's a whole bunch of people who come over to Xerox.

Yourdon: Interesting. That actually is part of a related question, which I hadn't really thought of when I started this whole thing— and that is, CIOs generally have a whole team of immediate subordinates that help them get their job done, and the question here is: as a CIO, what key qualities or characteristics do you look for among the people that form that team that you depend on?

Strassmann: Hard work. Long hours.

Yourdon: Okay.

Strassmann: When there is a crisis, they're always available.

Yourdon: Ahh, okay. Something I've heard that I didn't expect is CIOs telling me, "I want people on my team that I can get along with, because if you're going to be working hard, 12 hours a day, you want to have people you like."

Strassmann: Oh, you have to get along, but you don't have to be buddies, everybody's buddies. I don't believe in that.

Yourdon: Okay.

Strassmann: Everybody knew I was fair, but I was a bastard. I really was. I was driving to consolidate data centers at Xerox in order to come into a company that only 67 percent of its bills got out on time. Inheriting a data center run by local controllers and mash it all together in two years. You know, that took some muscle.

Yourdon: And in terms of looking for the people who were going to help you do that, then, you were mostly looking for people who would work really hard, be equally tough?

Strassmann: Yeah, you needed people who really go and work.

Yourdon: And who would be there if there was a crisis?

Strassmann: Yeah, you know, this is the military view. You must understand that if you were a commanding officer. You must understand that I am a military man. You know my military service? My father was a military man, one of the few Jews who had a command of a regiment in World War I.

Yourdon: Ahh, okay.

Strassmann: So, I go back. And in the military, when you go out there and there's a bunch of bad guys out there, you know the team spirit and the dedication and the commitment and the loyalties are very important.

Yourdon: That certainly does make sense. But let's go further with that. If you consider that sort of thing a priority, have you seen situations where some of the other business executives might misunderstand or feel differently?

Strassmann: Oh, absolutely. You know, there is an absolute classic thing against a controller and that never goes away. As a matter of fact, Harvard Business School has a case study of a division controller at Xerox versus Strassmann. There is such a case study.

Yourdon: Aha.

Strassmann: And this guy, who hoped to be the president at Xerox, his name was Engelman. He decides he's going to attack the IT establishment when I was ready to take computers away from these little places where they were accumulating their own enclaves of power. And I had none of that. Well, you know, it's nasty stuff, nasty stuff.

Yourdon: And so that just gets to be a power struggle?

Strassmann: Well, it has to be done. First, it has to be done in a very gentlemanly way. Never personalities.

Yourdon: Okay.

Strassmann: You never use personalities. You have to make sure you tow the line on HR-related issues in tough situations so that you are bulletproof if things get ugly. And there have been issues, including legal cases.

Yourdon: Mm-hmm.

Strassmann: And then you have to spend time with lawyers, because you have to spend time finding out what is feasible and what can be done and what accommodations can be made. This is a tough business. To be a CIO is a tough, tough business.

Yourdon: Yes. Certainly, I am coming to appreciate that more and more as I talk to people. Actually, that leads us to the next question, which is: it's a tough business, but if you succeed, then what? You know, you say you're still a CIO in a sense, and you've gone on obviously to kind of an advisory, mentoring, professorship role.

Strassmann: Well, what happened was I did my bit, 18 years at Xerox. And Xerox is going down the hill also.

Yourdon: Right.

Strassmann: Okay? So there's always a time to bail out. And then when you bail out, do you look for another CIO job or do you become a consultant? You know, the usual stuff? To become a consultant is death, I mean, that's death. A CIO who becomes a consultant, it hardly ever works. And I know lots of CIOs who have tried this thing and who just couldn't engage.

Yourdon: Well, but it sounds in your case that there were a couple of situations where you weren't a consultant in the traditional definition, but you contracted in to spend a certain amount of time doing consulting work.

Strassmann: Yeah, I spent a year with AT&T. The vice president of IT for AT&T hired me to do a specific job, and I spent a year there.

Yourdon: In a sense, General Motors did a similar thing.

Strassmann: I have never done what's called "spot consulting." Here and there I give a speech, or what-have-you, but I've never done what's called "taking consulting jobs." I look at the things. And this Defense Department thing just came over the transit. Now, I've done lots of things for the Department of Defense before. In other words, my approach is usually suitable for lots of things for lots of people.

Sometimes for no compensation. And sometimes it pays off and sometimes it doesn't. So, I did a number of things for General Motors and then I end up in the Department of Defense, and I stay in the Department of Defense. My biggest confrontation in the Department of Defense was with the controller of the Department of Defense because the moment I walked into the Department of Defense, I said, "We cannot leave IT under the controller."

[joint laughter]

Strassmann: I've done the same thing over and over again. There's a procedure for doing this thing, and there were a number of reasons to yank it out from the controller, because the controller didn't really control anything. The controller just controlled capital budget, which was not the issue. So, the thing is yanked out and put into a separate organization. It gets a very high position, by the way. You know, I don't even want to brag about the kind of position I had. So I do my Department of Defense job. And then, of course, we were going to do it for eight years, but time runs out because of the election. So Clinton comes in—I will not work for Clinton or any of his appointees, which by the way turned out to be a disaster anyway. So, I go off and then look around, and then some people say, "You know what? We would like you to do some teaching for us." So I start liking the academic thing. The academic thing gives you a tremendous amount of freedom.

Yourdon: Right.

Strassmann: You go somewhere with a card, "I'm a consultant." You know, that's terrible. If you come in as a distinguished professor, it's, "Okay, well." It's the same person, but it's different. So I do this, and then one day I get a phone call from NASA. "Umm, we have a problem with NASA. We have a new administrator." "Who is the new administrator?" Well, the controller from the Department of Defense now becomes the administrator of NASA because NASA has deep financial problems, so they yanked out the financial guy and put him in charge of NASA. Stupid thing. "And [laughter] he thinks very highly of you. Would you come down and just review the situation?"

So I go down to NASA, arrive early in the morning. . . I know that these people always work early in the morning, so I arrive early in the morning. Very important thing, by the way. The key levels in the government, people start working at 7:00 or 6:45.

Yourdon: Ahh.

Strassmann: Oh yeah. They show up early. They show me the whole thing. Then I have lunch. After lunch, they say, "The administrator would like to see you." So I go in and there is my friend, Sean O'Keefe, the administrator: "Oh, so nice to see you. I'm so glad you came. Please tell me what you have seen." And I just dump it on him. I said, "You guys are so screwed up. You guys don't know what you're doing. You are wasting money. You are spending money with Peat, Marwick, [Mitchell & Co.], a billion dollars on something that could be done on a small computer." They had a big SAP program, which can suck in an enormous amount of money without ever showing any results.

Yourdon: [laughter]

Strassmann: So, Sean O'Keefe sits there and all of his guys, they're all lots and lots of smiling. And I just say, "Look guys. I don't know what I can do for you guys because you have made a commitment, you have a contract, you are going to be spending a billion dollars on something totally useless. The various centers are totally independent computers. I don't know what to do for you." So after I finish this thing, O'Keefe turns around and says, "Well, Strassmann, you come here and you straighten it out."

I said, "Well, you know, guys, I just finished six years in Washington. You don't want me to come to Washington."

"Well, we're going to make it attractive for you."

I said, "Well, you know, I will have to talk to my wife. Let me go home and think about it."

So O'Keefe, who is a really sharp diplomat says, "Well, if you go home, you'll never come back. You know what? I'm going to make a bet with you. I'm going to offer you the job of CIO of NASA, and if you accept, I'm going to have a badge from NASA for you by five o'clock this afternoon."

And this is like three o'clock in the afternoon. Now, I know enough about Washington to know that that can't be done.

Yourdon: Right.

Strassmann: You know, you have civil servants and on and on. It's what's called a "senior executive position."

Yourdon: Right.

Strassmann: And I'm stupid. I'm really stupid. This is a smart Irish man. And he says, "I'm going to put you on my payroll." And so I said, "Okay, sure. If you can do it by five o'clock, I'll take the job," sort of laughing, like, "No way." Sean O'Keefe picks up the phone. Lawyers, personnel people start walking into the room. They all said they were just waiting. The whole thing was a setup! At five o'clock, I had a badge as the CIO of NASA!

Yourdon: That's amazing.

Strassmann: Now, you know, and this is my clear adversary, who I've been fighting tooth and nail. He lost the battle, because we took IT out of the controller's department in the Department of Defense. You know, that's a 30-billion-dollar piece of money.

Yourdon: Yes.

Strassmann: So then I'm stuck for a year. I say, "Okay, Sean, I'm going to give you a year." I'm just giving you vignettes of what ... it's a game.

Yourdon: Is it a game you would recommend to other successful CIOs when they feel that they've reached the end of their journey?

Strassmann: Of course. Absolutely.

Yourdon: So never become a consultant, but look for interesting assignments.

Strassmann: Look for assignments that you can leverage. And there are several assignments that can be leveraged. And never work for Peat, Marwick & Mitchell,[3] or Deloitte. They burn you up.

Yourdon: Have you seen CIOs trying to move up to the next level, [to] CEOs?

Strassmann: Oh yes, oh yeah.

Yourdon: Are there many success stories?

Strassmann: Oh yes, there are many, quite a few. And the reason is that these guys are inside the power structure, and they create alliances and they are acceptable. And they have become politically acceptable. They also know a great deal about the company, because as a CIO you really learn the company, particularly if you do it the right way—namely, you bore down and you see who connects, who talks to who.

Yourdon: And, obviously, more and more companies are beginning to realize that they live or die with their information.

Strassmann: Oh yeah. And so the CIO who is doing the right political moves and is doing the right homework, understanding the infrastructure and the way the blood vessels function, the nervous system ... this guy, after three or four years, knows a great deal of how the place operates because all the other guys are functional. They are marketing or they are lawyers or somebody else.

Yourdon: It was probably 20 years ago, I think, that John Reed became the CEO of Citibank and he came out of its IT department. I don't know if he had been CIO.

Strassmann: Yes, he was. I know John Reed. Oh, John Reed came to see me.

---

[3] Peat Marwick International merged with Klynveld Main Goerdeler to become KPMG in 1987.

Yourdon: He came out of the Sloan School.

Strassmann: Oh yeah. John Reed hired me.

Yourdon: Ahh, okay. I was just saying that he was the only example that I remember off-hand of somebody rising up through IT. There are probably lots more.

Strassmann: There are others, yeah, there are others.

Yourdon: There are probably an equal number of situations where the CIO feels just completely burned out because he's been fighting all those battles and maybe wasn't prepared for.

Strassmann: Oh, you don't fight battles. The answer is, you always pick your battles, and pick very few. And you always pick the battles that you know you cannot lose.

Yourdon: Oh, okay.

Strassmann: Because if you lose, you have to leave. The worst thing is for a CIO to lose a battle and stay around. He's a living dead guy.

Yourdon: Aha, okay. Well, for a long time, as you know, the life expectancy of a CIO has been about two years or even a little bit less.

Strassmann: Oh yes.

Yourdon: Now is that because they've lost battles?

Strassmann: No, no, no. There are lots of reasons, but let me tell you basically what the flaw is. The people who are hiring the CIO don't know what they want the guy to do. They haven't cleaned up the power structure. So they hire somebody with a totally mistaken idea of what this guy's supposed to do.

Yourdon: From the outside, usually?

Strassmann: Oh, from the outside. This is the two-year CIO. So they come in, the guy sits down, gets an office, and then he has to decide what to do. And then he has to scramble for everything. He does not know what his budget is; he doesn't know who's his rabbi. You know, you always need a rabbi.

Yourdon: Yes, yes.

Strassmann: So, after a year, the top executives look and say, "Well, we really didn't make the right choice. He's the wrong guy." He's not the wrong guy. The guys who picked him were the wrong guys because they've never done the work. They've never done . . . one of the things that your book can do is to bring into a CFO/CEO position a thinking of what it takes to make a CIO a success.

Yourdon: Okay.

Strassmann: You see, the CIO cannot be a success unless somebody wants him to be a success.

Yourdon: But that requires a fairly clear understanding of what the role needs to be and what that role needs to be.

Strassmann: Yeah. And then you hire the right person for that role.

Yourdon: Do you see many situations where the CIO rises up through the ranks, as opposed to being chosen and brought in from the outside?

Strassmann: Very rarely. It does happen. There are some exceptions. I had people working for me at Xerox because I had a real mean training school in the data center, and some of them worked their way up from shift supervisor to CIO.

Yourdon: Wow.

Strassmann: But they were exceptional. I mean, there are such cases.

Yourdon: Actually, there's a variation on that that I have now begun to see, and interesting that you should mention Citibank. Citibank is one of many large companies that has multiple CIOs. I have been trying to contact one particular CIO. Well, it turns out that he's not *the* CIO. He's one of ten.

Strassmann: Always, there are lots of CIOs around.

Yourdon: And especially with the big multinational companies these days. So maybe they're at the sub-CIO level and there's more of this rising up through the ranks. But if not, the question becomes, where do CIOs come from? They're not born into that role, so they have to make a jump. Maybe you jump from position X in one company to CIO in another company? Is that the more common way of doing things?

Strassmann: You know, it's very hard to generalize. I've jumped. You know, I've been with General Foods, Kraft, and Xerox. The Department of Defense and NASA. Five. Okay? So I've been in this business since, depending on how you count it, I've been in this business for 60 years. So I had 5 jobs in 60 years. On the average, you know, that's ...

Yourdon: That's a lot longer than average.

Strassmann: The question is, are these jobs additive? Or just musical chairs? One advice I would like to give to everybody, very important: When you are a CIO, you are also a programmer.

Yourdon: Aha.

Strassmann: You never let go of the craft. You never let go of it . . . I've published now 300 papers. I usually write papers because there's something I don't know about. And the best way to learn something is write a paper about it, as you undoubtedly know. The only person who ever learns anything is the professor, by the way.

Yourdon: [laughter]

Strassmann: The professor learns much more than the student. Guess why I'm teaching a course on cyber-operations?

Yourdon: So you can learn about it.

Strassmann: I am learning this stuff! I've spent the last two and a half months learning this stuff. So, so the craft . . . you must understand there's a fundamental craft that you have to nurture. You cannot let go of that.

Yourdon: Now, once you got into the business world, were there business mentors or role models that kind of gave you a sense of how to behave or, what was important versus not important?

Strassmann: I would say one of the great experiences was when I arrived at Xerox. I arrived on a Monday, reported to work at 8:30, and at 10:30 a gray-haired gentleman walked into my room and says, "I'm Joe Wilson [the CEO of Xerox]."

Yourdon: "Just call me Joe." I read that part of your book.

Strassmann: Yes, "just call me Joe." And it is that humility. See, there is a certain sense of decency and ethics which is very important. You know, it's power struggles, but it has been always decent, it always has to be ethical, it always has to be done with recognition of people. Now, I violated that maybe once or twice, and I'm really sorry about it—when I sort of acted harshly, retaliated against certain individuals. But that's not the way to operate.

Yourdon: Do you think that kind of behavior has largely disappeared in American business today?

Strassmann: Oh, American business, so far as I know, is extremely confrontational now. Too confrontational.

Yourdon: And certainly the kind of behavior you read about and hear about in Silicon Valley is kind of, you know, the epitome of the IT world. It seems like a lot of backstabbing and confrontational behavior.

Strassmann: Well, you know, Citicorp was just infested with that. I mean, it was a sick, sick situation.

John Reed hired three outsiders to come in and have a look at his place. We went around, visited lots of Citi locations. And we came back with a remark that the issue was not technology, because the technology was good, but it was the confrontation and the continual conflict which was tearing the place apart.

Yourdon: How long ago was this?

Strassmann: [1995], '96.

Yourdon: Interesting, interesting. One of the other things, of course, that is often true in the Silicon Valley kind of IT world is companies being run by very young and often somewhat inexperienced and somewhat immature people, who may not have learned proper behavior, by being part of an organization where they could watch others.

Strassmann: Oh, you learn your behavior from your parents, my friend. I mean, don't wait for corporations to straighten out your behavior.

Yourdon: Well, parents first and foremost, of course, but also your entire upbringing and schools and so on. You're right; it's not just in the business world. Although I think that people will often see a lot of bad examples in the business world. If you were brought up in a certain way and suddenly find yourself in a backstabbing culture, that's got to be a culture shock.

Strassmann: Yeah. My years with Kraft, by the way, were very nice. These were hard-working people. They were all milkmen starting local routes. Hard-working, hard-drinking, very nice people. It wasn't much money, but it was pleasant. It was very genteel.

Yourdon: Hmm, interesting. How is it by contrast in the military? I mean, the people who end up doing the computer stuff . . . some of them may have come into it right from university, but don't some of them come from a more traditional, West Point kind of culture?

Strassmann: Yeah, but let me tell you something. I find a larger collection of gentlemen of substance in the military than in corporate America. Particularly in the Navy.

Yourdon: Really?

Strassmann: Oh, yes. I mean, the rough kind of in-your-face approach is very much scoffed at. These guys will never make a promotion, because you've got to go through lots of steps before you get up to admiral. These are all gentlemen, every one of them. They may have different opinions, they may be backwards, they are obsolete, but they are gentlemen.

Yourdon: Now does this start at Annapolis and carry them all the way through?

Strassmann: They don't even get into Annapolis.

Yourdon: Unless they have that foundation. Oh, okay.

Strassmann: By the way, my grandson got a congressional nomination for Annapolis.

Yourdon: Congratulations!

Strassmann: But they decided he's a geek and he would only make ship captain, so they sent him to Carnegie-Mellon, and they are paying for him.

Yourdon: One last technical question and then I will leave you alone. One of the popular IT things these days is the agile development approach, which seems to also have some impact on project management. It's not just a technical way of developing systems. But have you seen any advantages or disadvantages of agile systems development from a management perspective?

Strassmann: [laughter] Let me say that the word "agile"—lots of things get peddled under that thing.

Yourdon: True.

Strassmann: The more I look at things, particularly in the last 20 years, the more I'm concerned not about the development, but the architecture, the design, you know, how are the relationships set today? Who's really deciding what kind of databases, what kind of metadata to put into place?

Yourdon: Okay.

Strassmann: You can do lots of agile development extremely inefficiently if the thing is not put together with any kind of a sense. Lots of little ants are moving all kinds of twigs all over the place.

Yourdon: [laughter] That's a nice metaphor. Okay.

Strassmann: I think that's great. But I have not spent time on that. I really have not spent time on that. I'm more concerned about the things which are not being done to make it even possible for people to do development.

Yourdon: Well, you're looking at things, as you said earlier, in terms of a 40-year or 50-year lifecycle. So it's one thing to move twigs around, but the twigs will get blown away in a windstorm.

Strassmann: See, one of the most important issues is, what will be the life of the code and how maintainable the code will be. Has this code been agilely developed for a one-year lifetime and then be junked and thrown away?

Yourdon: Some things are, but, of course, you and I are old enough to know that some things we thought would be thrown away in a year have lived 25 or 30 years, so that's the big surprise.

Strassmann: And the difference between what gets thrown away and what doesn't get thrown away: Has it been embedded into a framework? See, I'm very much concerned about data.

Yourdon: Okay.

Strassmann: And have these people really answered the question of how well this particular application gets the data securely? Now, the code itself—particularly if I have an infrastructure in place—infrastructure is a service, in other words, a cloud service which provides an infrastructure. The infrastructure, I don't have to do. If the front end you throw away every three months, I don't care.

Yourdon: Okay.

Strassmann: The problem is to stack. And the stack is data, communication infrastructure, the coding infrastructure, the interoperability, metadata, connectivity, the protocol. I mean, there's layers in a stack.

Yourdon: Right.

Strassmann: I don't mind if you throw away the top 5 percent every time you want. It doesn't matter. It's a button, just throw it away. Ninety-nine cents. That's all it was worth. The problem if you go with an application that will build an entire stack, or you go in with a big project that'll take a year and it will cost $10 to $50 million. That's not the way to do things.

Yourdon: So for things of that sort, do you feel we shouldn't be using the popular forms of agile at all?

Strassmann: Oh, you can use agile. And decide on what layer you're going to put it in.

Strassmann: You don't want to do agile on the infrastructure, for instance. You don't want to do agile on data. You just don't touch it.

Yourdon: Okay.

Strassmann: In fact, you have a totally different environment set up for control of data. And infrastructure in particular. You know, in the infrastructure you may have things starting on the Internet. And then because of latency, you may decide to put the data center capability, what's called "on the edge," to get you down to milliseconds.

Yourdon: Right.

Strassmann: You should be able to slide out of the stack the infrastructure, slide it on a different . . . without the upper layer or lower layer being affected. That's where the costs come in.

Yourdon: Right. Interesting. Well, that's, as you know, an area where there are huge battles being fought today, as was the case 20 years ago when my friends and I were introducing the structured methodologies.

Okay, well, I think I have covered just about all of the questions I had on my list, which I very much appreciate your taking the time to talk to me about.

Index

CPSIA information can be obtained at www.ICGtesting.com
Printed in the USA
LVOW081529211011

251567LV00001B/18/P